RISEN FROM THE ASHES

A History of Firefighting in Plymouth, Devonport and East Stonehouse 1673–1973

Finbar Nolan

Published by Jeremy Mills Publishing Limited

113 Lidget Street
Lindley
Huddersfield
West Yorkshire HD3 3JR

www.jeremymillspublishing.co.uk

First published 2013

ISBN 978-1-906600-91-4

This book is dedicated to the many generations of firefighters who have served the former three towns of Plymouth, Devonport, and Stonehouse. Their dedication and bravery in preserving life and property from fire should never be forgotten; some paid the ultimate price in serving their fellow man, especially during the terrible blitz on Plymouth. May their memory forever live on in the thoughts of firefighters today and in the future.

CONTENTS

FOREWORD

RALPH HAVERY OBE, FIFIREE
FORMER CHIEF FIRE OFFICER, CITY OF PLYMOUTH FIRE BRIGADE

HAVING SERVED AS the last Chief Fire Officer of the City of Plymouth Fire Brigade, from 1962 until 1973, and then as Chief Officer of Devon Fire Brigade (which became responsible for the fire protection of Plymouth) until my retirement from that brigade in 1978, I am delighted to have been invited to write the Foreword for *Risen from the Ashes*. The book has chronicled 300 years of firefighting history in the three towns of Devonport, East Stonehouse and Plymouth, up until the last days of the City of Plymouth Fire Brigade.

Tribute must be paid to Finbar Nolan for the tremendous amount of time and energy that he has devoted to the task. I am sure that fire buffs, not only in Plymouth, but far and wide, together with other people interested in the history of the City of Plymouth, will find much of interest in this work.

On reading the book, it becomes clear that the history can be divided into three main sections:

(i) from 1673 until World War II
(ii) from World War II until the formation of the peace-time brigades in 1948
(iii) from 1948 until the amalgamation of Devon County Fire Service, City of Exeter Fire Brigade and City of Plymouth Fire Brigade to form the new Devon Fire Brigade in 1973.

During the first period, fires appear to have been fought with large numbers of people, sometimes thousands, often supplied by the navy and army, but with very little and poorly maintained equipment and virtually no organisation or collaboration between the military and civil authorities: situations which had never been previously experienced anywhere in the world. Hundreds of fires burned simultaneously. At the same time, the City was being bombarded with high explosive bombs that killed or injured thousands of its citizens, thus creating more difficulties for the firefighters dealing with the already impossible task of containing the fire situation.

Various criticisms and recommendations were made at that time regarding the inadequacies of the fire brigade, both from lack of equipment and poor organisational aspects. However, I feel that given the extraordinary circumstances of the times, few if any, fire brigades in the UK would have been up to the challenges being faced in Plymouth. As a result, Plymouth Brigade, together with all other individual brigades, lost its identity and the National Fire Service was created some months later to deal with the wartime situation.

During the third and final period, 1948–1973, the functions of the fire brigades changed from being a purely firefighting service to that of an all round emergency service covering not only firefighting but also extensive fire prevention duties, involving inspection and certification of most types of premises to which the public had access, and also responding to any type of dangerous or emergency situation where their experience, equipment and instant availability could be of assistance.

With the large scale demobilisation of personnel from the National Fire Service in 1946, the new peacetime Brigade was formed by a nucleus of ex-regular and NFS personnel, greatly augmented by a supply of fit, disciplined young men who, after wartime service in HM Forces, wished to continue a service way of life and thus chose to make the Fire Service their new career.

Due to Plymouth being a garrison town for all three armed services, the Brigade was always fortunate in having such a ready supply of high quality and disciplined young men available to it. Such standards were readily absorbed by the other young recruits without a service background, which ensured the Brigade always had a workforce of the highest quality with a strong sense of duty and esprit de corps.

A good Brigade requires three main constituents:

(i) an adequate staff of well trained personnel
(ii) a good supply of high class appliances and equipment
(iii) a good Fire Authority, in our case the city council, to administer and finance its brigade.

We were very fortunate in having all three.

Ralph Havery OBE FIFireE
June 2012

INTRODUCTION

AS THE CITY of Plymouth has changed, so have the character of its fires, fire brigades and disasters. The challenges facing the modern firefighter are very complex compared to the firemen of yesteryear. Fire has played a vital role in man's development in history, ever since cavemen learnt how to harness it to cook food and keep themselves warm. But if you ignored it or were careless with it, then its fury could be, and often was, devastating.

Prior to the formation of insurance company fire brigades, the first being 'The Fire Office,' in 1680, fire wreaked havoc throughout the country. There was little or no means of dealing with outbreaks of large fires. Devon suffered some terrible losses during the eighteenth and nineteenth centuries. Places like Chumleigh, Chudleigh, Brandninch, Newton St. Cyres, North Tawton, Lympstone, Moretonhampstead, Stoke Canon, South Molton and Ottery St. Mary lost large proportions of their villages and towns due to the ravages of fire. The towns of Plymouth, Devonport (formerly known as Plymouth Dock), and East Stonehouse also suffered dreadful losses prior to the birth of organised fire brigades.

It is recorded that in 1673 a fire engine, complete with buckets, etc, was brought to Plymouth. This rather crude fire engine was known as a parish pump and relied on the Beadle and inhabitants of the town to fetch it and work it at an outbreak of fire. Parish pumps were often badly maintained and many fell into a state of disrepair due to lack of funds.

Insurance companies were growing quite concerned at the high losses they were incurring through fire and many of the companies formed their own volunteer fire brigades throughout the country. The West of England Insurance Company formed the first fire brigade in Plymouth in 1838 with Mr Walter Marshall as Chief Officer. The company was first established in Exeter in 1807 where its headquarters and fire brigade were located.

Other fire insurance companies who had their own fire brigades operating in Plymouth were The County Fire Office, with Mr John Carkeet as the Superintendent, and The Liverpool and London and Globe Insurance Company, with Mr Thomas Raddan as Chief Officer.

The West of England Fire Brigade served Plymouth for fifty-three years, whereas the County Fire Office Fire Brigade served for twenty-five years, and the Liverpool and London and Globe Fire Brigade served for just ten years.

A common practice in the years preceding organised fire brigades was that many insurance companies donated sums of money for the upkeep and maintenance of the parish pumps and ancillary equipment throughout towns and villages in the country. The above mentioned companies were the only ones to maintain actual fire brigades in Plymouth, contrary to what is written in other publications.

Plymouth Corporation formed a fire brigade in 1863 following the demise of the County Fire Brigade; they were assisted by the Police. In 1891, the Police took total responsibility for firefighting arrangements in Plymouth. Devonport and Stonehouse Fire Brigades operated until 1916 when they too were amalgamated into the Plymouth Police Fire Brigade. The Police remained in charge until 1941 when the National Fire Service was formed.

This historical account attempts to cover the firefighting arrangements, early fire brigades and some notable fires within the three towns from the very early days until 1st April 1973, when the City of Plymouth Fire Brigade was amalgamated, along with Exeter City Fire Brigade and Devon County Fire Service, into the newly formed Devon Fire Brigade.

I have included a section within this book on the fires and fire arrangements within Devonport Dockyard, as the Dockyard played a significant part in our fire history here in Plymouth.

Some of the tragic fires and other incidents contained in this historical account are taken from the newspapers of the day, and I have deliberately used the script format that the reporters used in writing the articles to emphasise how graphic their accounts were.

Upon reading this historical account, I feel sure that today's firefighters, policemen, historians and other interested parties will have a much greater understanding of the heroic figures who shaped our modern day fire brigade. Sadly, for some of our brave firefighters, they paid the ultimate price in doing so, especially during the terrible blitz on Plymouth during the war years.

Finbar Nolan
January 2012

CHAPTER ONE

THE EARLY YEARS

A SIGNIFICANT EVENT occurred in the premises of Mr Thomas Farynor, a contractor for supplying ship's biscuits to the Navy, in Pudding Lane, London, in the early hours of Sunday 2nd September 1666. A fire broke out in the bakery after Mr Farynor had retired for the night, and this was the beginning of The Great Fire of London. He was woken in the early hours by his assistant, who smelt smoke. They were trapped upstairs due to the smoke and flames now advancing into the staircase. Mr Farynor managed to escape with his family and assistant, via a garret window, and onto a roof of an adjoining house. Sadly, his house servant became the first casualty of the Great Fire, as she was reported to have perished in the flames.

The fire quickly spread to the Star Inn, which was behind the bakery, and its passage was fuelled by a vast range of combustible materials in its path. In the first instance, the fire was not considered too serious. The then Lord Mayor, Sir Thomas Bludworth, was sent for from his house on the other side of London; he duly arrived about an hour after the fire was first discovered. In his annoyance at being roused from his bed in the early hours, he was reported to have said, 'Pish, a woman could piss it out.' He then returned to his home.

The fire, however, quickly spread up Pudding Lane towards premises used as warehouses, which contained all manner of highly combustible items, such as oil, tallow, and fodder. The speed and intensity of the blaze was now causing mass panic, and there were hundreds of people in the streets, running or trying to save their belongings from the advancing fire. This sadly had little effect, and the fire raged with increasing magnitude.

The fire raged for four days and destroyed 13,200 houses, eighty-seven churches and forty-four Great Livery Halls within the City of London. It is reported that only six people lost their lives as a result of the fire, which is miraculous, considering the dense population and the high fire loading of the buildings at that time. Even though there were crude arrangements for firefighting in place, this catastrophe highlighted the inadequacies of the arrangements. During the years prior to the Great Fire of 1666, regulations in some areas of the country required that a barrel-full of water for quenching fires should be placed before the doors of buildings and bell-men rang their bells at night calling out – 'Take care of your bell and candle, be charitable to the poor and pray for the dead.'

In days gone by, people thought that tiny fiery lizards lived in fire and spoke of them as spirits of the fire. Such a powerful and destructive element must, in their imagination, be a god, and temples were built in its honour. For centuries, lamps dedicated to the fire god were kept constantly burning in the temples

Fire squirt being used at a fire. This method of getting water onto a fire was an early attempt at controlling a jet of water onto a fire. The squirt was a large syringe made from brass or wood and required several people to operate and keep it supplied with water.

This colourful gentleman was an officer with the West of England Insurance Company Fire Brigade c.1825.

and never allowed to become extinguished. The custom of keeping a perpetual fire both as a need and a ritual is one of the most ancient in the world.

Although fire proved a friend of primitive man, it also became his most feared enemy, as the events in 1666 proved. Following the Great Fire, arrangements for dealing with outbreaks of fire within the more populated areas of the country improved, albeit very slowly. In some regions, things did not begin to improve for another hundred years.

The three towns of Plymouth, Devonport and Stonehouse suffered great losses in the early days, but as the following historical account shows, the people took on the fiery fiend and eventually learnt how to subdue him.

Early accounts

The Plymouth and South Devon Records Office, which is located in Clare Place in Plymouth, is where I uncovered many old papers and town accounts, which enabled me to ascertain when the towns of Plymouth, Devonport and Stonehouse received their first fire engines, and how the upkeep and maintenance of the fire equipment serving the three towns were paid for.

One of the first records of an actual fire engine being obtained to fight fires in the town of Plymouth reads: '1673; a fire engine with buckets, etc, brought to Plymouth'. This was a very early manual Bagpipe type engine with buckets for supplying it with water from the various conduits or wells, of which old Plymouth had a number. It was an improvement on the old Syringe, or Squirt as it was known, and was able to pump much more water at one stroke of the pumping handle. It could not maintain a continuous stream of water, and was a very poor weapon for its purpose.

The engine first brought to Plymouth was known as a Parish Pump and was kept in a shed in the Barbican area of the town. In case of fire, the town's beadle or watchmen had to summon help from the inhabitants to haul the engine to the scene of fire. It is well documented that during the alarm of fire in those times, there were scenes of much disorder and looting. The labour employed to pump the engines had to be plied with ale at regular intervals, or else they refused to carry on. In later years, it was the practice in some areas of the country to issue the men employed to pump the engines with tokens, which were exchanged for money after the fire had been extinguished. This practice tended to eliminate blackmailing by the old beer-swigging scavengers. It took a considerable amount of effort and manpower to keep the engine working at a fire and without the assistance of the local population, the situation would be untenable. Volunteer fire brigades at that time tended to be quite small in manpower and their exertions were better applied to fighting the fire itself rather than pumping the handles on the manual pumps.

In the year 1677, it is recorded that a sum of £6. 1*s.* 0*d.* was paid out when Mrs Alice Allen's house was on fire. The costs were for repairing the buckets and looking after the engine and for the men's labour and other charges about the same. There are numerous entries in the record books where various persons were paid sums of money to maintain the engine and buckets belonging to the town. Unfortunately, the records showed that the engines and buckets were not serviced on a regular basis, and more often than not, they fell into disrepair and it cost the town council much more to have them repaired than having them serviced regularly. It was the custom at that time to invite the people of the town to contribute towards the upkeep of the engines and other plant. It is interesting to speculate whether the town's people paid willingly by voluntary subscriptions, rather than by the modern practice of compulsory payment through the council tax.

Another entry in the town's accounts for Plymouth showed that, in 1702, a new water engine and forty-four buckets were bought for the town. The cost of supplying the new engine and buckets and for mending the old engine and buckets amounted to £11. 0*s.* 2*d.* Part of this sum was again made up with voluntary subscriptions. Twenty-six years later, in 1728, two further fire engines were purchased at a cost of over fifty pounds; the engines were kept in the storehouse in Higher Lane on the Barbican. These engines were designed and built by Richard Newsham of London. They were capable of throwing forty gallons of water a minute to a height of seventy feet. The accounts showed that various people were paid, on an annual basis, to service and repair the fire engines and buckets. Records also show that once again, in 1761, two new fire engines were bought for Plymouth, presumably to replace the old ones which by then had fallen into disrepair. The Phoenix Fire Office was another provider of subscriptions. The Phoenix maintained fire brigades in various places around the country, and Plymouth, Devonport and Stonehouse received subscriptions at various times for either the repair of the town's engine or for the repair of equipment. Records showed that, in 1790, the Plymouth agency received twelve new leather buckets for the town of Stonehouse. In 1793, Devonport received £21. 0*s.* 0*d* towards the repair of the parish pump. Plymouth received a donation of £5. 5*s.* 0*d* as one year's repair grant for the town engine. Devonport received the same amount in 1840 towards the cost of new fire plugs and Plymouth was given £15. 15*s.* 0*d* as three years' subscriptions which were in arrears. The Phoenix Fire Office continued giving annual subscriptions right up to the end of the nineteenth century.

The formation of the Town Watch

In the year 1770, a Town Watch was formed in Plymouth, consisting of three officers and eighteen watchmen; one can well imagine that here was the genesis of both the Police Force and Fire Brigade, and the streets of old Plymouth were illuminated with 250 lamps. It must have been a queer sight to see the watchman, with halberd, lamp and bell, leading the crowd hauling the engine to a fire. During these times, an interesting local practice during an alarm of fire was that signal guns were fired, presumably from the ramparts of the Citadel and on ships moored up in the Hamoaze. Alarms were sounded on drums at naval and military establishments and a bell was sounded in the Dockyard. During the alarm of fire within the three towns, it was the practice to dispatch hundreds of soldiers or sailors to the scene of fire with the manual fire engines from their barracks, in order to assist the civil authority with firefighting, if required. Many of them were used to prevent looting and other general disorder, which was rife in those early years. At about the same time as the formation of the Town Watch, a new 2 ½ inch water main was laid to the Barbican at a cost of £68.19*s.* 5*d.*

One of the first fires in which the new engines were used was at a fire that occurred at the Royal Naval Hospital, Stonehouse, in May 1762. The naval hospital was built in 1759, and as with other military establishments, they had a fire engine based at that location and operated by the service personnel at that establishment during times of fire. The fire broke out at midnight in No. 12 block, and was caused by the boiling over of the carpenters' glue. The town's engines assisted the Dockyard engines and the hospital engine, which were already on the scene.

The minute book records that, on 26th April 1777, the Custom Board agreed to pay towards the cost of cleaning and using one of the Corporation's fire engines, if the engine was housed in the Custom House on the Barbican. The engines were then in a storehouse in Higher Lane.

In 1776–7, the Sun Fire Office began contributing £5. 5*s.* 0*d.* per year towards the upkeep of the Corporation engines. The Royal Exchange Insurance Office also began contributing towards the upkeep of the engines at this time, and by 1794, the Phoenix Insurance Company also began contributing towards their upkeep. The Phoenix Company also gave £21 to Devonport in 1793, towards the repair costs of their parish fire engine and, in 1796, they supplied twelve new leather buckets to East Stonehouse. This practice of assistance continued well into the late 1800s.

The year 1795 saw the building of the Royal Marine barracks at Stonehouse and, once again, there was a manual fire engine located there, primarily to deal with outbreaks within the barracks. History showed that it rendered valuable assistance outside the barracks on numerous occasions. Most government establishments had a means for firefighting, along with great numbers of soldiers or sailors billeted there. One of the primary reasons why the military were only too willing to assist in firefighting within the three towns was the fact that the government was afraid that any conflagration near to their establishments would endanger the country's defences. The dignitaries of the three towns were quick to seize upon this goodwill, and, as history showed, they dragged their heels and avoided their responsibility of providing adequate fire arrangements within the boroughs for many years.

Fireman of the Sun Fire Office c.1750.

On the evening of December 16th 1795, a dreadful fire took place on the Barbican in Southside Street, within the premises occupied by a Mr Douglas, a sailmaker. In a few minutes, the whole building was in flames, which extended to the houses adjoining and threatened the destruction of all the surrounding property. The fire continued for six hours with incredible fury, and assistance was given to the local force by the military, the Dockyard and Naval Hospital engines. It was providential that the tide was at flood at the time, or the damage would have involved the shipping in Sutton Pool. If Plymouth had not been a garrison town, and the assistance afforded by hundreds of military personnel at large outbreaks of fire was not there, then I am sure that Plymouth would have suffered the same catastrophic results, as was the case for other Devon towns mentioned earlier.

Following a calamitous fire on Bull Hill in January 1808, the Mayor, William Langmead, set up a fund for the poor sufferers of the fire. A handbill was published appealing for subscribers, as the losses incurred totalled £470, which was a substantial amount back then. Prior to the public meeting, a sum of £51 had already been received into the fund. It was common practice in those early days to ask for donations to assist poorer members of the community following destructive fires, as the average person could not afford to pay fire insurance premiums. The practice of failing to have adequate insurance against loss by fire was by no means pertaining solely to the inhabitants of the early days. It is still relatively common to find tenants in today's society, especially in the more deprived areas of the city, who don't have their contents insured against loss by fire or water. Whether this practice is by choice or circumstance, it is still quite alarming.

There was an outbreak of fire in Pembroke Street, Plymouth Dock, in 1810 and pans, pitchers and vessels of all kinds were brought into use to keep the parish engine going. The townsfolk worked furiously to keep the fire from spreading. They had to remove the roofs of several houses which were in danger, in order to check the fire spread. When fires occurred in the thickly populated areas of the towns, especially in the middle of the night, the general uproar and panic was incredible. Most of the poorer properties were rack rented, which resulted in large numbers of people dwelling in the same building, and history has shown that casualties were often high, as fire wreaked havoc within. The lack of a trained fire brigade with adequate means of dealing with an outbreak of fire at that time only stimulates our thoughts on how they coped. The town of Plymouth Dock was renamed to Devonport in 1824, and a large column was erected in Ker Street to commemorate this change. This column is still there today, alongside the magnificent Guildhall building. The fire station was attached to the Guildhall and housed the men and appliances of the Devonport Fire Brigade.

Organising fire arrangements

On 28th May 1819, a fire broke out in a property in Whimple Street, Plymouth, and the late arrival of the fire engines and the insufficient and unsatisfactory way in which the fire was dealt with prompted several respectable inhabitants of the town to write to the Mayor, Richard Arthur. They requested a general meeting of the inhabitants of the town to consider and determine a system of supplying and working the fire engines. It was thought that this might ensure promptitude, regularity and effective co-operation on the part of those whose more immediate duty it was to give assistance on such distressing occasions.

The general public meeting was held at the Guildhall on 2nd June, and it was quickly resolved unanimously, that the existing plan and arrangements in cases of fire were quite insufficient and very unsatisfactory.

The meeting again resolved unanimously that it deemed it expedient that a company of firemen should be forthwith embodied to act in cases of fire, to consist of a captain, two leaders and twenty-five men.

The meeting appointed a committee, consisting of the following gentlemen: Mr John Collier, John Prideaux, Henry Gandy, Thomas Jessop, William Hawker, Richard Baily, John Gullet, Charles Marshall, William Kerswell, Philip Smith, Dr Stewart, William Gregg, Jr, Richard Hamlyn, Robert Fortescue, John Gill, John Lee Stevens, Samuel Rowe, John Nicholls, William Patey, Robert Voisey and William Cole. Their brief was to consider the adoption of a system for the better supplying and working of the fire engines, and for employing such other measures as would ensure promptitude, regularity and effective co-operation on all such distressing occasions. For these purposes, they did forthwith confer with his worshipful the Mayor, and the Commissioners for watching and lighting the town, and the agents of the different insurance companies. Mr John Collier was voted in as Chairman of the Committee, with any seven being competent to act.

It is clear that this burst of concern and enthusiasm amounted to no more than empty words and promises, as once again, in April 1823, following several complaints about the state of the town's fire engines, the Mayor, (W. A. Welsford), chaired a meeting. The meeting consisted of several gentlemen, agents to the Commercial Union, Sun Fire Office, Phoenix Fire Office and the Eagle Fire Insurance

BOROUGH
OF
Plymouth.

Guildhall, May **29, 1819.**

SEVERAL respectable Inhabitants having represented to me, that from the confusion which took place at the **FIRE** last Night, in *Whimple-Street*, and the **INEFFECTIVE** state of the **ENGINES**, it is their opinion, that the present Plan and Arrangements, in cases of Fire, are quite insufficient and unsatisfactory ; and having requested me to convene a General Meeting of the Inhabitants of this Town and Borough, to consider and determine on the adoption of a System of supplying and working the Fire Engines, which may ensure promptitude, regularity, and effective co-operation, on the part of those whose more immediate Duty it is to give Assistance on such distressing Occasions :—

I do, therefore, hereby request a **GENERAL MEETING** of the Inhabitants of this Town and Borough, at the **GUILDHALL** thereof, on **WEDNESDAY** next, the Second Day of June Instant, precisely by Eleven o'Clock in the Forenoon, for the above Purpose.

RICHARD ARTHUR,

MAYOR.

Handbill produced in May 1819, calling upon the people of Plymouth to attend a meeting to discuss the state of the parish fire engines following a serious fire in Whimple Street.

Borough of Plymouth.

AT a GENERAL MEETING of the

Inhabitants of the Town and Borough of PLYMOUTH, convened by the Worshipful the MAYOR, by Publick Advertisement, and held at the GUILDHALL, of and within the said Borough, the Second Day of JUNE, 1819, in consequence of the late FIRE in Whimple-Street.

RICHARD ARTHUR, Esq.

MAYOR, IN THE CHAIR.

Resolved unanimously,—That as the Accident of FIRE, and the alarm and danger attendant thereon, are common to all the Inhabitants and Proprietors in this Borough, it is the common interest and duty of them all, to consult and devise such Measures as are most likely to prevent that Calamity; and to provide the means of arresting the same when it unfortunately happens.

Resolved unanimously,—That the present Plan and Arrangements in cases of Fire, are quite insufficient and unsatisfactory.

Resolved unanimously,—That this Meeting doth deem it expedient, that a Company of Firemen should be forthwith embodied, to act in cases of Fire; to consist of a Captain, two Leaders, and twenty-five Men.

Resolved unanimously,—That the following Gentlemen, viz.—

Mr. John Collier,
John Prideaux,
Henry Gandy,
Thomas F. Jessop,
William Hawker,
Richard Bayly,
John Gullett,

Mr. Charles Marshall,
William Kerswell,
Philip Smith,
Dr. Stewart,
Mr. Wm. Gregg, Jun.
Richard Hamlyn,
Robert Fortescue,

Mr. John Gill,
John Lee Stevens,
Samuel Rowe,
John Nicholls,
Wm. Patey,
Robert Voisey, and
Wm. Cole,

be appointed a Committee, to consider of the adoption of a System for the better supplying and working the Fire Engines, and for employing such other measures as will ensure promptitude, regularity, and effective co-operation, on all such distressing occasions. And that for these purposes they do forthwith confer with the Worshipful the Mayor, and the Commissioners for Watching and Lighting this Town, and the Agents of the different Insurance Companies. That Mr. John Collier be requested to accept the office of Chairman of the Committee, any seven of whom shall be competent to act; and that their first meeting be on Friday next at Eleven o'Clock in the forenoon, at the Guildhall of the said Borough.

Resolved unanimously,—That when the said Committee, in conjunction with the above-named Authorities, have matured a Plan, they do request the Mayor to publish the same for the satisfaction and information of the Inhabitants at large.

Resolved unanimously,—That the Thanks of this Meeting be given to DOCTOR BELLAMY, for preparing and bringing forward the aforegoing Resolutions.

Resolved unanimously,—That these Resolutions be signed by the Chairman, and published in hand-bills, to be circulated within the Town and Borough of Plymouth.

RICHARD ARTHUR, Mayor.

The Mayor having quitted the Chair,

A report following a public meeting in 1819. Here it can be seen that a nucleus for a fire brigade was to be formed; these men were drawn from several insurance companies operating within the town. They were to be known as the Fire Police, which had no bearing upon the police as we know it. Ironically, it wasn't until 1823 that they were actually set up.

Companies, to try to resolve the same problems expressed in 1819.
It was resolved that:

- Two good Fire Engines were necessary for giving efficient aid in cases of fire.
- That each Insurance Office, having agents established in this place, be requested to subscribe to the fund for carrying this object into effect, according to its inclination and ability.
- That four persons be appointed and called 'Directors of Fire Engines', for the purpose of superintending and carrying into effect the objects of this meeting. To that end, that they have the engines always kept in good order, so that they may be fit for use on any emergency, when they are to conduct the management of the same. The command, however, to devolve on the Director who shall first arrive at the spot where the engine is required, and that he shall be remunerated accordingly for his prompt attention and services on such occasions.
- That the keys of the Engine-House shall be kept in the Watch-House of the Guildhall, and the names of the Directors placed immediately over them, as well as a second list in the Council Chamber. Each Director shall also have a painted board over his door, with the words 'Fire Engine Director' thereon.
- That Messrs. Richard Sampson, Carpenter, of Westwell Street; Richard Jarvis, Carpenter, Broad Street; Christopher Davies, Sailmaker, of Southside Street; and John Williams, Printer, Old Town, were appointed as Directors.
- That the Corporation be requested to permit the engines to stand in the Guildhall Court, Gratis, and to give up their property in the present engines for the aforementioned purposes.
- That there are a Chairman and three managers, as a yearly committee.
- That Joseph Pridham, Esq. is requested to act as Chairman; and Messrs. Welch, Coryndon, and John Stevens as the committee of management for the ensuing year.
- That Mr Eastlake was requested to act as Treasurer for the same period.
- That the Committee of Management be requested to meet the Directors forthwith, and cause one of the engines to be immediately put in proper order.

With the above arrangements in place, there was a marked improvement in fire precautions within the town, notwithstanding that the entire committee of Directors, and the volunteers available to fetch and work the engines, were purely part-time, and, having never been trained in fire extinction, lacked a practical ability in firefighting. This newly appointed body was known as Fire Police, but in no way was there any connection with the Police as we know it, as history shows that police forces did not begin until 1829, when the Metropolitan Police were formed. There were several towns throughout the country that formed Fire Police from the amalgamation of fire insurance companies, the most famed being The London Fire Engine Establishment, formed in 1833, but they never used the term Fire Police at all. The fire engine and ladders of the newly formed Plymouth Fire Police were kept at the Guildhall, and the alarm of fire was given by the tolling of the session's bell. As stated earlier in this book, it was the practice in the early days to ask for subscriptions from the town or interested parties to help pay for repairs and improvements to the existing fire engines, hoses, and buckets belonging to the town. In the Plymouth Directory for 1830, there were reported to be thirty volunteer firemen available to fetch and work the engine.

Fire Engines.

Plymouth, 24th April, 1823.

AT a Meeting of several Gentlemen, Agents to Fire Insurance Companies, held at the Guildhall this Day, by desire of The Worshipful the Mayor, to take into Consideration the present State of the Engines, and to decide on the best Means of securing immediate Assistance to the Public in Cases of Fire;

The Worshipful the Mayor

IN THE CHAIR;

IT WAS RESOLVED;–

1.—That Two good Engines are necessary for the purpose of giving efficient aid in case of Fire.

2.—That each Insurance Office, having Agents established in this place, be requested to subscribe to the Fund for carrying this object into effect, according to its inclination and ability.

3.—That Four Persons be appointed and called "Directors of Fire Engines," for the purpose of superintending and carrying into effect the objects of this Meeting; and to that end, that they have the Engines always kept in good order, so that they may be fit for use on any emergency, when they are to conduct the management of the same:—The command, however, to devolve on the Director who shall first arrive at the spot where the Engine is required; and that he shall be remunerated accordingly for his prompt attention and services on such occasions.

4.—That the Keys of the Engine-House shall be kept in the Watch-house of the Guildhall, and the Names of the Directors placed immediately over them, as well as a Second List in the Council Chamber. Each Director shall also have a painted Board over his Door, with the Words "Fire Engine Director" thereon.

5.—That Messrs. RICHARD SAMPSON, Carpenter, of 1, Westwell-Street; RICHARD JARVIS, Carpenter, Broad-Street; CHRISTOPHER DAVIES, Sailmaker, Southside-Street; and JOHN WILLIAMS, Printer, Old-Town, be now appointed Directors.

6.—That the Corporation be requested to permit the Engines to stand in the Guildhall Court gratis; and to give up their Property in the present Engines for the aforementioned purposes.

7.—That there be a Chairman and Three Managers as a Yearly Committee.

8.—That JOSEPH PRIDHAM, Esq. be requested to act as Chairman; and Messrs. WELCH, CORYNDON, and JOHN L. STEVENS as the Committee of Management for the ensuing Year.

9.—That Messrs. EASTLAKE be requested to act as Treasurers for the same period.

10.—That the Committee of Management be requested to meet the Directors forthwith, and cause one of the Engines to be immediately put in proper order.

11.—That this Meeting do adjourn 'till this day Fortnight.

W. A. WELSFORD,
MAYOR and CHAIRMAN.

Handbill of 1823 calling upon the citizens of the borough to attend a meeting to discuss the state of the parish engines, and to try to establish a better system in raising a crew to deal with outbreaks of fire.

The Mayor received the following letter on 3rd May 1827:

> Sir,
>
> The committee of agents for Fire Insurances at Plymouth, having met this day at the Guildhall and taken the examinations of witnesses, is of the opinion that the Town's Engines are in good and efficient state, except the hoses. The agents unfortunately, have not sufficient funds to provide new hoses, and they beg to submit to the Mayor and commonalty (as they are now exonerated from the annual charges which they hence fore paid for keeping the Engines in repair, etc) the necessity of their contributing towards the new hoses, and issuing an advertisement calling on the inhabitants, who are equally interested in so desirable a measure to subscribe for the like purpose.
>
> The committee have also to add, they were of the opinion, that the Town Engine No1, was of considerable service at the late fire, and also in all respects efficient (except the bursting of the hoses) which were immediately replaced, and that the Fire Directors and Fire Men exerted themselves to the utmost in checking the flames and preventing a considerable destruction of property.

Once again, a handbill was produced and handed to the inhabitants of the town, inviting them to a meeting at the Guildhall, where hopefully, enough funds would be raised to purchase the new hoses. The meeting was not very numerous, though the subject to be considered was one of great public interest. The Mayor was called to the chair. A desultory conversation of some length ensued, during which it was clearly ascertained that the engines, with the exception of the hoses, were in excellent repair, but the hoses were in an inefficient state, in fact they were almost useless. A motion to the following effect was moved by J. Collier, Esq. and carried unanimously: that the fire engine hoses, being in a very bad state, it is expedient, forthwith, to place new ones on their stead. That the expenses which will be incurred for that purpose, amounting to about one hundred pounds, be defrayed by a public subscription and that the inhabitants at large be [sic] requested to contribute towards a sum to be so appropriate. Nearly £40 was subscribed at the meeting, the Corporation heading the list with a donation of £10.

It was observed by a gentleman present at the above meeting that not more than one half of the property in this town was insured, and it was also stated that the town, if the size of the houses recently built be taken into consideration, had doubled in size since 1800.

The next big fire took place in Catherine Street, Devonport, in 1828. Not a soul was in the street when it began, and the watchman did not raise the alarm, nor did the engine arrive until the flames had spread to the adjoining premises. The Citadel engine was summoned, and promptly arrived with several hundred soldiers. For some time, the district was threatened with destruction, and the troops experienced utmost difficulty in preventing the crowd from plundering the deserted shops.

The borough engine and ladders were kept at the Guildhall, and in case of fire, application for their use was to be made to James Day and Richard Ellis, the Borough Beadles. The Plymouth borough water supply was greatly improved in 1827; the small lead pipes were replaced with large iron pipes. Fire plugs were fitted on these mains; these were the forerunner of modern hydrants, and consisted of sockets inserted into the cast iron mains, with a tapered wooden plug driven in to hold back the water until required. The firemen had a most difficult job to force their standpipes down into the socket once the plug had been removed, as, since no control valve was fitted, a good drenching was guaranteed.

An outbreak of fire, at once tragic and pathetic, destroyed the residence of Fort Major Watson, in the Plymouth Citadel in 1836. The roaring and crackling of the flames in the early morning aroused a servant, who ran to the door to raise the alarm. Some of the inhabitants managed to escape by jumping from the windows, through the flames, but the Major, a tall and heavy man, fell into the furnace within as he was preparing to jump. Two of his daughters were shrieking for help, when the floor collapsed and carried them with it. The Citadel engine, along with a large body of soldiers, and the town's engine, with a willing workforce of policemen and others, fought the fire, which was extinguished after several hours.

BOROUGH of PLYMOUTH.

Guildhall, May 19th, 1827.

THE Committee appointed by the Inhabitants of the Borough of Plymouth aforesaid, to superintend the management of the Town's Engines, having represented to me that the Leather Hoses belonging to the Engines are nearly worn out, and will very shortly become altogether unfit for use; and having at the same time recommended that a Meeting of the Inhabitants should be forthwith convened to raise a Fund by Subscription, for providing NEW HOSES, and putting the Engines in repair, to render them completely serviceable for the preservation of the Inhabitants, and their Property, against injury by Fire.

I do therefore hereby request a GENERAL MEETING of the Inhabitants of this Town and Borough, at the GUILDHALL thereof, on THURSDAY next, the 24th Day of MAY Instant, precisely by 12 of the Clock at Noon, for the above purpose.

Richard Arthur,

MAYOR.

W. HAVILAND, Printer, &c. Bedford-Street, Plymouth.

Handbill produced in May 1827 calling for a meeting of the people of the town to discuss the need for new hoses and repairing the old fire engine.

An early drawing of insurance company firemen fighting a fire c.1760s.

The remains of the Officer and his children were found in a heap, as though they had been consumed in each other's arms.

Even though the police reorganised arrangements for firefighting in 1836, with one superintendent, three inspectors and twenty-seven constables, they only took part responsibility. In 1887, Supt Frederick Wreford was appointed as Superintendent of the Fire Brigade, with Inspector J. Hill as his deputy and Mr McKeer as Inspector.

The inhabitants of the three towns relied heavily upon the military and Dockyard engines, along with the hundreds of soldiers and seamen who would attend with the engines to render assistance to the local firemen. As well as the three towns, another unofficial town lay behind the vast walls of the Royal Dockyard; as well as all the places of work, there were numerous places of residence, and quarters for officers and seamen. In order to protect our nation's defensive assets, the Admiralty supplied its own arrangements for dealing with outbreaks of fire within the walls of the Dockyard.

CHAPTER TWO

FIREFIGHTING ARRANGEMENTS IN DEVONPORT DOCKYARD

IN 1829, SIR Robert Peel had formed the first police force in England – the Metropolitan Police. Four years later, in 1833, the Admiralty introduced a Dockyard police force to police the Royal Dockyards and establishments. They were not used at Plymouth until 20th May 1834. This new force was formed by reorganising and remodelling the existing collection of warders and watchmen currently employed within the Dockyards.

For the first time, uniforms were worn: a stovepipe hat and blue frock coat with silver buttons, which was cut away at the front from the waist downwards. The trousers were of white duck in the summer, but darker and warmer during the winter months. The police carried warning rattles to raise any alarms; these were forerunners to whistles. They also carried truncheons, ornately decorated with the Sovereign's coat of arms, and the man's police number.

In the event of fire, these policemen, along with the local workforce of the Dockyard, hauled the manual fire engines to the scene of operations, and got to work with quenching the outbreak. This was quite a labour-intensive procedure, as a bucket chain gang had to be formed to feed the fire pump with water. Numerous men were also required to pump the fire engines, which was an exhausting job, and often done in shifts. The fire pumps had to be positioned very close to the outbreak, as the distance from the pump to the fire was often restricted due to lack of fire hose and this often proved a perilous operation.

Many of the military establishments in and around the three towns had manual fire engines at their disposal, and these were often summoned to render assistance at outbreaks of fire within the Dockyard. These were usually accompanied by several hundred soldiers or sailors, who were used to assist in firefighting or to control the gathering crowds in order to prevent looting and other disorders, which was very common practice among the less well off inhabitants, especially within the streets of the three towns. Large crowds would gather at the Dockyard gates during outbreaks of fire, and the soldiers were sometimes stretched to maintain good order.

The three towns of Plymouth, Devonport, and Stonehouse did not have any organised fire brigades in the early days, only parish pumps, which were operated by volunteers. The pumps were more often than not in a state of disrepair and unusable. They relied heavily upon the military establishments in the area to assist them during outbreaks of fire.

In 1838, the West of England Insurance Company formed a fire brigade in Plymouth, with Mr William Marshall appointed as Chief Officer. The County Fire Insurance Office also had a fire brigade formed at this time, with their agent, Mr Carkeet, as their superintendent; this insurance brigade ceased in 1863. Whilst these brigades served the three towns, they were still assisted by the military at large outbreaks of fire. Assistance was often reciprocated, as these insurance brigades also assisted at outbreaks within the Dockyard and other military establishments. The valuable assistance rendered by these brigades at the Great Fire in the Dockyard in 1840 was well documented.

The policing of the Dockyard often gave cause for concern, and many complaints were received against the Dockyard Coppers. Superintendent T. M. Mallalieu of the Metropolitan Police conducted an enquiry into their activities. The result of his enquiries revealed that, in his opinion, the Dockyard police force was badly trained, and consequently, it was disbanded.

An act of Parliament laid down in 1860 stated that the Metropolitan Police would carry out the policing of all Royal Dockyards in the country. The control of policing within Devonport Dockyard was transferred on Monday 22nd October 1860 to the Metropolitan Police, under the superintendence of Mr Bray, a former Chief of Police at the House of Lords, and a former detective in attendance on Her Majesty Queen Victoria. The number of constables who came from the Metropolis numbered thirty-four, and about another thirty were retained from the disbanded Dockyard police force. Those policemen formerly belonging to the Dockyard police, but disqualified from entering the Metropolitan Police, were re-employed as labourers within the Dockyard.

Firefighting arrangements within the Dockyard still relied on the local artisans and labourers, supervised and assisted by the police, to deal with outbreaks of fire. The overall responsibility was in the hands of the Admiral or Captain Superintendents of the admiralty or military establishments.

Even though the Metropolitan Police did not have overall responsibility for firefighting arrangements until 1897, they were still expected to drill and practise on a quarterly basis, and to maintain the fire pumps within the Devonport and Keyham Yards.

In 1863, the Admiralty purchased the first steam fire engine for Devonport Dockyard. This was a Merryweather steam engine, which won first prize at the international competition held at the Crystal Palace that year. The fire engine was named the Sutherland, after the then Duke of Sutherland, and was capable of throwing a powerful jet of water to over 160 ft. This steam fire engine was taken out of service in 1905, but was used once again in 1918 after undergoing a few alterations, along with a new boiler being fitted.

In a copy of a handbook issued by the Metropolitan Police in January 1868, for fire brigades within naval and military establishments at Devonport, the following details were recorded:

> The following details are not intended to supersede those of 1864, which form part of the general instructions for Police of Her Majesty's Naval and Military Establishments (except so far as the local distribution of the plant is concerned), but rather to ensure a more thorough acquaintance with the water supplies, and underground arrangements connected therewith. To provide for the efficient co-operation of the establishments in case of an alarm of fire, or when Police are ordered out for necessary practice. With this important auxiliary aid, the Commissioner expects the Police to become thoroughly efficient, and prepared for any emergency.
> Superintendents or chief officers of Police in charge are to make application to the Admiral or Captain Superintendents. In Military Stations, to the Superintendent or chief resident officer, on such days as it may be desirable to practice, and the inspecting Superintendent will have the whole plant of the establishments brought out for practice quarterly, reporting on these occasions specially to the Commissioner.
>
> Richard Mayne,
> Commissioner of Police of the Metropolis.
> January 3rd, 1868.

The fire plant at Devonport and Keyham Yards at that time was:

Devonport Yard

- Nine manual engines
- Twenty-five hose-reels
- Twenty ladders
- Eighteen fire hooks
- One fire escape

Keyham Yard

- Five manual engines
- Fourteen hose-reels
- Six ladders
- Twelve fire hooks

Auxiliary Aid

- Steam fire engine in charge of Chief Engineer, but kept in constant readiness day and night for either Yard in the Police engine house.

Devonport Yard

Water supplies in the two Yards were very good, as besides the unlimited amount of sea water available, there were, entering the Devonport Yard from the Granby reservoir, two pipes, one of six inches and the other of four inches diameter, filling the reservoirs near the Church. The one to the north side held 1,557 tons, the other, on the south side, held 1,860 tons, making a total of 3,417 tons. The average pressure from them was about fifty feet head. This was the ordinary supply, but in case of emergency, there was the nine-inch main pipe of the town, which also entered the yard at the gate. This was led from the high level reservoir at Stoke, which was 150 feet above the level of the sill of the Dockyard Gate. This was connected with nine-inch service pipes of the Yard. In case of fire, the six- and four-inch pipes would supply the reservoirs, and the water in the nine-inch pipe of the town would directly charge and supply the nine-inch service pipes of the Yard.

To convey the water through the Yard, there were two main services of pipes, one of twelve-inch pipe (with its branches), which completely ran through the Yard, and on which were 167 fire cocks and ten stop cocks. The other composed of nine-, six-, and in a few cases, four-inch pipes, with its branches, and on which were 159 fire cocks and nineteen stop cocks, making a total of 326 fire cocks and twenty-nine stop cocks. The fire and stopcocks had iron coverings, and their situation was indicated by large letters and figures on the nearest fence or building.

Keyham Yard

The water supply of this Yard was contained in three reservoirs near the terrace. These reservoirs each held 807 tons. One was fed with salt water (pumped by steam power), the supply being inexhaustible; the other two were fed with fresh water from the leat of the Devonport Water Company at the bottom of Haddington Road, entering the Yard under the East boundary wall near St. James's Church, by a four-inch pipe.

On the salt water pipes, there were forty-seven fire cocks and thirty-five stop cocks, and on the fresh water pipes, there were sixteen fire cocks and twenty-six stop cocks, making a total of sixty-three fire cocks and sixty-one stop cocks.

Directions of the Admiral Superintendent as to the Auxiliary Aid for Police in case of Alarm of Fire in Devonport and Keyham Yards.

By Day

1. When the gate bell rings quickly at any other time during the working hours than the usual ringing for going out or coming in, the labourers employed under the Boatswain, as previously told off for this purpose, are to proceed to the police engine houses, keep silence and await instructions from police.

2. That the labourers belonging to the Yard should, in addition to working the manual engines, work the fire ladders, fire hooks, and fire escapes; and that the ladders, hooks, and fire escapes should be used at every quarterly practice of fire engines.

3. In case of fire occurring during the dinner hour, the bell will be rung in the usual manner for fire; all strangers, women and children, are immediately to leave the Yard.

4. The Smiths, Hammermen, and Boilermakers, who dine in the Yard, are to proceed to the police fire engine house, to transport the engines to wherever ordered by the police. They were required to work them in relays under their officers, keeping silence and good order.

5. Any other person found to discontinue his work, whether established or hired, without permission, will be suspended for the first offence, and discharged for the second.

6. Whenever there is an alarm of 'Fire Stations' in the Yard, all persons in the offices are to remain at, and continue their usual duties, waiting for orders from their officers.

7. Permission is not given to any one to leave the offices to go and look at the proceedings, be they real or for instructional exercise.

By Night

1. In the event of fire occurring after the working hours, the Police will send to the Admiral Superintendent and Resident Officers, and make the night signal (two rockets fired together, continuing the same until answered by two blue lights from the flag ship) without delay for assistance from the ships in harbour. They will also give immediate information at the Raglan Barracks, where a fire party is nightly told off.
2. The Yard bells are not to be rung, nor the gates thrown open for the admission of people, without express directions from the Admiral Superintendent. The boats from ships of war are to be allowed to land men sent to assist at the fire, under the directions of the Police.

The Chief Engineer of the Yard was responsible for keeping the Sutherland steam fire engine in a state of immediate readiness around the clock. The police firemen were responsible for keeping hot coals burning in the No. 1 Engine House at all times, and in the event of the steamer being required, the hot coals were then shovelled into the fire box of the fire engine, and she was steamed up and ready to work within minutes. The Superintendent of Police would immediately send for the Chief Engineer, who would work the engine, and the Admiral Superintendent would order a driver and two horses to get the steamer to its working position.

In 1868, the Yards at Devonport and Keyham, along with the Royal William Victualling Yard, and the Royal Naval Hospital at Stonehouse, had the following plant at their disposal in case of fire:

Devonport Yard

No. 1 engine house, near the main gate:
- One steam fire engine (Sutherland)
- Seven manual engines

No. 2 engine house, North end of yarn house:
- Two manual engines

Keyham Yard

No. 1 engine house, main gate:
- Three manual engines

No. 2 engine house, South end of quadrangle:
- One manual engine

Royal William Yard

No. 1 engine house, near main gate:
- Three manual engines
- One hose reel

No. 2 brewhouse Arcade:
- One hose reel

Royal Naval Hospital

No. 1 engine house, rear of Captain Superintendent's Office:
- Three manual engines
- One hose reel

No. 2 near Agent's Office:
- One hose reel

Gun Wharf, Devonport

Police engine house, main gate:
- Three manual engines
- Two Hose reels

Royal Magazine and Laboratory, Bull Point, Devonport

Engine house, main gate:
- One manual engine
- One hose reel

Basin steps magazine:
- One hose reel

Water-gate laboratory:
- One hose reel

As well as the plant located within the fire stations, there were numerous hose reel stations, ladders, and fire hooks, distributed throughout all these establishments. At each of these establishments, several of the manual fire engines were to be kept fully kitted and in a state of readiness, should there be a request for assistance in the towns outside of their walls. Requests for assistance at fires outside of these establishments were first to be sought from the Admiral Superintendent, or Chief Officer of Yards.

The original Rope House and Great Square Storehouse, which were located in the original Yard, were reputedly destroyed by fire around the year 1769. The attempts to quell the conflagration proved very ineffective due to the crude fire apparatus available at that time, as well as a lack of properly organised firemen. It is interesting to note that at that time the extent of the Dockyard was only seventy acres.

In 1799 the original Dockyard chapel was destroyed by fire, and in 1817, at a cost of £24,000, a new church was built to replace the burnt out chapel. Sadly, this church was to meet a similar fiery fate, this time at the hands of the enemy during an air raid on the Dockyard in 1941.

Great changes were taking shape in the early years of Plymouth Dock, as in 1824, by Royal approval, Plymouth Dock changed its name to Devonport. To mark this momentous change, a one-hundred-foot column was erected at a cost of £2,750. This column is still there today, at the end of Ker Street, beside the old Guildhall.

By 1837, about twenty-five per cent of the Navy consisted of steam vessels, and the only steam yard was at Woolwich. This yard was hard pressed to meet with the demands of the Admiralty, and it was deemed necessary to establish further steam yards at Devonport, Portsmouth, and on the Mediterranean island of Malta.

The new steam yard was to be built at Keyham, and excavations began in 1844. Before the commencement of work, the large powder magazine at Keyham point was re-located to Kinterbury. Because it was not large enough to store the entire contents of the old powder magazine, the surplus was stored on five men-of-war, known as powder hulks, which were moored in the Hamoaze.

The new steam yard was opened in October 1853, even though it was not completely finished. So then they had the original dockyard to the south and the new steam yard to the north, with part of the town of Devonport separating the two yards. This arrangement was to prove very difficult in future years. The Dockyard police establishment was increased to cover the new yard, and two new fire engine stations were built, one near the main gate and the other at the south end of the quadrangle.

The two separate yards were clearly inconvenient, as in 1854 excavations were begun on a tunnel to join the two yards. Work was completed in 1856. At that time, a footpath ran through the tunnel, which was used by both pedestrians and horse and carts alike. This situation remained until the arrival of the steam railway in the Dockyards.

In 1851, the Dockyard police firemen moved from their old and cramped station, which was located beside the smith's shop on the dockside, into a new large fire station, which was near to the main gate in the original dockyard. The Policemen, performing fireman duties, were billeted above the stables and engine house, which were located on the ground floor. The station was on the top of a hill overlooking the site of the Great Fire, which occurred in the Dockyard in 1840. This building is still there today and was used as a fire museum from 2000–2010.

The Metropolitan Police firemen at Devonport Dockyard had their busiest year in 1882, with six major fires. In the March edition of the *Fireman* magazine for 1887, it showed that Devonport Dockyard had the Merryweather Sutherland steamer; three Merryweather large double cylinder steam fire engines and two small Valiant steam engines. Keyham Yard had two Merryweather medium double cylinder steam fire engines.

In 1896, a further 114 acres of land was procured, and work began on the extension to Keyham Yard to the north. After ten years of work, the Prince and Princess of Wales officially opened the extension on 20th February 1907. The new extension to the yard cost the nation £6,000,000.

Firefighting arrangements improved with the arrival of another new steam fire engine, a Merryweather Gem, bought for the Keyham Yard. Local arrangements were still in place for the fire brigades of the three towns to render assistance within the yards. By this time, each of the three towns had their own fire brigades, and the need to rely on the dockyard to provide fire pumps and manpower was drawing to an end.

A pair of Merryweather Gem steam fire engines outside of the Merryweather factory in Greenwich in 1900. One is destined for Devonport Dockyard and the other is for the Dockyard in Gibraltar. © Ron Henderson

It must be borne in mind that fire brigades, and their methods of dealing with outbreaks of fire, were still very crude, and in the early years of the fire brigades being formed, water damage played a major role in the extinction of fire.

After the First World War, the Metropolitan Police at Devonport Dockyard were under pressure to return to the metropolis, and the Admiralty instituted a force to be known as the Royal Marine Police, to replace them in the Royal Dockyards. This was not completed until 1934. Again, this police force was responsible for firefighting within the Dockyard and other naval establishments.

The newly appointed police force was hardly established before the outbreak of the Second World War was upon them. Their restrictive practice of recruiting policemen from Royal Navy and Royal Marine pensioners showed its weaknesses. It became necessary to enlist a new section of the force, known as the Royal Marine Police Special Reserve. Problems still existed with manpower, and a third force, the Admiralty Civil Police, was formed, and anyone, regardless of former military service, could join.

The Dockyard, along with the City of Plymouth, suffered terrible damage, with a large loss of life during the war years. Mr Albert Townshend, the Second Officer with the Exeter Fire Brigade, was seconded to the Admiralty in 1940, to reinforce and reorganise the police firemen within the Dockyard, and he became their Chief Officer. Before that, he served in Brighton for twelve and a half years, and rose to the rank of Acting Relief Sub Officer. In March 1935, Albert was appointed as Second Officer of the Exeter Fire Brigade; he was thirty-four years old. The following year he was awarded a silver medal by the Society for the Protection of Life from Fire, along with five other members of the Exeter Fire Brigade for gallantry displayed at the Guinea Street fire in Exeter in February 1936. Sadly, Mr Townshend was killed in North Yard, as a result of enemy action, in April 1941; he was thirty-nine years of age. Mr Townshend, who was born in Brighton, was eventually laid to rest in the Brighton and Preston Cemetery in Sussex. Devonport Dockyard was an important target for the German bombers, and numerous fire teams were put in place to help deal with the many outbreaks of fire that occurred following the air raids. Fires raged for days, both in and out of the dockyard, and the combined efforts of all the firefighters were pushed to the limits in order to provide adequate firefighting arrangements. Reinforcement firefighters were brought to Plymouth from all over the country to assist Plymouth in its time of need. Sadly, many of the firemen lost their lives during the Blitz on Plymouth and its Dockyard at Devonport.

Following the end of the war, the arrangements of policing the dockyards was reviewed, as the Admiralty found itself with three police forces, each with different conditions of service and discipline,

Mr Albert Townshend: he and five other firemen were awarded the Silver Medal by the Society for the Protection of Life from Fire, for their gallantry at a fire in Exeter. He became the Second Officer of the Exeter Fire Brigade in 1935. He was sent to Devonport Dockyard in 1940 to become the Chief Fire Officer; sadly he was killed by enemy action in North Yard, in April 1941.

but all under the same chief constable. In October 1949, the three forces were disbanded, and the new Admiralty Constabulary was formed.

Once again, the policemen performed fireman duties within the Dockyard. This time the firemen moved from the old station in South Yard to a new station at Albert Gate. The last fire engines to be at this station were a Dennis F12 Pump Escape and an Austin Towing Vehicle.

Following a change in policy within the Admiralty Constabulary, it was deemed that the Admiralty Police were no longer responsible for firefighting within the Dockyard, and the responsibility was handed over to the City of Plymouth Fire Brigade in 1969.

Dennis F12 pump escape (42 RN 75), seen on her way to retirement following the demise of the Dockyard Fire Brigade in 1969.

CHAPTER THREE

NOTABLE ACCOUNTS OF FIRES ATTENDED WITHIN THE ROYAL DOCKYARD AT DEVONPORT

THE EARLY YEARS of the Dockyard's history were marked by numerous fires and other tragedies. In 1691, the naval ship *Kent* exploded *en masse,* whilst firing a salute to the Admiral, in the Sound. Little or nothing could be done to lessen the impact of the disaster, and many seamen lost their lives at the time of the explosion, or in the immense fire which followed. In the same year, the *Exeter* exploded whilst at anchor in the Hamoaze, and the seventy-gun *Harwich* was wrecked off Mount Edgecumbe, with the loss of all hands.

On 2nd July 1761, reports were coming in of five separate fires being discovered at the same time within the Royal Dockyard. The fires quickly got a hold, and within a short space of time, there was a huge inferno. Once again, the primitive fire appliances proved vastly inadequate in dealing with such an outbreak, and damage was quite extensive. Arson was suspected but not proven, and damage was estimated at £49,900.

A second serious fire occurred in the Dockyard on 27th July 1770, causing considerable damage; once again arson was suspected. The art of fire investigation at that time was rather restrictive compared to the highly technical means afforded to the modern fire brigades of today, and the conflagration remained recorded as suspected arson, but not proven.

A further two attempts were made to maliciously set fires within the Dockyard, but were frustrated by vigilant watchmen. A Native American, James Aitken, a well-known arsonist, attempted to scale the Dockyard wall, but was put to flight by a watchful sentry. He made a second attempt to enter the Dockyard a short while later, but was again intercepted and put to flight. Thoroughly discouraged by his lack of success at Devonport, it was known that he made his way to Portsmouth, and was accredited to setting fire to the Ropery there. In 1775, the *Torbay*, which was anchored in the Hamoaze, burnt to the waterline despite all efforts to save her.

In January 1779, a watchman near one of the Hemp Houses put another unknown arsonist to flight. He made his escape, via a rope, over the Dockyard wall, which he used to gain entry. The would-be arsonist, in his haste to escape, left behind a basket containing an assortment of fire-raising materials, and a dark lantern.

Another large fire occurred in the year 1794 on the newly captured French warship *La Coquelle*, which was secured alongside the *Endeavor* in the Hamoaze. The fire broke out in the gunroom of the French ship and quickly spread throughout her lower decks. Within a short space of time, both she and

In 1796 an explosion of immense magnitude totally destroyed the naval frigate Amphion, which was anchored in the Hamoaze. Aboard the ship were over one hundred invited guests, including women and children, saying their goodbyes to the crew, who were about to sail on a mission for the Admiralty. It was reported that 300 people were killed instantly during this tragedy. © Chris Robinson

the *Endeavor* were blazing furiously, and despite valiant attempts to save them, they were left to drift to the muddy shoreline, where they both burnt out.

A most frightful and devastating tragedy occurred on 22nd September 1796, aboard the naval frigate *Amphion*, which was anchored in the Hamoaze. The ship was under sealed orders to leave on a mission for the Admiralty, and a leaving party was in progress. There were over one hundred invited guests, including women and children, saying their goodbyes to the crew. In an instant, the happy throng was giving forth terrifying screams, as a vast explosion ripped through the ship and transformed it into a giant holocaust. The ship quickly fell apart in the raging fire that followed, and within a very short time was totally destroyed. There was nothing that could be done to assist them, as the whole tragedy took only minutes to conclude its grisly task. Three hundred souls were reported to have perished in an instant, and only a few people survived. A Court of Inquiry was convened at a later date, and it was reported that a short time previously, the ship's gunner had been caught smuggling a bag of gunpowder ashore to sell, and that another bag of powder had been found, with its top disguised with ship's biscuits, ready for removal.

In 1813, two government ships, the *Captain* and the *San Josef* were secured together in the river Tamar; suddenly the *Captain* was seen to burst into flames. Help was quickly on hand, and after great physical efforts by the local workforce, the *San Josef* was towed away from the blazing *Captain*. So fiercely did the *Captain* burn that the night sky was illuminated brightly, and the Dockyard was bathed in artificial daylight. Despite all further efforts, the *Captain* was destroyed.

Two workers were killed at Kinterbury powder magazine on 26th January 1821, when a massive explosion destroyed the magazine. The victims were an elderly man and a young boy. Other members of the workforce escaped with minor injuries. So violent was the explosion that it was heard as far away as Liskeard, and a stave of a powder barrel was picked up in a street in Torpoint shortly after the explosion.

The Great Fire of 1840 in Devonport Dockyard

The biggest and most destructive fire within the Dockyard occurred on 27th September 1840; this fire was to be known in later years as 'The Great Fire of 1840'.

At six o'clock on the evening of Saturday 26th September, Mr Spiers, the carpenter of the ship *Talavera*, having finished his day's work, reported to the Admiral Superintendent to inform him that all was well on the ship. He then left the Dockyard and went home for the night. It was a still night with just a gentle breeze blowing from the north-west. The silence was only disturbed by the footsteps of the occasional sentinel doing his rounds. The Captain of the Guard, in the course of his rounds, passed the ill-fated *Talavera* at three o'clock. In addition, at half past 3 a.m., Inspector Carlyon patrolled past the ship; all was quiet at that time.

The *Talavera*, a ship of seventy-four guns, was under repair in the forward section of the Union Double Dock; behind her in the other dock was the *Mindon*. The Head Dock where the *Talavera* was lying was a roofed dock. The roof was constructed of Riga fir timber covered with paper, tarred and painted. The dock shed was 260 feet long, 125 feet at its widest point, and fifty feet above the level of the coping. The *Mindon*, a ship of seventy-four guns, was in the stern dock. The dock was not roofed at that time, as the original roof was blown off during a gale in 1836.

To the right of the covered head dock was a large work shed known as Adelaide Row and Gallery. The building was 200 feet long, and was used as a shipwright's work-shed, and a store house for trophies of war, such as figureheads and relics. The building was covered in a gable roof, open at both ends, and covered with tarred paper.

The *Imogene*, a ship of twenty-eight guns was lying in the oldest dock in the Yard, to the right of Adelaide Row. This dock was built in 1688, and was roofed in 1823. The dock was 240 feet long and 125 feet wide, and was thirty-nine feet high above the coping. The roof, like the roofs of the Adelaide Row and above the *Talavera*, was covered in tarred paper. Under this roof was stored about 1,000 deals of timber, which were the means of spreading the fire to the timber shed. To the right of the *Imogene* were the timber shed, sawpits, and other buildings.

At about quarter past 4 a.m., a policeman on his rounds saw smoke issuing from the stern ports of the *Talavera*. He immediately sprung his rattle to raise the alarm, whilst the sentinels fired blank cartridges. A messenger was quickly dispatched to the police station at the entrance to the Yard. Within ten minutes of the discovery of the fire, a fire engine was taken from the engine house and brought to the scene of operations. No sooner had the men began to pump the handles of the engine, than the thick black smoke gave way to a body of flames burning furiously through the lower deck ports on the larboard side.

The fire soon spread to the wooden standards supporting the shed, and within minutes, the fire spread along the horizontal beams creating a perfect arch of fire, before bursting through the combustible paper and tarred roof, lighting up the night sky. Hundreds of local residents and artisans employed in the Yard crowded by the Dockyard gates. Because it was impossible to subdue or check the spread of fire by the handful of men in the Yard, the alarm bell at the gate was rung furiously, and messengers dispatched to summon assistance from various establishments throughout the three towns. Within a relatively short space of time, the Royal Artillery, the 11th Regiment and the 65th Regiment arrived with their engines, along with a large body of men to work them. The West of England Insurance Company Fire Brigade, from Plymouth, soon arrived in fine style, with four horses pulling a magnificent and powerful manual engine; the brigade was under the command of Mr William Marshall, the Chief Officer.

The County Fire Insurance Office Fire Brigade was next on the scene, with Mr Carkeet as the Superintendent; again, this brigade came from Plymouth. Officers and men from the ship *Ordinary* brought fire floats, which were moored in the Hamoaze, to the scene. Fire engines, accompanied by hundreds of soldiers, seamen and marines, were brought to the fireground from all the military establishments in and

A scene of much activity and uproar at the Great Fire of 1840 in the Dockyard.

Small boats seen in the bright light of the Great Fire in the Dockyard in September 1840.

around the three towns. Within an hour from the alarm being sounded, thirty-six engines were playing on the fire.

The *Talavera* was now a burning mass, and the blazing dock shed soon ignited the vast quantity of timber adjoining the ship, which, in turn, seized upon the Adelaide Gallery. The Gallery not only contained the relics and figureheads of the fleets, but was full of deals and chests of tools belonging to the workforce. The fire spread at an alarming rate and the paper and tarred roofs of the Adelaide Row and frigate dock, where the *Imogene* was lying, was soon ablaze. The figurehead and bow of the *Minden* was also on fire. It was feared that the whole establishment was to perish in this conflagration.

The firemen directed their efforts into saving the *Minden* and preserving other buildings, as well as trying to check the progress of the fire by dragging combustible material away from the path of fire. They tore down the piles of timber, and threw them into the tidal basin to form firebreaks. The heat being generated by the fire was so intense that other buildings were badly scorched.

The sagacity displayed by the many horses employed in dragging away heavy timbers was incredible. They worked bravely amid the terrible heat and choking smoke. Shortly after the fire had broken out on the *Talavera*, the bow of the *Minden* ignited. Fortunately there was no shed above this ship, yet she was given up as lost. However, the bravery and determination of some of the workers saved the *Minden* from the same fate as the *Talavera*. The sluice gates to the docks were opened, and being high tide, the water rushed into the docks and because the 'Minden' had unplanked sections to her hull, the water soon filled her hold. The large amount of water jets being played upon the burning, hissing bow allowed an engine-man from the Dockyard to enter the burning ship and play a jet of water in such a manner as to check the flames' progress. With the assistance of the ship's carpenter and a few brave seamen, they rigged hand pumps, stopped the scupper holes, and flooded the main deck. Because of the fact that *Minden* was within twenty feet of the *Talavera*, it was a miracle that the ship was saved. Without the brave exertions of a few artisans, seamen and marines, the miracle would not have happened.

On the larboard side of the burning mass lay the *Canopus*, a ship of eighty-four guns, captured from the French. There was barely seventy feet between her and the head dock and the whole area was strewn with timber. The fact that the dock where she was lying had a roof covered with copper sheets instead of tarred paper saved the structure from a similar fate. The burning flakes which fell upon the roof did not pose an immediate danger.

Other ships which were lying nearby were towed to safety by the steamer *Carron*, and tied off to the *Spartiate*, lying in the Hamoaze. All efforts were now aimed at stopping the spread of fire, and not at trying to extinguish individual fires. Had the flakes of burning material, which were floating in the air like fiery birds, fallen on other fragile and combustible roofs within the area, then the nearby town of Devonport would have been in grave danger.

The sight and sound of the whole spectacle struck terror into all those spectators who clamoured to the Dockyard walls or lined the shores across the Tamar to witness the conflagration. The sounds of crashing timbers, the crackling and roaring of the fiery beast consuming all before it, the shouting of the firemen and artisans, and the hissing of burning timbers being hurled into the basin made for an audible spectacle. All this against a backdrop of bright light, heavy dense smoke and leaping shadows, which was mirrored in the calm water of the Tamar in front of the Yard.

By nine o'clock next morning, the Great Fire was got under control, but the *Talavera* and the *Imogene* were just hideous burnt out piles of blackened timber. Both were burnt to the waterline. The whole appearance of the Yard was that of utter devastation, shrouded with rising smoke and steam. With blackened faces, the hundreds of gallant firefighters were exhausted from their extraordinary efforts throughout the night. The fire engines pumped throughout the day to completely extinguish the fire, and to damp down the huge piles of charred debris strewn about in the four acres involved in fire.

There was much speculation as to the cause of the fire: even though arson was strongly suspected, it was never proven.

A. The *Talavera*, a ship of seventy-four guns, in which the fire started. The dots on each side of the docks denote the standards which supported the roofs; these were totally consumed in the fire. So intense was the heat that huge chunks of the dock, which were constructed of Portland stone, spalled off and crashed down into the dock.

B. The *Minden*, a ship of seventy-four guns, was taken into the stern dock at the same time as the *Talavera* was taken into the head dock. The gates which separated the two docks were already defective, but they were totally destroyed. The gates at the entrance of the stern dock were unaffected by the fire; the fire engine floats were stationed outside these gates and they supplied a good quantity of water to some of the fire engines at the stern of the *Talavera*.

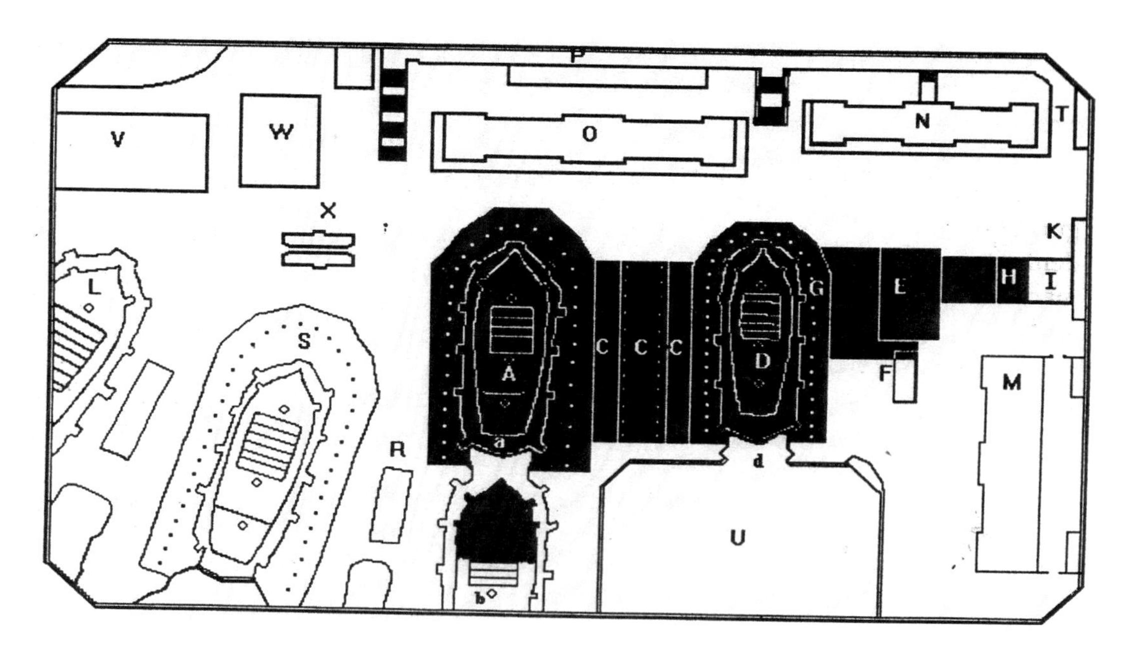

Plan of fire spread following the Great fire of 1840 in the Dockyard. The shaded areas show the extent of the fire.

C. Adelaide Gallery and Row, built in 1826 as a shipwright's work shed. Named after the then present Queen Dowager and used as the repository of the trophies, figureheads, and relics of the wars.

D. The *Imogene*, a ship of twenty-eight guns, completely gutted by the fire, along with the covered South dock. There were 1,000 deals of timber stored in there, and those were the means of extending the fire to the timber shed. The gates at the entrance to the South Dock were badly damaged by fire, and were reported unrepairable.

E. Timber Shed and Store, a wooden building with tarred paper roof was totally destroyed by fire. This store was only about twenty-five feet from the roof of the *Imogene*.

F. Brick built offices of the foreman of the float, which was only partially affected by fire.

G. There was a large quantity of deals piled up on the open ground between these buildings, which assisted the spread of fire to buildings E and F. The completely wooden building at E spread the fire into building H.

H. Saw Pits. The fire spread was effectively halted here, due to pulling down part of the Saw Pits, which created a fire stop, and prevented the fire reaching the timber pound I, next to building M. Several fire engines were gainfully employed here, playing vast quantities of water onto the timber pound. Had the fire breeched this area, the combustible buildings in its path would have put the town of Devonport in grave danger, as the distance was only about thirty feet from the combustible stores.

L. *St George*, North New Dock.

M. The Rigging House, a small limestone built building with slate roof, approximately fifty-five feet long and eighteen feet wide. More fire engines were at work here preventing the fire from entering the building. The sterling efforts made in preserving this building were paramount in preventing the destruction of the storehouses to the south of the Yard.

N. Officers' Offices. These buildings were badly scorched by the fire, and the radiated heat cracked the windows.

O. Joiners' Workshop and Clock. This building was only forty-five feet from the burning *Talavera* and the head dock roof. The firemen played jets of water onto this building to act as a water curtain. Men scaled the roof in order to throw water up to the cupola of the clock in the centre of the building, as there were great fears that the structure would catch. The heat was still very intense despite the water curtain. A lot of the lead on the roof melted and the clock face became red hot.

R. A Fire Engine House and Store. Only the direction of the wind prevented this wooden building meeting a similar fate to buildings on the windward side.

S. The *Canopus*. Had the wind been blowing from the South West, this roof also, and the *Canopus*, could well have been destroyed. The copper covered roof and the side of the building suffered severe scorching, but did not ignite. Had it done so, it would have endangered the *St George*, a ship of 120 guns, which was lying in the North New Dock, only seventy feet from the *Canopus*.

U. Boat Basin, in which all the extinguished timber was thrown.

V. The Smith's Shop.

W. The Fire Engine House and Store.

X. Suppling Kilns.

Further accounts of fires at Devonport Dockyard

Shortly before eleven o'clock on the night of 25th November 1864, the firing of guns from HMS Adelaide, the guard ship, aroused the inhabitants of the three towns. This unusual event, as may be imagined, created much alarm and it soon became generally known that there was a fire somewhere, but as to where the fire had occurred was unknown at that time. Within a short space of time, it became apparent that there was a fire within the Dockyard, as the Dockyard bell was being rung furiously, and alarm guns were firing. Thousands of people flocked to the Dockyard. The only visible sign from the outside was a dull red glow in the direction of the sawmills.

One of the Dockyard manual fire engines, manned by the police, was got out and taken to the scene. A good supply of water was obtained, and some of the firemen gallantly climbed onto the roof of the burning building in order to pour a continuous stream of water over the roof. This proved to be very effective, as it saturated the old timber roof and held the fire in check. Another manual fire engine arrived soon after the first one, and got to work in close proximity to the other engine. About five minutes after 11p.m. the fire engine from Raglan Barracks arrived, in charge of a detachment of the 2nd Queen's Own Regiment, in the command of Major Rock, closely followed by about 600 men of the same regiment. There was a delay in being admitted into the Yard, but once they were in, they set up on the north-west corner of the building, directing a hose through the windows of the building, which, by that time, was threatened with entire destruction.

Whilst all this was taking place however, orders had been given to place the steam fire engine Sutherland in working gear. It took about twenty minutes to get steam up, and almost simultaneously with entry of the 2nd Queen's engine, it steamed down to the place of action. Within a short space of time, it directed two powerful jets of water through the windows at either end of the building. As soon as the Sutherland was set to work, there was a visible effect produced upon the flames, which degenerated into a mass of black smoke.

At a quarter to twelve o'clock, the engine from Mount Wise Barracks arrived, in charge of about seventy engineers, under the command of Lieut. Fellowes, and set to work from the higher end of the western side. The West of England engine soon followed the engineers, but its services were not needed. By one o'clock, the fire was completely extinguished, but the engines continued pumping for some time afterwards to allay any fear of a fresh outbreak.

All the officials connected with the Yard were early on the spot, and every one worked right heartily to stop the progress of the fire; this practice was normal in those days. There were several detachments of men from the different regiments and garrisons, ordered to the Yard to render assistance, but they experienced appalling treatment, and complained bitterly. When they arrived, the Dockyard gates were closed against the public. The manner in which they were jostled about by the police and other military was disgraceful. Three soldiers of the 6th Regiment were stationed at the side entrance with fixed bayonets, and as the crush from behind was becoming rather severe, they presented their bayonets, making it by no means comfortable for those in the front ranks. There was general chaos at the Dockyard gates during times of fire, as the unruly mobs that always gathered, and the military, were often caught up in the disorder. The origin of the fire was unknown, and this was the first fire of any magnitude since the Great Fire that caused such devastation in September 1840.

A serious fire occurred aboard HMS *Agincourt* on 15th May 1873, while lying in dry dock, Keyham Yard, Devonport, with 300 men on board. Just before nine o'clock, a seaman was painting the lower gunner's storeroom, when he slipped and fell off his ladder, upsetting the oil lamp onto a heap of tow used for cleaning the ship's guns.

The flames quickly took over and a serious fire ensued. He raised the alarm. Within fifteen minutes, the Dockyard steam fire engine, the Sutherland, was alongside and steamed up, and drew water from the basin. The firemen also connected fire hoses to the fire plugs along the dockside and began pumping volumes of water down onto the fire.

The Metropolitan Police firemen, under the command of Supt. Wakefield, worked intensely to fight the inferno. The store where the fire broke out was sealed off, and the room was filled with water, to the level of the manhole. Many of the workmen still on board, along with a few firemen, were overcome by thick smoke below deck, and had to be dragged out by the other firemen.

As soon as the alarm of fire was given, the *Agincourt* hoisted signals, and Admiral Sir Henry Keppel, GCB, Port Admiral; Sir William King Hall, KCB, Supt of Dockyard and Capt. Fellowman, CB, quickly arrived on board. When all the danger had past, a court of enquiry was held, the result being declared as an accident. In consequence of the fire engine having been taken through the town, from Devonport to Keyham, the news of the fire spread quickly, and a crowd of several hundred assembled around the gate into Keyham Yard.

In 1879, the Thetis, which was berthed in Keyham Basin, became involved in fire. Once again good work was done by the firefighters, but they could not prevent the ship from suffering serious fire damage.

Shortly after four o'clock on the afternoon of 8th February 1882, dense volumes of smoke were seen issuing from the return junk and hemp store in Devonport Yard. The building was entirely constructed of wood, 140 feet long, twenty feet wide, and about thirty-five feet high. It was packed full of old junk, rope, and canvas returned from ships paid off, and awaiting conversion for Yard service or sale by auction as condemned stores. An alarm was very quickly raised, and the whole of the extensive appliances kept in the Yard for use in case of fire were hurried to the scene.

Despite the excellent organisation, and appliances, that enabled over six tons of water per minute to be discharged within so short a period upon the burning mass, it was obvious that, from the highly inflammable nature of the store, and from the firm hold the fire had obtained, the building and its contents were doomed. As the Rigging House, which was crammed with many hundreds of tons of tar, and the Sail Loft, containing thousands of pounds worth of sail canvas and manufacturing sails, were in close proximity to the raging inferno, it was considered advisable to order up the tugs. The whole of the available afloat service from the ships in harbour and the steam and manual fire engines from Keyham Yard were summoned. A large contingent of 500 seamen, marines, police and military were ordered to the fire. This was in addition to the 700 men on the books of the Yard, having regularly assigned fire stations and duties. All officials, naval, military and civilian, in the port, were, within a short period, offering their assistance to Captain A. J. Chatfield, Captain of steam reserve, and for the time being, acting Admiral-

The Merryweather Sutherland fire engine in the Royal Dockyard at Devonport in 1863; note the firemen with their stovepipe hats. Their fire tunics were red in colour.

Superintendent, who, with Mr Wakeford, Superintendent of the Metropolitan Police, took command of the huge firefighting force.

At a quarter to five, and within thirty minutes of the conflagration being discovered, the flames broke through the roof and lit up the Yard and harbour with a lurid glare. The immense bodies of water, however, being projected from every direction began to tell, and by sheer weight kept the seething mass within its own limits. As darkness closed in, it was evident that the surrounding buildings and contents would be saved, with the destruction being solely confined to the store in which the fire occurred and its contents, which were valued at £20,000. By six o'clock, the whole of the supplementary staff were dispensed with, and the firefighters, who were operating the manual and steam fire engines, were ordered to remain on duty for the night to flood the ruins. The cause of the outbreak was undoubtedly due to spontaneous combustion, the old hemp having frequently been found at almost combustion point, and, but for the ready means and exhaustless water supplies at hand, together with the tireless actions of the firefighters, the whole of the vast range of store houses would have been razed to the ground.

Storehouse Completely Gutted

Another fire in the Dockyard in June 1894 was attributed to the act of a workman leaving an unextinguished pipe in his coat pocket. The first notification of the outbreak was given at about 10.30 p.m., when a policeman belonging to the Devonport Borough Police, while patrolling his beat in the vicinity of Mutton Cove, perceived smoke issuing from the quadrangle. He hastened towards this area of the Yard, and having satisfied himself that one of the immense stores was on fire, made contact with the Metropolitan Police headquarters via a break glass fire alarm, and summoned help. Meanwhile the fire was making rapid headway, and the first firemen to arrive at the scene were faced with a huge wall of flame. The Commander-in-Chief at Mount Wise was contacted, and he ordered the general alarm be sounded. This was the successive firing of guns from HMS Devastation, the port guardship, and elsewhere. This alarm stirred the residents of the three towns, and caused great excitement.

While this was going on, the initial steps to deal with the fire had commenced in earnest, and a copious supply of water from the dockyard hydrants sent several jets of water upon the burning mass. The firemen seemed to be fighting a losing battle, as the large amount of water being played upon the fire had very little effect, the fire having plenty to feed upon.

The Dockyard steam engine, Sutherland, which was kept in a state of readiness twenty-four hours per day, was quickly horsed, and taken to the scene of the fire. The manual fire engines had previously been doing useful work under the very shadow of the burning building. It was decided to call on the Government tugs, *Aetna*, and *Scotia*, to render assistance, and they quickly took up their positions in the basin and began to deluge the building with huge amounts of salt water. In all, there was one steam fire engine, two manual engines, thirteen hose-reels and two admiralty tugs at work in quenching the flames. The Dockyard police were assisted by hundreds of bluejackets, who worked with commendable alacrity. From the outset, there was very little chance of saving the building, one of the few all-wooded buildings in the Yard, many of the older buildings having been replaced by more substantial erections. The fire was brought under control just after midnight. Throughout that time, both Devonport and Stonehouse Fire Brigades, with their steam fire engines, were in readiness outside the dockyard gates should they be required.

A Merryweather Hatfield trailer pump delivered to Devonport Dockyard in 1910. © *Ron Henderson*

The scene outside the dockyard gates was one of great unrest. The firing of the alarm guns brought crowds of people from all over the three towns, but they behaved dreadfully. By then there was a seething mass of people in Fore Street. There were equal amounts of soldiers and sailors, as well as civilians, who were very unruly, and fights were breaking out between all who were the worse for wear after drinking. The situation was so serious that the military were forced to drive the crowds back by brandishing their weapons with fixed bayonets. The scene had not been equalled in Devonport for many years, and it was most fortunate that the injuries were no more than bruised heads and torn clothing.

Devonport Yard had, by the year 1896, three large Double Vertical Merryweather steam fire engines, while the Keyham Yard had a Merryweather Medium double cylinder steamer. The Merryweather Sutherland was finally retired from active service in 1905, and was returned to Greenwich where it was re-boilered and refurbished, and kept in Merryweather's museum. In 1924 the Sutherland was gifted to

the Science Museum in London, where it was put into store at the former Royal Air Force establishment at Wroughton. It is still there today, and is reputed to be the oldest steam fire engine in the world.
The respective police-firemen of both Plymouth and Devonport Dockyard were tested to extremes on 15th July 1920, when a serious fire broke out in the clothing store in Mills block, Royal William Yard. The fire broke out at 12.30 pm, and the alarm was sounded. Plymouth firemen rushed to aid the Dockyard firemen, and Marines from the barracks at Stonehouse, hauled their manual fire engine to the scene to assist the firemen.

The Merryweather Sutherland steam fire engine after it was re-boilered and overhauled back at the Merryweather factory in Greenwich in 1905. This prize-winning fire engine was originally purchased for the fire brigade at Devonport Dockyard in 1863. © Ron Henderson

The fire was brought under control at 4 p.m. Despite valiant efforts of all in attendance, extensive damage was sustained to the building. The Dockyard also provided four tugs, which enabled the firemen to attack the fire from the tidal basin.
Another destructive fire occurred in 1921, this time to the No. 1 Storehouse, which was part of the Factory Block at Keyham. This original old building, which had wooded floors and staircases, sustained serious internal fire damage before being brought under control by the Dockyard and civilian firemen. The cause was believed to have been spontaneous combustion in a bale of cotton waste.
The whole of the Dockyard suffered greatly during the Second World War, and many of the details are still regarded as classified and therefore not for publication. During the hostilities, firefighting arrangements were put in the hands of the Admiralty. In the autumn of 1940, Mr Albert Townshend, former Second Officer of Exeter City Fire Brigade, was appointed as Chief Fire Officer of the Dockyard.

Sadly, as stated earlier, his association with the Dockyard was short lived, as he was killed as a result of enemy action soon after his appointment. Following the cessation of hostilities, the RN fire service was disbanded and the Royal Marine Police again filled the role.
The aircraft carrier *Implacable* suffered a serious fire in 1952; once again, the gallant efforts of the Dockyard and local authority fire brigades prevented an even more serious fire.

The Dockyard Police Fire Brigade lasted into the era of the Admiralty Constabulary, and many will remember the fire station to the side of Albert Gate. Firefighting arrangements for the Devonport Dockyard were eventually handed over to the City of Plymouth Fire Brigade in 1969, thereby ending

Devonport Dockyard Metropolitan Police Fire Brigade outside their fire station in the Keyham Steam Yard in 1903.

Smoke seen billowing from the windows of Mills block, Royal William Yard, in July 1920. Several fire floats, as well as the land brigade, managed to stop the spread of fire, which originated in the clothing block.

a relationship of over 100 years with civilian firemen. How strange it is to note, that in the early days of the three towns, the townsfolk of Devonport were very reliant upon the Dockyard firemen and their fire engines, and now the situation was to be reversed.

Plymouth's First Effective Fire Brigades

Prior to the formation of Fire Insurance Offices, the only form of compensation for someone's loss by fire was by a charitable collection taken from the townsfolk or wealthy businessmen within the community. The first Fire Office was opened in the Metropolis by Nicholas Barbon and a couple of partners in 1680; The fire insurance company was called the Fire Office. Other fire insurance companies were established within a short space of time, and business was on the increase in London.

Line up in Devonport Dockyard in 1942. The lorry to the left was full of hose and other pieces of equipment, and also towed a trailer pump. In the centre is the Merryweather Salamander pump escape, and on the right is the Leyland 100-foot turntable ladder. This TL was loaned to the Plymouth fire brigade after the war.

The Albion Merryweather Salamander seen in Devonport Dockyard in 1942; on this occasion it was crewed by naval personnel.

The Fire Office formed a fire brigade during its first year of business, and their firemen were dressed in bright livery. They were initially recruited from Thames Watermen, of which London had thousands; most plied their trade on the river Thames as operators of water taxis.

Dennis 'N' type motor pump fitted with a 500 gpm pump. This appliance was delivered to Devonport Dockyard on 4th October 1915. This was the first type of a motorised fire engine produced by Dennis brothers. © *Ron Henderson*

Merryweather Hatfield 1,000 gpm motor pump based in Devonport Dockyard. Note the huge diameter suction hoses. © *Ron Henderson*

Merryweather Greenwich Salamander with a Merryweather Telescala escape ladder (FMG 681), delivered in 1936. © Ron Henderson

By the 18th century, there were numerous Fire Offices operating their own fire brigades within London and other cities throughout the country. Some fire offices would fix metal badges, known as Firemarks, to the insured properties. This really was no more than fancy advertising, which might persuade others to insure their properties through the same office. There exists, in many historical books, a fact that states that insurance companies would only attend and extinguish fires in buildings currently insured by them, and where their mark was affixed. This is largely a myth, as apart from their early beginning, which was true of some companies, there is nothing to substantiate this claim in later years in any of the research carried out on the insurance offices. The company firemen wore brightly coloured uniforms with very ornate badges fixed upon the sleeve, or in some cases, on the breast. Great rivalry existed among the different fire brigades during their early years, and in a lot of cases, monetary rewards were offered for the first three fire engines to reach the fire.

Insurance company fire brigades were by now operating in towns and cities throughout the length and breadth of the country. These men were mainly volunteers, who had employment elsewhere, and were summoned in case of fire, similar to volunteer or retained firemen today. Not all insurance companies maintained their own fire brigades, but many would donate sums of money, on an annual basis, to various places around the country, for the maintenance of the fire plant. Some companies also donated leather fire buckets and hose, and sometimes they provided funds to purchase new uniforms.

It is recorded that in the year 1776 various Plymouth insurance offices began to contribute sums of money each year towards the upkeep of the Corporation fire engines, and for the repairing of buckets and hose.

With the reorganisation of the police force in Plymouth in November 1836, to comprise a superintendent, three inspectors and twenty-seven constables, much better fire protection was afforded the three towns and district, although the City Fathers still failed to realise their responsibility to safeguard the lives of the public. It was left to fire insurance companies to equip fire brigades, or provide their own brigades, and for a quarter of a century the duty of providing protection from fire was discharged by them without cost to the ratepayers.

It would appear that the first effective firefighting service in Plymouth was formed in 1838, when the West of England Insurance Company formed a fire brigade there, with their agent Mr William Marshall elected as their Chief Officer, Supt J. E. Adams, Foreman J. Swigg, twelve firemen and two torch boys. Among the personnel forming the brigade were: Chief Officer W. Marshall, Second Officer C. J. Brooks, Foreman J. Swigg, Firemen J. Bailey, J. Voden, W. Crocker, W. Voden, J. Good, G. Glanville, W. Brian, J. Cornish, G. L. Philp, and torchboy J. T. Crocker. The fire station was in Cornwall Street and their main appliance was a Shand Mason thirty-man manual pump, christened Firefly. Their cover extended to a radius of about twenty miles around Plymouth. Their uniform consisted of a leather helmet, blue coat with red adornments, plush green velvet breeches, thigh length leather boots, belt and tomahawk. On the breast of the coat was a brass plate depicting the company coat of arms, and the fireman's number.

In those distant days, the West of England Fire Brigade must have made a thrilling picture as they dashed along darkened roads, with torch bearers standing on the front of the engine holding lighted torches to light the way, their appliance swaying along behind four galloping horses with postillion riders.

The first fire call attended by the West of England Fire Brigade was on September 17th 1838, at Hill's Shipbuilding Yard at Cattedown. The engine was horsed from the Globe stables in Frankfort Square. The West of England Fire Brigade turned out to all fires within the area, and did sterling work at all of them, dispelling the myth that insurance brigades only dealt with fires in buildings displaying their fire mark, and only insured by that company. The West of England Fire Brigade in Plymouth was highly commended in a book *Fires, Fire Engines, and Fire Brigades* written by Charles Young in 1866, and was described as one of the most professional brigades in the country. However, Charles Young went on to say that the brigade had been subjected to constant annoyance and interference from the police, and other paid servants of the public, who were unable, it seems, to understand or appreciate the spirit which actuates a volunteer. This line of conduct unfortunately, was not only confined to Plymouth, or the paid servants of the public, as many examples of harassment frequently occurred in London and elsewhere.

On the death of Mr William Marshall in February 1882, the agency was taken over by Mr W. Derry, and the fire station was transferred to Station road, (Union Street). Mr C. J. Brooks had then become Superintendent of the brigade and Mr W. Crocker the Foreman. Mr Crocker and four men, lived at the station. To commemorate their Jubilee, the brigade was supplied with new uniforms at the end of 1888. The leather helmets were replaced with brass fire helmets, and their brass breast badges were removed. Eventually the brigade was disbanded in 1891, after fifty-three years' service. Further tributes to this fine and respected fire brigade can be found later in this book.

The West of England Fire Brigade attended hundreds of fires in the three towns, including the Great Fire in the Dockyard in 1840. Some of the other notable district fires attended were:

Marley House, Brent, 1840
Langdon Hall, Wembury, 1843
Turpin's Stables, Plympton, 1852
Cann House, Tamerton Foliot, 1862
Brent Flock Mills, 1863
South Devon Powder Mills, Millbrook, 1864
Littleton's Farm, Saltash, 1867
Langdon Farm, Wembury, 1868
Cargreen Manure Works, 1870
Trematon Farm, Saltash, 1871
Hamlyn's Wool Factory, Horrabridge, 1871
Spurrell's Farm, Eggbuckland, 1871
Kitley Stables, 1873
Yealmpton Mills, 1879
Loughter Mills, Plympton, 1884

The County Fire Insurance Office also had a Volunteer Fire Brigade in Plymouth, which was established in 1838, with Mr John Carkeet of Woolster Street as their agent and superintendent of the fire brigade. This small brigade also attended many fires in the area, and they were also present at the Great Fire in the Dockyard in 1840.

This brigade was disbanded in 1863, and soon afterwards, the Borough Corporation formed their first fire brigade in Plymouth. They took possession of the fire engines and equipment, which was gifted to them by the County Fire Office – a generous contribution to the newly formed brigade.

Another insurance company to establish a fire brigade within Plymouth was the Liverpool and London and Globe Insurance Company, whose headquarters and fire station was in Westwell Street. Their Chief Officer was Mr Thomas Raddan, a Shoeing Smith, the second officer was Mr Kempe, and six of his employees made up the rest of the brigade. The insurance agents for Plymouth were Messrs Plimsaul, T. W. Bastow, Gibson and Harris.

The Liverpool and London and Globe Fire Brigade was the first brigade within Plymouth to have a steam fire engine. They had a Merryweather 350 gallon per minute pump, and the engine was horsed from the Royal Hotel stables, which was nearby. Among the fires they dealt with was one at Snawdon and Northey's furniture works in Union Street in July 1873. While pumping from the dam, a large trout came through the main, and the fish was kept, and preserved in spirit for many years in the office of the West of England Insurance Company. The brigade was short-lived, and they were disbanded in 1876.

Members of the Liverpool and London and Globe Insurance Fire Brigade aboard their steam fire engine near to their headquarters in Westwell Street c.1875. I apologise for the poor quality of this photograph, but this is the only known picture of this brigade in Plymouth, and I consider it worthy of inclusion.

In 1888, the Western Insurance Company came to Plymouth to set up business. Even though they did not maintain their own fire brigade, they did present Plymouth Corporation Fire Brigade with a new Merryweather steam fire engine, which was handed over with considerable ceremony. The presentation was made in Guildhall Square and invites were sent to fire brigades in Devon and Cornwall, and dignitaries of the three towns, along with high ranking officers of the Military and Admiralty. The ceremony was precluded with a powerful demonstration of the steam fire engine, which won praise and approval from all present, including hundreds of local residents, who clamoured to witness the spectacle.

CHAPTER FOUR

DEVASTATING FIRES WITHIN THE THREE TOWNS

Fatal fire in Devonport

IN THE EARLY hours of January 1840, smoke was seen issuing from the cupola of the Royal Hotel, Devonport. The seat of the outbreak was a bedroom occupied by Colonel Horndon, of Callington. The West of England brigade, and pumps from the Royal Dockyard and Raglan barracks were summoned, along with the parish pump, which was hauled to the scene. Upon arrival, it was noticed that a serious fire could be seen through several of the upper windows. Hanging out of one of the windows was the Colonel himself, in a dreadful state of alarm. Before the Colonel could be reached, the floor dropped, carrying the aged occupant with it. Guests and servants lost their way in the corridors, and it was only the shouts of the rescuers that enabled them to escape, blackened and burnt, to the open air. Bursting through the roof, the flames shed an illumination over the town, and, with the collapse of the walls, the parish pump was buried beneath the debris. Once again, the West of England men performed admirably, and they were duly assisted by the men from the Royal Dockyard, their brave exertions preventing further loss of life in what was a bad fire.

Norley Street fire

On Wednesday 16th March 1849, shortly after nine o'clock at night, an alarm of fire was given in Norley Street Plymouth. Flames were seen issuing from a workshop occupied by Messr Rundle, cabinet makers, situated at the back of extensive premises in that street, and adjoining the wall of a large chapel in Ebrington Street, home of the Plymouth Brethren. Within a short space of time, the County Fire Office and the West of England Fire Brigades were on the spot with their respective fire engines. The former, under the judicious management of Mr Carkeet, took up a position in Ebrington Street. The firemen carried the hose through the chapel, and full command of the fire was had. A good supply of water was immediately obtained, and the effects of their powerful engine on the fire was soon visible. Indeed, it was admitted by those who took an active part during that evening, that it was chiefly down to the good positioning of the County engine that the flames did not extend much further, and that greater damage was not sustained.

The West of England engine took its station in front, and after some little delay from want of water it commenced pouring a vast column on the fire, under the able directions of Mr Marshall, thus checking the spread of the devastating element towards the front of the house and adjoining premises.

The Customs House and Citadel engines were brought to the scene with great promptitude. Both rendered good services, and with the joint efforts of all the brigades, the fire, which burnt very vividly for nearly two hours, was got under control. The workshop and all the property in it were destroyed. The back of the house adjoining was also seriously damaged. Glass in several of the windows of the chapel was shattered, due to the radiated heat. In addition, the tenants of the property lost a considerable amount of their furniture and belongings.

There were upwards of twenty children, besides adults, in the house. Most of the former were in bed when the fire was discovered. Fortunately, nobody sustained any personal injury, though the loss of furniture and belongings was severely felt. The Officers and men of the 28th Regiment were also quickly on the spot, after the alarm was given. Too much praise cannot be given them for their promptitude and energetic services. W. Burnell, Esq., the Mayor, and Mr Gibbons with the police were also present, rendering every assistance. The general inhabitants of the neighbourhood appeared to vie with others in their endeavours to render efficient aid.

It was supposed the fire originated by the igniting of shavings in the shop, after the men had left work. Mr Rundle was insured with the West of England Fire Office, and Mr Southall, the owner of the premises, with the Globe Fire Office. This was further proof to dispel the myth of insurance company fire brigades only putting out fires in premises insured by themselves.

No sooner had all the interested parties of the fire in Norley Street returned to their respective fire stations and barracks, than another alarm of fire was received. The firemen, barely rested, were called out again at two o'clock in the morning of the 17th March, to premises in Union Street. The fire was in the valuable property of Mr Ponsford Fisher, a tallow chandler. Flames were issuing simultaneously from every quarter of the factory, the contents of the workshops and stores being of combustible materials – tallow, oil, cotton, etc. The West of England engine, with Mr Marshall, was first to arrive, having being taken there by the Plymouth Police, under the direction of Inspector Cole (Mr Gibbons and several others being absent and at the assizes). Within eighteen minutes of the alarm being given, this engine was in full play, an ample supply of water having been obtained. It was admirably worked, and great praise was later heaped upon the police and fire brigade for the efficient way they went about their work.

The County Fire Office Brigade, under the superintendence of Mr Carkeet, whose zeal nothing could exceed, and the Royal Hospital, Royal Marine, and Citadel engines, quickly followed, and were also quickly in full play. By their united efforts, the raging fire, which was subdued within two hours, was confined to the building in which it commenced. Great fears at one period were entertained, not only for the safety of Mr Fisher's dwelling house, from which it was at one time contemplated to make separation, by pulling down a portion of the outbuildings which connected to the premises, but also the Brewery, the Central Hall, and other valuable property which surrounded it. But fortunately, from the judicious management observed, and from the very able and powerful assistance rendered, the destructive element was kept down. Nothing could exceed the awful appearance of the fire, when at its greatest height: the horizon was most brilliantly illuminated for a great extent, and lurid flames would sometimes be seen to shoot into the air, carrying with it dense columns of smoke. This would be followed by flakes of bright flame rushing up from the glowing embers. In fact, at one period, the entire site of the workshops, lofts, etc., looked as one immense burning cauldron, the fierce flames almost appearing as if nothing could subdue their raging.

The 28th Regiment, under the command of Col. Messiter, and the Royal Marines, commanded by Col. Mitchell, with a division of men from HMS *Agincourt*, were soon in attendance, and rendered great aid. Captain Toup-Nicholas and Lieutenant Pulloh, from the Royal Hospital, were also present, and gave the most efficient services in directing the energies of the men to the proper quarters. William Burnell, Esq., the Mayor of Plymouth, kindly rendered his assistance, as well as the Stonehouse Police, who were also very active.

It was never established how the fire started. The whole of the property in the warehouse was destroyed, but it was pleasing for the reporters to be able to report that there was no serious injury or loss of life.

A letter was received by Mr Marshall, of the West of England Fire Brigade on the 22nd March, five days after the fire, from Captain Superintendent Toup-Nicholas, RN Hospital. He praised the actions, bravery, and efficiency of the men under his command, stating that all of his men, especially firemen Good and Bailey, should receive some sort of reward for their actions. It isn't known whether or not these men were indeed rewarded, but this was just one of the numerous accolades that the men of this brigade received during its existence.

Terrible fire and loss of life on the Barbican

A report in the *Plymouth, Devonport, and Stonehouse Herald* for 10th June 1848, describes a fatal and disastrous fire, which occurred in No. 2 the Parade, on the Barbican. The premise in which the fire commenced belonged to Mr Samuel King, who, with his wife, occupied a portion of the upper part of the house. The other tenants being Mr Issac, a Jewish man who carried on the business of a waterproofs manufacturer, with his wife and children; Benjamin, a Jew and general dealer; and a seaman named Hammond, with his wife and children.

Shortly after four o'clock in the morning, a tremendous noise was heard in the neighbourhood, as if a number of cannons had been discharged, and within a minute, flames were seen issuing from the lower part of the house. The alarm soon spread, but before a dozen persons had congregated, the entire front appeared in a complete blaze, the raging element spreading with an indescribable rapidity.

Mr Issac, and a porter named Witheridge, had been decanting a quantity of combustible oil into cans in the ground floor shop when an accident occurred, causing the combustible liquid to catch on fire. Mr Issac, on seeing the danger, ran upstairs and alarmed the other residents and his wife and children. The lodger, Benjamin, escaped half naked into the street, but unfortunately, the other persons, from the delay of only a minute or two, were cut off from reaching the lower part of the house and became trapped.

By now, several of the neighbours were in the street, having being woken by the initial explosion and subsequent screams of the trapped persons. A couple of men, Mr J. Stevens and Mr Buckingham, were dispatched to Mr Carkeet's premises in Woolster Street, for the County fire engine, which they brought to the Parade in a very short space of time.

A ladder was procured from a nearby builder's yard, and was placed against the front of the building. One of the trapped residents, Mr Samuel King, climbed onto the ladder and began making his way down. About thirty feet from the ground, the ladder broke, and he fell to the street below, among the burning embers. Although badly injured and suffering terrible burns, he survived.

While this distressing scene was passing in front, a more appalling affair was to be witnessed at the back of the house. Here, at the windows, were seen Mrs King, Hammond the seaman, his wife, and four children, the flames flirting around them in every direction, most piteously beseeching help. Their cries for help became even stronger and more harrowing, as all hope appeared to be cut off. At last, after a delay of a minute or two, another ladder was procured and placed against the only window accessible, scarcely eighteen inches wide. Through this small aperture, about forty feet from the ground, Mrs King first got out and was saved. Mrs Hammond followed, with a three year-old child in her arms. Then Mr Hammond, with another child of about thirteen years old, also got down the ladder. They were at great risk from the flames, being all more or less burnt.

By this time, the fire had extended, and was burning with such intense fierceness in every direction that those supporting the ladder were enveloped in flames, and were obliged to retreat from the spot. Conscious that there were still two persons in the house, the children of Hammond, several attempts were made, but it was clear that all efforts would be in vain. The fire had reached the window, and amidst the heart rendering cries of the affected parents, the children perished; the floors and roof falling in soon after.

Within a short time after the alarm had been given the County, West of England, Custom House, Distillery and Citadel fire engines were in full play. The power of the West of England fire engine, under Mr Marshall's directions, which had seen the inevitable destruction of the house where the fire originated, was directed to preserve Mr Stevens' house, and fortunately, they were successful.

Street fire escape which was kept in various locations in the town. This particular escape was located in the Barbican area c.1870, and was manned by an Escape Fireman, who used to live nearby and was responsible for getting the escape to a fire.

The police, under the directions of Mr Gibbons, the intelligent Superintendent, were very early in attendance, and on this, as well as on other similar occasions, their services were most valuable. The 35th Regiment, under the command of Colonel Wilson from the Citadel, worked tirelessly in pumping the military engines, and keeping control of the crowds of onlookers. The fire raged with intense violence for nearly two hours, until at about half past six, it was clear that the fire was got under control.

A number of men were employed during the morning, in search of the bodies of the unfortunate sufferers. At ten o'clock, they were found lying close together on the remains of the bed, which, no doubt, had sunk through the floors with them. They were dreadfully burnt, presenting a most distressing spectacle.

Fire and loss of life at Cattedown

The Plymouth firemen were once again called to a most destructive fire, with loss of life, on Thursday 3rd March 1853, in the premises of Mr Ellis, a rope maker, in the Cattedown area of Plymouth. The premises consisted of a dwelling house, stores and ropewalk, about 200 yards in length.

It appears that about a quarter to twelve o'clock, Mr Ellis had returned home after an evening out, when, on opening the front door, a volume of fire instantly burst forth. He immediately raised the alarm, which aroused Mr Henry Macey, another resident in the house, his wife, and five of their children, who chiefly through the exertions of the husband were safely rescued from their perilous position.

The burning house, however, still contained another of Macey's children, a fourteen-year-old daughter, who slept in the upper part of the house, and the father again entered the blazing house, in the hope of rescuing her. The wife and other children were then removed to a neighbour's house, and nothing more was thought of Macey for an hour or so. When enquiries were being made, and he not being found, it was conjectured that he had fallen a victim to the flames, which unhappily proved to be true. During an examination the following morning, of the ruined remains of the dwelling house, the discovery of some human bones, blackened and charred by the fire, left no doubt, that Macey, in an endeavour to save his other child from a fearful death, perished with her in the attempt.

In the meantime, two powerful fire engines arrived with the County Fire Office Brigade, commanded by Mr Carkeet. A good supply of water was obtained and the engines were soon at work upon the fire. Within the hour, the other fire engines and men in attendance were: the West of England Fire Brigade, under Mr Marshall; the Citadel fire engine, with a strong body of officers and men, and the engine from HM Dockyard with Sergeant Cox and a number of the police force. There was no more thought of Mr Macey until his frantic wife pleaded with the firemen as to his and her other daughter's whereabouts. By now the whole of the complex was burning fiercely, including the thatched ropewalk, which contained one hundred barrels of tar. Despite the united exertions of all the men, the premises were burnt to the ground.

The cause of the fire remained unknown, but it was believed to have originated in the dwelling house. Had the return of Mr Ellis to his home been delayed a few minutes longer, the whole family of the poor Macey would have perished. With the house being filled with smoke, they would surely have been suffocated before the fire reached them.

His daughter was a girl about fourteen years of age. Their remains were found at some distance from each other. It was conjecture that when the unfortunate man reached the bedroom in which the child slept, he discovered that she had gone into some other part of the house. While searching about for her, he was suffocated himself.

Devonport enjoyed immunity from big fires until February 1855, when Mr Hudd's spirit stores in Fore Street caught fire. It was impossible to work the parish engine, in consequence of the want of water, and the flames were reaching to the opposite side of the street, roofs and walls soon crashing there as well. The West of England Brigade, the County Fire Office Brigade, and military engines were soon on the scene and a reasonable water supply was obtained. The firemen worked in freezing conditions, and a piercing wind blew in furious gusts. Frost coated the hats of the firemen, and icicles formed on the scorched timbers. Luckily, no lives were lost, and no major injuries were reported, but once again, the fire and the destruction it caused won the day, and the firemen, who were chilled to the bones, were left to damp down the smouldering ruins.

Terrible fire in Southside Street

Shortly after midnight on Monday 5th April 1859, a fire was discovered in a house in Southside Street, occupied by a greengrocer named Mr Stevens. It appears that a daughter of Mr Callard, a fish dealer, of Stokes Lane, had been sent out to get some supper drinks. On passing Mr Stevens' house, she saw an unusual light in the shop, and, on further examination, discovered that the place was on fire. She rushed back to her father, and Callard immediately proceeded to the spot and roused the inhabitants. By this time, the flames had spread very considerably, and it was with no small difficulty and danger that many of the poor persons who lived in this and the adjoining houses escaped with their lives. After the alarm was given, Callard was exceedingly active, not only in rescuing the women and children from their impending danger, but in saving the furniture, clothes, etc. He was ably assisted by Mr Martin, of the Parade, whose laudable exertions merited much praise. The town engine, under the management of Mr Carkeet, was soon on the spot, closely followed by the West of England and their active fire brigade. The Citadel and Dockyard engines were also present. It was soon realised that the water mains were dry, despite the fire plug being opened.

The flames spread rapidly, and before the engines could be got to work, the house was in a complete blaze, and the fire had extended to the adjoining house, which led to the old Mitre Court. Detachments of the 2nd Warwick Militia, under the command of Captains Digby and Carew, Lieutenants Vaughton and Grieves, and the 2nd Battalion of the 17th, under the command of Lieut. Colquhour, Ensign de Bros and Quartermaster Faulkner, rendered more valuable services, not only in pumping the engines, but in the preservation of order and the protection of the property. Mr Superintendent Codd and the police were early on the spot. The Custom House engine was also brought to the scene, but was not got to work. The engines, after obtaining a supply of water, played with good effect. The flames were fortunately prevented from reaching Mr Walling's premises to the west, or Mr Glover, the grocer, to the east, though the latter premises were slightly damaged by the ignition of a beam which joined the Stevens house.

It was evident, after the engines had been in play for some time, that the fury of the fire was being overcome, and at two o'clock there was no further fear that the fire might extend. The damage sustained was, however, very extensive. Mr Stevens' house was completely destroyed, and the Royal Oak beer shop, adjoining, shared the same fate. Mr Stanbury's bakery sustained considerable damage. Mr Stanbury had his stock insured with the British Empire Mutual Fire Office, for a sum of £100, but his loss far exceeded that amount. The houses destroyed were the property of Mrs Bayly, a widow of the late Mr Bayly of Stonehouse, and were insured with the Phoenix Fire Office for a sum of £1,700. A large number of poor persons suffered losses which were of the most serious importance to them, and which some never redeemed by their own exertions, and were glad to find that a relief fund had been set up for them.

Large fire in the centre of Plymouth

A huge and most destructive fire took place in the very midst of the busiest part of Plymouth on 17th April 1861; a range of buildings was burning furiously. There had not been a big fire of any significance within Plymouth for two years, but this conflagration was to test the skill and resilience of all the firemen and military that attended. The following report was printed in the *Western Daily Mercury* on the day following the huge fire:

> It is not often that we are called upon to record, amongst the multitude of events, pleasant and calamitous which transpire from day to day in the three towns of Plymouth, Devonport, and Stonehouse, and a catastrophe as sad as a destructive fire. The beneficent law of compensation would seem to have special instance of its universal operation in this locality. For while we are exposed to losses of life and property to a great extent by water, probably no town or towns of equal size and population in the United Kingdom, can be said to be more exempt from the terrible effects of fire. But a painful exception to this rule occurred yesterday, within a few yards of the office of the *Western Daily Mercury*, and in the very midst of the busiest part of Plymouth. During four hours in the height of the day, the fiery scourge extended itself from point to point of a combustible stack of buildings filled with materials of the most dangerous kind, at such a time devouring all before it. Since the total destruction of the Flour Mills of Messrs Hurrell and Crossin, on Tavistock Road some years ago, no similar event of equal magnitude with that which we have now to record, has taken place. When, however, it is remembered that no fire of any importance whatever has occurred within the borough for fully two years, there is much room for congratulation than that of yesterday was not even more extensive.
>
> The scene of the fire was the space between George Street on the South, Courtney Street on the West, Frankfort Street on the North, and Frankfort Lane on the East. All our Plymouth readers were familiar with the elegant shop of Mr Madge, cabinet maker and upholsterer, on the North side of George Street. But all will not have been so well acquainted with the premises in connection with the establishment in which the labour was performed which resulted in the contents which adorn the furniture emporium to the front. The range of buildings contained many shops, warehouses, stables, hotel, and spirit store, workshop and timber yard, and various offices. The fire was thought to have started in the carpenter's workshop above the shops. Many of the buildings involved were made of wood, which added to the rapidity of the spread of fire.

Police hose reel as used extensively by the Police Fire Brigade in Plymouth. These reels were located throughout Plymouth and could be easily brought to the scene of fire. A standpipe would be set into the water main and the hose would unreel from the hydrant to the fire.

Before long, the alarm spread throughout the town, and thousands of people flocked to the spot. A body of policemen, under the direction of Superintendent Codd, Inspector Damerel, and Sergeants Murch and Coombe, arrived very shortly, and within a few minutes, the new engine of the West of England Fire Brigade was brought into the street (this was a thirty-man manual engine from Merryweather's). Unfortunately, the great essential, water, was not forthcoming, and for some time the supply was dependant on contributions from neighbouring tanks and wells. In the emergency, the tank of the *Western Daily Mercury* was found useful, and the employees, and many others, rendered service by carrying the water in buckets, to the spot. The reason for the shortage of water was that nobody knew the whereabouts of the fire plugs, and the men from the water works company were called to find the plugs.

By now, the fire was spreading furiously. In quick succession, the County Fire Insurance Company's engine and the engines from the Royal Victualling Yard, the Naval Hospital, the Marine Barracks, the Citadel and the Custom House were brought to the scene by the military, the marines, and the police. The blaze was out of control and spreading at an alarming rate before the fire plugs were found and an adequate supply of water was procured. The Mayor of Plymouth, W. Luscombe, Esq., arrived at the scene, accompanied by the magistrate of the borough. Three hundred marines were mustered at the barracks and marched to the scene, calling for the Millbay engine on their way. By four o'clock in the afternoon, the fire was virtually extinguished, but the engines continued to pour vast amounts of water onto the smouldering ruins.

All afternoon, the avenues leading to the site of the conflagration were crowded with spectators, who would barely break the restraint imposed on them by the soldiers, who stood, with fixed bayonets, at every corner, and who lined the principal streets. This restraint was not without its beneficial results, for it prevented the undue crowding and interference of the populace which too often accompanies catastrophes of this nature. One question, which suggests itself in the review of the catastrophe, is why the fire plugs could not be found, and the water turned on in cases of danger, by the police. It was the practice in other towns to affix a sign to the wall opposite each fire plug, but not so in Plymouth and the civic dignitaries were urged to address this matter with urgency.

It is very interesting to note that the problems and delays in locating suitable fire plugs were not only confined to the above reported fire. Ever since the introduction of a fire brigade in the borough of

Plymouth in 1838, there had been numerous fires where the same delays were reported. There is no direct evidence to show that action to remedy the problem was immediately forthcoming, as further reports of the same situation appeared in newspapers in the years which followed. Today, there are still walls and buildings throughout the older parts of Plymouth which have a white metal plate with the letters 'FP' on them; this was the marker to denote that the fire plug was close by. Nowadays, of course, every fire hydrant has an indicator plate associated with it, detailing its exact location, which makes it easy for the firemen to locate them.

Burning of a government ship in Plymouth Sound

The denizens of Plymouth, Stonehouse, Devonport, and the surrounding locality had been visited with their full share of conflagrations that appeared to abound throughout the country, with all the accompanying alarm, excitement, danger and, in some cases, pleasure. The Millbay Soap Works, the rope manufactory at Teats Hill, the stabling premises in Union Place and the bakery in Saltash Street, which were all attacked and reduced to ruin within a remarkably short space of time, still remained on the landscape as blackened and charred ruins, as if they were monuments to the fiery monster. Rising above the waters beneath the heights of Jennycliff Bay were to be seen the masts of the *Lady Franklin*, the American vessel burnt and sunk in the Sound towards the end of 1861. Again, on 23rd February 1862, another wreck, inferior to none of these in dimensions or importance, was seen the following morning from the Stonehouse and Plymouth side, and from the waters of the Sound itself, lying beneath the shadowy woods of the Mount Edgecumbe domain.

The ship *Paragon*, of Whitstable, a finely built schooner of about 200 tons burthen, left the basin of the Royal William Victualling Yard at Stonehouse, ran down Sutton Pool and through the harbour entrance, round St Nicholas Island (Drake's Island), and out to sea. She had on board 1,400 bags of biscuits, which she chartered to convey to Deptford for the government. There was a very strong wind blowing, which had increased to gale force, and to get up the channel with a head wind such as had been blowing for a couple of days, was a task so difficult that more nautical men than the master of the *Paragon* declined to attempt it. The consequence was that a fleet of vessels returned to the Plymouth waters and anchored in the Sound, the Cattewater, and surrounding places of safety. Amongst them came the Whitstable schooner and dropped her anchor in the comparatively smooth water before the aforementioned island and Mount Edgecumbe, near the bridge of rocks. There she was seen, riding at her ease during the late morning.

About three o'clock in the afternoon, some of the men working in the Victualling Yard observed that streams, and then volumes, of smoke were issuing from the *Paragon*, and their curiosity was immediately excited with reference to the cause. They watched the vessel, and shortly she was seen to part from her anchor and drift before the wind with foresails set and Union Jack reversed. The breeze carried her almost directly to the west, and her speed increased. In a very brief space of time, the schooner ran aground in Barn Pool. Within a few minutes, a boat crew left the stricken ship and came straight to the Victualling Yard, reporting the fire, and solicited the aid of the authorities, who responded immediately.

Captain Wheeler, master attendant of the Yard, ordered out a boat crew, and proceeded in charge of them to the opposite side of the water where the vessel was stranded. Immediately afterwards, the large steam tank *Minx*, which was used for the purpose of supplying water to vessels in the Royal Navy, was sent over, and poured a body of water upon the flames, which had by this time, for the afternoon had advanced to nearly five o'clock, obtained possession of the schooner. About the same time, the government steam tugboat *Theis* left the Yard, with Mr Currie, the Captain-Superintendent of the Victualling Yard, Mr Allen, the harbourmaster, and other gentlemen on board.

One of the Yard's manual fire engines was also loaded onto the boat, with a party of firemen to work it. The efforts of the men on board were directed mainly to salvage work, in saving as much of the ship's cargo as they could. They succeeded in rescuing about 400 or 500 bags of biscuits out of the 1,400 on board, but the fire, which was spreading rapidly, put paid to any further salvage work. The *Zephyr*, another government steam tug, and the *Pike*, a steam tender to HMS *Adelaide*, steamed down the harbour to the same spot to assist in operations there.

The united efforts of everyone on board the fleet of vessels were, however, unavailing, so far as subduing the flames were concerned. The flames had obtained too strong a hold upon the *Paragon*, having spread from the stern, where it originated, to the bow, and enclosed within its power the whole of her hull. Fortunately, the sails and rigging were saved, in addition to the portion of the cargo already mentioned. About half past six, therefore, the several tugs, boats, floats, etc., drew off the scene, and left the schooner to the uninterrupted course of the flames.

Night closed in, and the darkness added to the appearance of the conflagration. The lurid light thrown up against the sombre sky conveyed the knowledge of the fire far and wide across the countryside and waters. Thousands of people from all parts of the three towns and their suburbs turned towards the rendezvous indicated by the startling beacon light. The thoroughfares leading to the more prominent points of the coastline were crowded, the multitudes all moving in a similar direction. Paradise Walk, leading from Stonehouse Hill to the Mount Wise steps, and skirting Stonehouse Pool, became a resort of great favour. Hundreds of persons congregated at every turning where the burning mass could be seen. Upon Mount Wise itself, even upon the heights of the flag-staff, amongst the excavations and masonry of the new fortification, the people were collecting in groups. Although little could be seen from there, great volumes of smoke, tinged with a ruddy light, rose above the ship. By far the greatest concourse wended its way down Durnford Street, at the extreme end of Stonehouse, and took up a position at Devil's Point, beneath the ramparts of the fort. Seen from this point of view, the spectacle was extremely fine. The eye, alighting first upon the galaxy of lights suspended from the rigging of the fleet of wind-bound ships in the Sound, passed rapidly across Drake's Island and the wooded slopes of Mount Edgecumbe.

Partially illuminated now by the glow from the harbour side, the eye fell suddenly upon a blazing pile, rising from the water's edge immediately beneath one of the most sheltered and luxurious woods of the Mount Edgecumbe estate. The flames were rolling along the decks in brilliant waves, bursting from the vessel's sides, climbing the bare masts and wrapping themselves around the scorched yard arms that were standing. The pyre was reflected in the sea beneath and the second picture rose and fell with the turbulent billows. The wind was still rising and the generally quiet surface of the Sound and its many bays was broken and disturbed. Across the wide sweep of water between the spot where the vessel lay and the opposite shore, a full, strong light was thrown, increasing into brilliancy or decreasing into comparative gloom as the flames re-asserted or relinquished for a time their mastery. About half past eight, the masts fell, and nothing remained but the half-burnt hull of the ship. From that hour until midnight, the conflagration continued, with more or less violence, gradually consuming the remaining timbers of the ship, and exhausting it. The crowds of watchers continued to be reinforced until a very late hour, and the last of the sightseers, driven home by a drenching shower of rain, left the fire at its work.

The *Paragon* had discharged a cargo of rum at the Yard a few days previously; she was only insured for about £700, and the origin of the fire was never known. The firemen at that fire were on a hiding to nothing. Firefighting at sea is a most perilous activity, as you cannot guarantee your escape should things go badly wrong. The best option they had was to stand well back and pour water onto the fire. Without the modern day, hi-tech equipment and personal protection, the firemen of that time relied on their courage and tenacity at major fires.

Disgraceful action by Marines at a large fire at Millbay

Firefighting is not an exact science, and therefore every fire is different in its own way and behaviour, but one thing that appears to be standard at every fire in the early days of the volunteer fire brigades and amateur firemen is the huge amount of water damage that was done to unaffected stock and belongings, during the course of fire fighting. As a result of the high fire loading of the old buildings, along with the absence of modern building materials and regulations, fires often spread with alarming speed. The early firemen did not have breathing apparatus and hand-controlled branches, so it was very often the case of directing large volumes of water through windows and other openings. It was also the practice, in the early years, to tear down thatched and tarred roofs of adjacent properties, to try to prevent fire spread.

Within the area of the three towns, which were garrison towns, there was never a shortage of soldiers and sailors, who were brought to the fire ground, along with their barracks fire engines, to render assistance to the town's firemen during alarms of fire. Overall, the military afforded valuable service, but there were occasions when their presence created havoc.

During a large fire in a mill in the Millbay area of Plymouth in June 1862, about 300 Marines were marched to the fire, bringing with them their fire engine. Already at the scene were the engine and twenty men belonging to the South Devon Railway Company. The powerful engine and men of the West of England Brigade, and the County Insurance Fire Brigade were also in attendance. Whilst all these men, along with a large number of Marines, worked tirelessly and proficiently, there was a body of Marines who wreaked havoc in the Washington Hotel, which was near to the building involved in fire. There was very little danger of the fire extending into that property because of the thick stone wall which separated them. The Marines, however, no doubt excited by the drink they expected to find, determined in their own minds that all the houses were to be burnt down, and also resolved to possess themselves of the liquor under the specious pretence of saving the property. Mr Ryder, the owner of all the houses and the furniture of the Washington Hotel, implored with them to desist, saying that he preferred the whole to take its chance.

This building was in fact, the second house from the burning mill, so that there was still one house to take fire before it could be at all placed in jeopardy. The Marines, however, were determined to have their own way, forced an entrance and proceeded to the work of devastation. The classical laws of meun and teum are always laxly observed at a fire, but here they were utterly disregarded. To save the beer, wine and spirits from being spoilt, the men drank them themselves. They turned on the taps on their first entrance and thus gained a plentiful supply of liquor. They met Mr Rowley on the first floor, who attempted to prevent their denuding the rooms, but his efforts were in vain. They pushed him aside and threatened if he offered further obstruction to save the things by throwing them at him. Once possessed of the rooms, they carried on the strangest vagaries under the same pretext. For fear of doing them injury, they tenderly attached cords to the mattresses and bedding, and let them down, but the doors they unhinged, and these, together with the chairs, and everything breakable, they threw out of the window. Valuable marble fireplaces were ripped from the walls and thrown out of the window, smashing into little pieces in the street below.

Not a single door was left in the hotel, and several complaints were made to the police and to the military officers present, but no steps were taken to prevent the proceedings until all was completed. Some of the roughs who are always present on such occasions followed the example of the military, and one or two were sent off to the police station for, as the police graphically termed it, 'helping themselves'.

Historic Cann House destroyed by fire

Not all the large fires were contained to within the three towns, however, as on the 28th July 1862, an alarm was received that there was a large fire at Cann House, in the village of Tamerton Foliot, which was about five miles outside of Plymouth. This beautiful house was the country seat of Mark Grigg, Esq., the head of the firm Coates, Williams, and Cox, of the Plymouth Gin Distillery.

Cann House was situated on the left of the Plymouth highway, near the entrance to the village of Tamerton Foliot. The village is in the heart of a deep valley, and Cann House was a charming rural retreat, of semi-Italian design, and thatched. The exterior had been recently decorated, and the interior was in perfect and finished condition. Sadly, the house was destroyed by fire. The first alarm of danger was given about half past three, by a hedge trimmer working there. The news was carried to the village, and within a short period, numerous men from the village arrived to lend assistance. A horseman was dispatched to Plymouth to raise the alarm. Meanwhile, great difficulty was experienced in obtaining water, so the villagers concentrated on saving the contents of the house. The roof was by then well alight, and the fire was spreading rapidly. Most of the important pieces of furniture, paintings and silver plate were removed to a place of safety by the workforce. By the time the West of England Fire Brigade arrived, the building was beyond saving; therefore, all efforts were directed to preventing the spread of fire into the outbuildings. The County Insurance Fire Brigade arrived at half past four, but there was no means of working their fire engine due to the lack of a good water supply.

At five o'clock, the house, stables and coach house were in ruins, a heap of smouldering embers. Mr Grigg, Esq. expressed his gratitude to all the villagers, whose efforts saved all but a few pieces of silver plate from the burning building.

The year 1863 was quite a significant year for the fire brigades in Plymouth. As well as some destructive and fatal fires within the three towns, there was the demise of the County Insurance Company Fire Brigade and the formation of the Plymouth Corporation Fire Brigade. The following pages contain reports of significant events which occurred during 1863.

Late arrival of fire engines causes much criticism

January 6th 1863, saw the destruction by fire of the magnificent buildings of the Plymouth Theatre and Royal Hotel, located in the midst of Plymouth. The Royal Hotel and Theatre formed an extensive and elegant fabric, which was finished in 1813, at a cost of £60,000. The north front was 270 feet long, and had in the centre a magnificent portico of the Ionic order, under which was the main entrance to the theatre and Assembly rooms. The hotel occupied the entire eastern front, and had an Ionic portico, a choice example of Grecian simplicity.

At about twelve o'clock, the alarm was given that the theatre was on fire. The air was thick with the taint of charred wood, and flickers of fire could be seen through several windows. The onlookers in the streets observed the fire getting a good hold and were alarmed that no fire engines or police were on the scene. The first fire engine to arrive, after about fifteen minutes, was that of the West of England Fire

Great fire which destroyed the Theatre Royal and Royal Hotel in Plymouth on 6th January 1863.

Brigade, and for nearly an hour, that was the only fire engine that was on the fireground. Here, in the centre of a town with a population of 150,000 inhabitants, it seemed ridiculous that only one solitary fire engine was fighting a losing battle with the vast fire. The huge throng of onlookers, who were by then very angry and disorderly with the lack of action, could only watch with horror as the fire ripped through the building, virtually unchecked. The effort of the one fire engine being played was totally inadequate.

Eventually, there could be heard the rattling of wheels upon the cobbled streets, as a large contingent of Marines arrived with their engine. The mass of men in white short smocks busied themselves before the hotel, amidst the mocking and jeering of the disorderly crowd. By now, troops were arriving from all quarters, but despite their late efforts, they were of little use. Marines, with bayonets fixed, surrounded the fireground in order to keep back the angry and violent crowd. Consensus suggested that their efforts would have been better employed in saving the contents of the buildings, rather than shouldering their arms and angering the onlookers.

Mr Newcombe, who was the manager of the theatre, discovered the fire just before midnight. A smell of fire was discovered during the night's performance, and was fully investigated, but no fire was found. At eleven o'clock, the audience had left the theatre. The smell of fire was again apparent, and this time Mr Newcombe personally made a tour of inspection. When all seemed secure, the manager then left the premises. Mr Newcombe still felt apprehensive, and presently returned, and again, went through the entire building, with the exception of the property room, out of which Mr Purvis, a confidential servant, and a very careful man, came and assured Mr Newcombe that all was well there. They both left the theatre, locking the door behind them, no sign of fire being observed.

Mr Newcombe then retired to his house at Balmoral Place, the Hoe. He was so unsettled, and his mind was still on the subject that, just before twelve o'clock, he took the theatre key in his hand and opened his door with the intention of going down to the theatre to inspect the premises yet again. A messenger met him at his door, which confirmed his fears that the theatre was on fire. Messengers were dispatched to the various engines, and the fire escape, which was stationed close to the theatre, was planted against the building, and was made available to a small extent in hoisting the hoses of the engines when they arrived.

Leather fire helmets belonging to Firemen No. 6 and No. 7 of the West of England Insurance Company Fire Brigade c.1860.

The first engine to arrive was that belonging to the West of England Company, under the calm and efficient charge of Mr William Marshall. That invaluable engine arrived about 12.15 a.m. and took up its station on the Athenaeum side of the theatre, where a good supply of water was obtainable from the first fire plug opened. The hose was first brought round to the box entrance, beneath the central portico, and the firemen were enabled to advance several yards into the building and play upwards, although scarcely reaching the property room, where the fire originated. In about a quarter of an hour, they were beaten back from that position by the collapse of the internal staircase. The next engine to arrive was the small South Devon Railway engine, under the direction of Mr Cockshott. The Royal Marines, together with their engine, arrived to rousing jeers, at one o'clock. Next came the Citadel engine, with forty-two men: this engine took up its position by the Mayor's new clock tower (Derry's Clock), where a good supply of water was obtained. The next engines to come to the spot were two belonging to the County Fire Office, of small size, from the Exchange. The town engine was accompanied by Mr Welsh and managed by Mr Carkeet, the agent of the County Insurance Company.

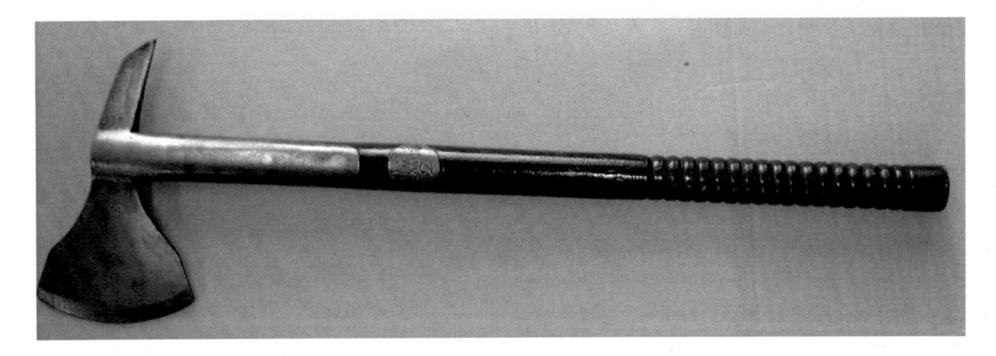

West of England axe c.1850; this was originally a naval boarding axe, but was adopted for use in the West of England Insurance Brigade. It was carried in a pouch which was on a shoulder belt.

The other engine, a larger one, was also under Mr John Carkeet's direction, and played on the western end for a short period, and was then removed to the front of the Royal. The smaller one was posted in the stable yard at the back of the hotel, and rendered essential service by playing into the blazing billiard room. The firemen stood resolutely and bravely on the first floor window, and did very much to save the hotel from complete destruction. Other fire engines, which eventually arrived, were engines from the Royal Victualling Yard, manned by a detachment of Royal Marines; the engine from the Royal Naval Hospital, and a small Merryweather Valiant steam fire engine, accompanied by 100 men, from HMS *Virago*. At about four o'clock, an engine from Raglan Barracks arrived with a large detachment of the 2nd Regiment. The crowd's anger at the delay of sufficient fire engines arriving early enough was slowly subdued throughout the early hours, as great feats of heroism were displayed by various firemen, which won the acclaim of the multitude.

Fatal explosion and fire in Stonehouse Lane

At twenty-five minutes past two on the morning of 10th March 1863, a huge explosion took place in King Street West, also known as Stonehouse Lane, which caused the deaths of six persons. The explosion and fire occurred in the house of Mr Morris Lawrence and Son, firework makers, who were probably at the time of the accident engaged in making articles which were intended to contribute to the pleasure and enjoyment of other people. As, however, both the father and son were killed, the circumstances which led to the explosion were never established, but it was almost certain that it was a case of fire caused explosion, rather than explosion caused fire, as an application of a naked flame was involved. One can surmise that, owing to the late hour, candles were certainly used to supply a working light, and it was indeed likely that a candle was accidentally knocked over, thus igniting gunpowder, which in turn created a mass explosion.

Mr Morris and his son carried on the business of pyrotechnists, in a small, mean-looking and somewhat wretched house in that part of King Street West, number 103 to be precise. The population there was very dense, consisting for the most part of the poorer classes of the Irish people. Lawrence, who was a good firework maker, was well known at the different country fairs, and also at the Plymouth market, which he used on regular occasions. He was doing a very good business, having received numerous orders for the supply of fireworks which were to have been used the following day.

Three duty policemen, Sergeant Murch, P.C. Elson, and another supernumery policeman, were walking up the street. They saw and heard the windows and shutters of Lawrence's house, which were blown right across the street, accompanied by a huge fireball and the house was in flames. The explosion had burst the door and windows open, and had also blown up a portion of the upper part of the small house, in which, unhappily, there were many people.

Sergeant Murch immediately began alerting the neighbours in the adjoining houses, while the other two policemen went off to summon the fire brigade. Two men, named Oliver and George Harris (who was a well known silly person, called Button George), made good their escape by jumping out of the upper window. Both men sustained terrible injuries in hitting the pavement below, and were eventually carried off to the South Devon and East Cornwall Hospital. Oliver was badly burnt, and George had multiple injuries caused by the fall. Another man, called Smith, got out through the attic window, and somehow managed to scramble across to the next attic window, on a deeply sloping roof with no ledge on which to rest his feet, and thus managed to affect his escape. Another man, named Lismore, escaped by jumping out of the window, but his poor wife and children, who were also endeavouring to make good their escape, were unsuccessful. The mother and her three children sunk into the flames, and in a few minutes they ceased to exist, having been burnt to death. Mr Lawrence and his son, who was a married man, were also burnt to death.

Morris Lawrence and his wife Fanny. Morris was burnt to death, as were his son and four other tenants, in a terrible explosion and fire, in a house in Stonehouse Lane in March 1863. Mr Lawrence was a renowned firework manufacturer, and the explosion occurred in the early hours, during the making of fireworks. © Michael Lucas

The West of England Fire Brigade was first to arrive, superintended by Mr Marshall, the Plymouth agent, with their powerful engine. These were soon followed by the engine from the Royal Naval Hospital, with a number of policemen and naval officers. Mr Hodge, the town surveyor, Mr Superintendent Freeman and Sergeant Thomas were also quickly on the spot. Everything that could be done was done to extinguish the flames. Mr Carkeet of the County Fire Office attended, but seeing that the fire was in no danger of spreading, decided not to call out his fire brigade. Within an hour or so, the flames were extinguished and the grisly task commenced in entering the burnt-out house to recover the bodies. The firemen soon picked up the remains of the six persons who perished in the inferno; so burnt were they that they resembled pieces of charred wood. They removed the remains to the deadhouse (mortuary) in Westwell Street. Mrs Lawrence, the wife of the elder Lawrence, had recently taken apartments nearby, because the house was so crowded. She was left a widow with seven children at home and three away, besides the son who had died in the fire.

Destructive and fatal conflagration in Devonport

Devonport was, on Saturday 25th May 1863, visited with a conflagration more extensive than that of any fire in the last twenty years. The first alarm was raised shortly after nine o'clock, when the inhabitants of Princess Street and its neighbourhood were startled by a loud explosion. The explosion proceeded from the house occupied by Mr William Emmett, a grocer and provision dealer, doing an extensive business at No. 70 Princess Street. Several persons at once rushed to the spot, but were met by dense volumes of suffocating smoke, which belched forth from the apertures of a cellar underneath the shop. There was stored there a large quantity of turpenzine, a substitute for turpentine, as well as other spirits. The explosion and fire was caused by Mr Emmett going into the cellar with a lighted candle to draw off a gallon of turpenzine for a local painter. The container of liquid had been leaking, which resulted in a mass of flammable vapours being present, and once the naked flame was introduced, a violent explosion occurred, combined with a fierce fire. Mr Emmett stood no chance and almost certainly died during the explosion.

In the meantime, Mrs Emmett ran upstairs to bring down two of the children who were in bed, but could not return. Her egress was barred by the dense smoke and flames which poured up through the house. A man named Gilbert, living at No. 10 Princess Street, became acquainted with the perilous situation in which Mrs Emmett was placed by seeing her screaming from a first floor window. He procured a builder's ladder and promptly rescued Mrs Emmett. He then returned to the first floor in search of her two children, whom he found in bed in a back room, unaware of their danger. He conveyed them to safety through the window, and gave them to a neighbour. Had they remained in the house a few minutes longer, they would have shared the same dreadful fate as their father.

As soon as the fire was discovered, P.C. Selby, who was on his beat, sprung his warning rattle and alerted the neighbourhood. Messengers were immediately dispatched for the Dockyard engines, manned by the Dockyard police under Inspector Beard. But unfortunately, as it often happens, on the arrival of the engines, no one knew the locality of the fire plugs, the police being in entire ignorance of the situation. There was a considerable delay before water supplies were obtained from fire plugs located in Marlborough Street and Fore Street, both a considerable distance from the fire. This water supply was used to feed the Dockyard engines. The borough engine obtained a supply of water at the corner of Tavistock Street, and was kept at work throughout the night. During the course of the fire, further fire engines and manpower arrived on the scene. These were: The West of England Insurance Company; the Gun Wharf engine; the Raglan Barracks engine; the Citadel engine; the Victualling Yard engine; two engines from the Royal Naval Hospital; the Granby Barracks engine; the Stonehouse Barracks engine; the Globe engine; the Millbay Barracks engine; the Mount Wise Barracks engine.

Accompanying the above-named engines were hundreds of soldiers and sailors, along with their commanding officers, who worked to obtain water supplies, fight the fire, and control the crowds of onlookers in the streets. In addition to the powerful engines already in attendance, the following ships in harbour sent their small fire pumps and additional manpower: HMS Cambridge, two engines, with 150 men; HMS *Warrior*, two engines, 200 men; HMS *Indus*, two engines and 150 men, and HMS *Adelaide*, two engines, 200 men.

Great assistance was also rendered by seamen from the ships *Edgar*, *Canopus*, *Orantes*, *Alert*, and *Implacable*. Armed parties of the Royal Artillery, Royal Marines, and Queen's Royals were also in attendance; large bodies of borough police were also on the spot. The sights and sounds of all these engines being hauled through the cobbled streets to the scene of operations must have been very exciting; the West of England fire engine was brought to the spot by four horses, who must have been very scared as they hauled the engine through the narrow, smoke-laden streets.

The radiated heat from the conflagration was intense, and the bravery of these fine animals was indeed worthy of praise. Several houses and shops were by then well alight, and the flames were being fanned by a stiff breeze. Houses in Tavistock Street, Fore Street and Catherine Street soon caught fire due to the flakes of fire being carried on the wind. At one point, the entire neighbourhood was under a severe threat, and only the valiant efforts of the firefighters prevented an even bigger tragedy. There were many narrow escapes, and about six houses, including Mr Emmett's house, burnt uncontrollably until well after midnight. The fires were eventually got under control and finally extinguished. During Saturday evening, much uneasiness was felt for the safety of Mr Emmett, and a great many feared that the poor gentleman had perished in the flames. Next morning, after the fires were extinguished, labourers set about digging through the charred timbers and rubble in the search for the missing man.

Their fears were soon realised, as about eleven o'clock, his badly charred remains were located among the debris in the area, which was once the cellar. Bearing in mind the severity of the fire and the close proximity of the houses in the narrow streets, together with the density of the populous living in the area, with many houses being rack-rented, it was most fortunate that Mr Emmett was the only fatality on that fateful night.

It is interesting to note that the eldest of the rescued children, John Emmett, was honoured in January 1884 by the King of Spain. John was awarded the Knight of the Order of Isabel la Catolica, for services rendered to the Spanish Government in the West Indies in 1878.

CHAPTER FIVE

PLYMOUTH ENTERS THE STEAM AGE

The County Fire Insurance Office Fire Brigade disbands

A MILESTONE IN the history of fire brigades in Plymouth was reached in the summer of 1863, as the County Fire Insurance Fire Brigade, which was then based in Athenaeum Place, was finally disbanded. They formerly occupied a small station in Woolster Street. This Fire Office Brigade had attended all major fires within the three towns since 1838, and their Superintendent, Mr John Carkeet, and his men afforded most valuable service to the communities of the area over the years. Very little is recorded about the history of this small volunteer brigade in Plymouth, unlike in bigger towns throughout the country. Their short-lived occupation was undoubtedly appreciated by the townsfolk and the civic dignitaries. The only organised fire brigade left operating in the borough of Plymouth at this time was the fire brigade from the West of England Fire Insurance Company. The Corporation still relied heavily upon them and the military for fire protection.

Plymouth Corporation Fire Brigade formed

Following the demise of the County Fire Office Fire Brigade, the civic dignitaries were compelled to address the issue of fire protection for the borough. For the past year or so, there existed friction between the Mayor and the military Commander-in-Chief of the Western District, concerning the control of the persons employed in extinguishing a fire which occurred in a manufactory at Coxside. Inasmuch as the town had mainly to rely, in case of fire, upon naval and military aid, it was not surprising that there was a disposition to ignore the civil authority. The upshot of the difference of opinion was that the Council resolved to call a fire brigade into existence, and to appoint as its head, an officer, who should be competent to direct operations in case of fire, to drill the members in their various duties, and, in short, to superintend the whole department.

Suitable persons were advertised for, and out of thirty-five or forty applicants, the Watch Committee unanimously selected Mr Walter Lethbridge. Prior to the appointment of Mr Lethbridge, the means for saving life and property from fire, beyond that at the command of the naval and military authorities, consisted of an engine and brigade belonging to the West of England Insurance Office. Upon Mr Lethbridge's appointment, which was on 11th August 1863, his brigade consisted of two engine directors, nine firemen, and a foreman of fire escapes. Mr John McKeer, one of the engine directors, later became the brigade Superintendent, following the resignation of Mr Lethbridge in 1886. The Corporation acquired the fire extinguishing appliances of the County Fire Office, consisting of two or three old hand machines, which were worked by some seven or eight firemen. The first Plymouth Corporation Borough Fire Brigade had its fire station in Tavistock Road, not far from where the central library is now situated. This brigade turned out with two manual fire engines and one fly escape, the escape being of the type used by The Society for the Protection of Life from Fire, a body operating mainly in London.

Mr Walter Lethbridge, Superintendent of Plymouth Corporation Fire Brigade, which was established in 1863.

After a time, some much needed improvements were made. One of Shand Mason's thirty-man manual fire engines was bought, and later on, this was supplemented by six hose-reels. These were wheeled carts which had several lengths of hose, rolled, ready for use, along with standpipes and branches, which could be used directly from the street fire plugs.

The hose reels were stationed at the following places: Harbour Avenue, on the Barbican; the Octagon police station; the Guildhall; Fire Brigade Station and the Workhouse. Two patent fire escapes were also added to the original plant. One was at the Guildhall and the other at Alton Terrace, Tavistock Road. From reports in later years, it was said that the Plymouth Corporation Fire Brigade was one of the most cheaply run Corporation departments, and attained a state of efficiency unsurpassed by that of any other town of similar size. The three towns remained free of any further large conflagrations for the remainder of 1863.

Extensive fire and accidents at Devonport

The town of Devonport was once again visited by the fiery foe on 22nd June 1865, when a fire was discovered at five o'clock in the morning in the premises of Mr Galpin, grocer and tea dealer, of Catherine Street. This fire resulted in the destruction of the interior of the house and adjoining property. Within a short time of the fire being discovered and the alarm being raised, a body of borough policemen, under Superintendent Lynn, arrived. A hose-reel and manual fire engine was brought to the scene from the Dockyard, accompanied by thirty men from the Metropolitan Police Force, under the supervision of Supt Baxter and Inspectors Irwin and Williamson. A fire plug was opened up near the building, and via the fire engine, several hoses were playing upon the fire. Another Dockyard engine was brought to the scene, and was stationed in Dockwall Street. By this time, the fire had a good hold of the outbuildings at the rear of the premises. At this point another engine arrived from the Mount Wise barracks, with a detachment of Royal Engineers. They could not locate another fire plug, so they proceeded to dig up the road to expose the water main, where a standpipe was driven into the main, drenching all who stood around the pit.

By six o'clock in the morning, there were hundreds of soldiers and firemen at the scene. There were detachments from the 28th Regiment, the 6th Regiment, Marines from Stonehouse, and another engine and detachment of men from Raglan Barracks. The men of the 28th Regiment were employed in pumping the engines, while other soldiers were busy keeping order among the huge crowd of spectators that had formed.

The West of England Insurance Fire Brigade arrived next and took up a position in Dockwall Street; they were courageously led by their active manager Mr Marshall. The hoses at play were making considerable progress upon the fire. Further contingents of sailors were dispatched from their ships, which were moored in the Sound; others remained on standby should they be required.

Fire mark of the West of England Insurance Company, who began trading in 1807; there were numerous variations to the fire mark of this company.

Shortly after six o'clock, and in spite of the plentiful supply of water poured on it, the fire had made great headway, and the adjoining houses stood in immediate danger. That occupied by Mr Lawry, the proprietor of an expensive drapery establishment, caught fire, and Superintendent Lynn, with commendable presence of mind, and at great risk to himself, ascended a ladder, and with an axe, knocked away the portion of wall that had caught fire; his actions checked the progress of the fire. By eight o'clock, the fire was completely subdued and several military engines had, by that time, returned to their barracks. Three firemen were slightly injured during the firefighting when a ceiling came crashing down and buried them beneath the rubble. They were quickly extricated by their fellow firemen, and apart from cuts and bruises, they were unharmed.

Disastrous fire at candle company, Coxside

In the early part of the 19th century, the manufacture of candles was often carried out in the homes of the tallow chandlers. The Victorians soon invented a much more mechanised way of manufacturing candles, and in 1859, several of the small chandlers joined forces, and formed the Plymouth Steam Candle Company, in Manor Street. In 1861, the New Patent Candle Company Ltd was formed, and they took over the former soap works in Sutton Road. The soap works had burned down in 1850, and was later rebuilt. Sadly, fate saw to it that the rebuilt manufactory suffered the same fiery destruction under its new owners.

This picture appeared in the London Illustrated News *in 1866, showing the fire brigades of Plymouth fighting a huge fire at the Patent Candle Company at Coxside. The Borough Fire Brigade are seen here, and they were assisted by the West of England Fire Brigade.*

A large number of men were employed on these premises, and work was carried out both day and night throughout the whole week, up to Saturday evening, when the fires were extinguished in the engine room, and further labour was suspended until the Monday morning. A watchman was employed there to inspect the works before leaving in the morning, to check everything was safe. He left the works at five o'clock on Sunday morning, not long before the fire was discovered. Mr Young, who discovered the fire, dashed to the home of the works foreman, Mr Bingham, who lived a couple of minutes away. A runner was sent to summon the town fire brigade; by now the flames had taken hold of the whole of the building. The Marines at the Citadel could see the huge fire, and the firing of guns commenced to draw wider attention to the fire. Mr Marshall, Superintendent of the West of England Insurance Fire Brigade, was alerted to the fire, and he quickly rounded up his men and began their dash to the scene, with four grey horses pulling the large manual engine.

The fire, which was fuelled from the cotton, tallow, palm oil and the stock of candles in the works, was by now raging, sending a large column of smoke into the air. Upon arrival, the West of England brigade took up a position near the corner of the Sugar Refinery, while the town engine, under the command of Mr Walter Lethbridge, was stationed outside the main entrance, and they tried to prevent the fire from reaching the Soap Works. Two firemen from the West of England Fire Brigade were badly injured when a roof collapsed on them. They were Fireman Walter Bawden and Fireman George Philp. Both men were taken from the scene to hospital for treatment. Fireman Philp was the most severely injured, and he was rushed down to have immediate surgery.

Further fire engines from the military establishments were also brought to the scene and they took up positions at strategic points. The Royal Artillery engine was working in Shepherd's Lane, when they became aware that a further property, belonging to Messrs Edward James and Sons, who manufactured matches, was in danger of being engulfed due to the fiery brands which were being carried by the wind. They quickly hauled their engine, via Jubilee Street (Exeter Street), to the north of the St John's bridge area and played water onto the building.

In all, there were nine manual fire engines at the incident: the Town Brigade; the West of England Brigade; the Royal Artillery engine and men; four engines from the Royal Marine Barracks; the Royal Naval Hospital engine, and one from the Royal Naval Victualling Yard. About an hour after the arrival of the first fire engine, several fire floats were taken to Sutton Pool, where they did great service in pumping water to the various fire engines.

The local press made an issue that one of the town's fire engines, which was kept at the Old Soap Factory, remained there as there was no hose kept at the site. The various fire brigades eventually got on top of the situation, and special praise was afforded to the town brigade and the West of England brigade for their bravery, energy and efficiency.

The original cost of the ruined building was £21,000; it was later purchased by the Victoria Soap Company for the sum of £6,000, and they spent £3,000 on additional boilers and other valuable machinery. The whole of the property, with the exception of the walls, had been destroyed. The works was once again rebuilt, but lasted only until the afternoon of Tuesday November 15th 1870, when it once again suffered a most destructive fire.

Fires still continued to rage in and around the three towns, and among those which tested the various fire brigades and their aging manual fire pumps, were large fires at the S. Down Powder Works, Millbrook, in 1864; Catherine Street, Plymouth in 1865; Old-Town Street, Plymouth in 1865; Public House, Devonport in 1865 and Tavistock Road, Plymouth, in 1866.

First steam fire engine for Plymouth

Plymouth was indebted to the Liverpool and London and Globe Fire Assurance Company for a most important addition to the protection of the town, by the introduction of one of Merryweather's light steam fire engines, which made its first appearance in public on 24th April 1866. It was drawn through the streets of Plymouth by four horses, accompanied by the newly formed Insurance fire brigade. The engine was a perfect model in itself, being a facsimile of the one which was awarded the first prize at the Cologne competition in 1865. It weighed twenty-five cwt, and when working at full power, was capable of throwing a jet of water 160 feet high, emitting 250 gallons per minute. The boiler was fitted with water and steam spaces, and from its peculiar construction was almost unequalled for the speed in raising steam. This, of course, was a most important element in a fire engine, as the best chance of success lies in attacking a fire in its earliest stages. The pumps were double-acting in their suction, as well as their delivery powers, and were so constructed that it could pump gritty water without harming the pump.

The trial of the new engine was arranged for late in the afternoon, at the scene of the late disastrous fire at Price's Candle Works at Coxside. Those present at the demonstration included Messrs. J. Plimsaul, T. W. Bastow, Gibson and Harris, agents for the company in Plymouth; Mr Hodge, town surveyor; Mr Walter Lethbridge, Director of the Plymouth Borough Fire Brigade; and Mr James Compton Merryweather, from London.

The engine was brought up in front of the ruins of the buildings, and a fire was lit. Within minutes, a pressure of 60Ibs was obtained, and the new engine commenced working, and displayed wonderful powers. The engine was named The Torrent; this was to be a most valuable acquisition to the fire service in Plymouth.

As well as the new steam fire engine, the newly formed fire brigade of that insurance company consisted of six volunteers, and had Mr Raddan as their superintendent. The fire engine station was located in Mr Bastow's premises in Westwell Street, where horses were always ready at hand to convey the engine to any required fire. A big advantage was the fact that the Superintendent and four of his men lived almost next to the station, so that, in fact, they were regarded as sleeping at the station, which would hasten their turn-out when they were required.

New steam engine's baptism of fire

In the early hours of 14th August 1866, the brigade rendered tremendous service, along with other fire brigades, at a very destructive fire in a tanyard situated in Tavistock Road. The fire broke out in a coach house owned by Mr Caleo Trotter. A member of the borough police force called Monkley, who lived in

Group of West of England Insurance Company Firemen. c.1860.

the vicinity, was aroused from his sleep by the shout of 'Fire'. He ran to the burning coach house, which contained some valuable horses, a brougham, complete sets of harnesses, and a large quantity of hay. Monkley managed to lead the horses to a place of safety before the fire really got a hold and spread to a large building next door, which was used as a store for wool and hides.

The West of England brigade was first on the scene, commanded by Mr Marshall, and took up a position near the fire plug at the corner of Tavistock Place. The water was soon turned on and the hose was passed up the street, through the passage of a house, into the yard, and commenced to play on the southern end of the burning building. Next came the borough brigade with Superintendent Lethbridge, Mr McKeer and Mr Blackmore, who took up a position immediately in front of the main entrance, and attached their hose to the fire plug at the corner. The stream of water from the nozzle was so feeble that it was comparatively useless. While more efforts were being made to obtain more water, the steam fire engine belonging to the Liverpool and London and Globe came up, drawn by two horses, with Mr Raddan and his men.

Once a water supply was obtained, the steamer supplied two powerful jets onto the fire. Further assistance arrived shortly afterwards, with the Citadel engine, manned by a party of Royal Artillerymen, and detachments of the 65th and 80th Regiments, which also arrived to assist. A large number of Marines were also on the spot, and together with a party of sailors from the Cambridge, they rendered efficient service, and exhibited great courage, as they risked life and limb to salvage many of the contents from the conflagration.

The small fire brigade of the Liverpool and London and Globe Assurance Company, together with their much admired fire engine, earned the praises of the crowds for their efficient service at this fire. The brigade attended numerous fires in and around Plymouth throughout its existence, but sadly, this brigade only lasted for ten years, as they were disbanded in 1876.

Great fire at Snawdon's workshops in Stonehouse

One of the most disastrous fires ever known in the neighbourhood of Plymouth broke out in the early morning of July 22nd 1873, at Stonehouse. The conflagration, for no less a name can be applied to this unparalleled local misfortune, resulted in the destruction of an immense amount of valuable property. At about four o'clock in the morning, a passing road sweeper noticed smoke issuing from the premises occupied by Mr John Snawdon, a cabinet maker and upholsterer. The road sweeper used his brush to bang on the door to alert the slumbering family, whilst shouting out the alarm 'Fire'. Two policemen, who were on their beat in the street, also rushed to render assistance, while another member of the public raced off to raise the alarm at the various locations where a fire engine was housed.

The first fire engine to arrive on the spot was the one from the Naval Hospital, with Sir Henry Keppel and other officers and men. The Naval Hospital was only a few minutes' walk from the fire. Next came the West of England engine, in the charge of Mr Marshall, the engine from the Victualling Yard, an engine from the Royal Marine Barracks, and the steam engine and brigade of the Liverpool and London and Globe Insurance Company, under the superintendence of Mr Raddan. There were also large detachments of officers and men from various regiments, a number of Metropolitan Policemen from the Dockyard, and a posse of civil police. All rendered good service, in either crowd control or firefighting; the crowds were kept at a respectable distance by soldiers with fixed bayonets.

The fire had spread with alarming speed, and there was a big delay in obtaining a good water supply to feed the fire engines. It took a good thirty minutes before each engine was playing with effect upon the fire. There was a strong wind blowing, which constantly changed direction, helping to spread the fire far and wide. Shortly after six o'clock the wind turned again, sending a sheet of fire, some 150 feet in length, and fifty feet high, over the tops of the houses, and caught the building yard, belonging to Mr James Taylor. The yard contained a large amount of timber, which was soon blazing out of control. Further properties, including the Mechanics Arms, Chiswick Ale Stores and several other houses were soon burning furiously. Nothing could exceed the fury of the fiery element, and bursting from Mr Taylor's yard, it flew into his house, and in the space of an hour, that building was, like the others, completely gutted.

There was but a very small diminution in the extent of the fire until nearly nine o'clock, and then the first sensible decrease was felt. The flames were beginning to be subdued; the smoke was not so dense. The combined efforts of all the engines were concentrating upon the smouldering block of some ten houses, but any hope of saving them had long gone. A wall, some seventy feet high, belonging to Mr Snawdon's premises, was altogether left to its fate, and it looked rather shaky.

Throughout the whole time, everyone who could work, did work, and that with a will and a heartiness that spoke exceedingly well for all parties concerned. Men united with officers, in their attempt to assist; officers, whilst not relaxing discipline, fraternised with the men, in doing all they could for their civilian brethren. The gallant firemen also were deserving of the highest praise, and they exposed themselves to many risks of a peculiarly dangerous character. Mr Marshall, chief of the West of England Fire Brigade, suffered serious head injuries when a ceiling and joists fell on him. He was treated at the scene and then conveyed to his home.

At 3 p.m., all danger was at an end, and the scene of operations was scaled down to a few pumps that continued to damp down the smouldering ruins. The thoroughfares leading to the fireground, from Battery Street and Union Place, were battened up to deter the public from visiting the area of devastation.

Seven people killed in Union Street disaster

One of the saddest fatalities to have occurred in the three towns for many a year happened on 15th September 1873, at Stonehouse, when four men and three boys were ushered into eternity with an awful suddenness. The ruins of the recent fire at Mr Snawdon's property in Union Street, Stonehouse, which occurred back in July of that year, was the scene of this dreadful accident. The fire, one of the greatest seen in the locality for many years, completely gutted seven houses, and amongst the walls left standing

A Harrowing scene in Union Street, Plymouth, in September 1873, where seven people were crushed to death following the collapse of a gable end wall. The original building had previously been involved in a big fire which resulted in this wall being left standing in a dangerous manner.

was one between Mr Snawdon's cabinet making premises and Mr Steven's glass and china warehouse. It was this wall that fell, and smashed out of all recognition, four men and three boys, who were working beneath its shadow. The wall ran from Union Street to the rear of the premises in Union Place, and was nearly fifty feet high and carried five floors. It was built two feet thick, up to the first floor, and then for five storeys, it was about eighteen inches thick. For a run of about sixty feet this wall fell, cracking between the chimney breasts, and breaking off where the thickness of the wall was two feet thick.

Just before eleven o'clock that morning, this immense wall, measuring close upon 200 tons, came to the ground with a tremendous crash. Eight men and boys were at the time working at the foundation of a cross wall, that was to have formed a fire proof wall separating the cabinet makers' shop in Union Street from the dwelling house in Union Place. The foundation of this wall had nothing to do with the accident, for the men were working several feet off the wall that fell. By this enormous mass of wall, the eight were completely buried; seven met with instant death, and the eighth miraculously escaped with his life, even though badly cut about his head. Several men on the works witnessed the accident, and there was no lack of willing hands to dig the remaining seven fellows out. It was a full two hours before this gruesome task was completed, and the mangled bodies were then carried into Mr Taylor's yard, which was opposite.

Had the tithe of the wisdom exhibited in the pulling down of this wall been shown in respect of the wall which brought about this dire disaster, there can be no doubt that this sad calamity would have been averted. There was every reason to believe that all the deep sorrow and distress had been brought about by a reckless disregard of human life. The outcome of an over-weaning desire to save a few pounds by retaining the wall; this was not a case of everyone being wise after the event.

The West of England Insurance Company Fire Brigade in Plymouth in 1886. The Chief Officer, Mr Charles Brooks, is seated wearing civilian clothes.

All except those who were interested in retaining the wall seem to have felt certain that some such dire calamity as this would result, and this view was expressed, on more than one occasion, to the owner. The dangerous condition of the wall was palpable; the fire had weakened it considerably; a high wind was blowing at the time of the accident, and this was the immediate cause of the fall. The storm of the previous night, too, no doubt, tried the masonry, but to allow a wall fifty feet high and seventy feet or more long and not two feet thick to remain in this position, without any support whatever, presented to the practical mind, a most reprehensible action. Indeed, it appeared that in addition to the warnings of friends and neighbours, the dangerous condition of the wall was made the subject of notices to the owner by the local board. It was said that Mr Snawdon, to whom the wall belonged, or Mr Blight, the contractor, of Princess Street, had received verbal notice by the board as to the danger of the wall, and on the following Friday, this notice was repeated in writing. The unfortunate victims of this terrible accident were John Stratford, Richard Harvey, Francis Bennett, Dennis Sullivan, James McCarthy, William Voden and Edward Newbury.

Death of Fireman James Bailey

One of the oldest firemen belonging to the West of England Insurance Company Fire Brigade met with an untimely end in March 1874. James Bailey, who incredibly, was seventy-three years of age, had been a fireman in the West of England since its formation in Plymouth in 1838. On 21st February, he was called out with the brigade to a fire aboard a small vessel, the *Margaret Holton*, moored at Admiral's Hard, Stonehouse. In the darkness, James Bailey fell over the quay, and fell fifteen feet into the dry dock, where he suffered serious injuries. He sadly succumbed to his injuries and died in the South Devon and East Cornwall hospital on Monday 9th March. Mr Bailey had attended all the fires that the West of England were called to over the past thirty-six years, and had been exposed to incredible dangers on many occasions; it was ironic that he was to lose his life on what was, by his standards, a routine fire.

It is incredible that a man of seventy-three years of age was still actively involved in firefighting; such was the loyalty and dedication of the volunteer firemen of the West of England brigade. His funeral, which took place on Saturday 14th March, was a fitting tribute to the memory of the brave man who lost his life while engaged in the noble and hazardous calling. Hundreds of people congregated along the route of the procession as a mark of respect, which began at the fire station in Cornwall Street. His coffin was carried on the hose box of the West of England engine; on the pall rested his axe, helmet and accoutrements. The procession was led by the West of England Brigade; next came the town brigade fire engine, under the direction of Mr McKeer, and the men of that brigade, and following on was the mourning coach containing the family of the deceased.

The Liverpool and London and Globe steam fire engine, under the direction of Mr Raddan and his men, came next. The men of the West of England brigade walked on either side of their engine, acting as pallbearers. The procession made its way to the Plymouth cemetery where Mr Bailey was finally laid to rest.

John Good, a fellow fireman of the West of England Fire Brigade, who, along with James Bailey, was a founder member of that brigade back in 1838, wrote the following lines in respect of the loss of a close friend; the spelling and grammar is as it was written:

LINES
By a West of England Fireman on the death of a comrade

Oh! rest, Bailey, rest, neath your laurels of fame,
Won by duty and danger, mid smoke and flame.
I've stood by his side, from the year Thirty eight,
To that terrible night he met his sad fate;
And as valiant and true I have found him to be

As those to have conquered the brave Ashantee.
All honour to those who have fought in the field
The foes of old England, and made them to yield;
But their heroes are those who best can destroy,
But where we appear we give peace, hope, and joy,
And when the grim foe we have laid in the dust,
Feel our action was good, our cause it was just.
In that fatal night, he was called from her side,
Who for forty odd years had been his own bride;
Ever willing to go, he left his poor wife,
And in leaping to save, he lost his own life.
Let those who have means keep the wolf from her door,
And give to his widow a mite from their store.
May all those who have felt the help and the aids
In the hour of need, the fire brigades
Give and encourage, and we'll all risk our lives,
If mercy be shewn to our children and wives.

J. Good, West of England fireman,
Engine Station, Cornwall Street, Plymouth
March 18th 1874.

Brass breastplate for Fireman No. 7 of the West of England Insurance Company Fire Brigade. These badges were not used on the Plymouth uniform after 1890, as new uniforms were issued to the brigade.

CHAPTER SIX

CHANGES TO FIRE COVER

THE EAST STONEHOUSE local board finally decided to form a volunteer fire brigade, and in 1875 Mr F. Taylor was appointed as Chief Fire Officer. The brigade was made up of well-known local residents. The fire engines were of the manual type, and they had a Street Fire Escape, similar to the fire escapes used by the Corporation Fire Brigade in Plymouth.

Some members of Stonehouse Fire Brigade c.1895.

The brigade attracted much criticism as to the plant in their possession, and this was highlighted at a meeting of the Stonehouse Fire Brigade and local board in November 1878. The meeting was originally called to nominate new members to fill the vacancies which had occurred within the brigade. Complaints were heard about Mr Taylor, the captain of the fire brigade. It was alleged that he did not attend to his office in a proper manner, as the Fire Escape, which they owned, was in a bad state of repair, and as such might lead to serious injury, if not fatal consequences. It was decided that it should be examined by the board. Mr Thuell motioned that a Second Officer should be appointed in the absence of the Captain, as everyone was inclined to take the lead, resulting in chaos and disorder. Mr Lee was nominated as the candidate for the position.

Leather helmet and fire mark of the West of England Insurance Company.

The London and Liverpool and Globe Fire Brigade disbands

The year of 1877 saw the disbandment of the Liverpool and London and Globe Fire Insurance Fire Brigade, which operated from their headquarters and their fire station, which was located in Westwell Street. Insurance companies throughout the country were beginning to dispense with their fire brigades towards the end of the 19th century, as the local authorities finally began accepting responsibility for providing adequate arrangements for dealing with fires in their towns and cities. This process was very slow and it wasn't until the year 1929 that the last insurance fire brigade actually disbanded, in Worcester.

The Liverpool and London and Globe Fire Brigade, together with their steam fire engine, had performed valuable service to the people of the three towns for the past ten years. With the demise of this short-lived insurance brigade, the borough of Plymouth, however, was still protected by the following fire brigades: The West of England Insurance Company Fire Brigade, with their large manual engine, stationed in Cornwall Street, and the Plymouth Borough Corporation Fire Brigade, who had been given the steam engine by the outgoing Insurance brigade to bolster their fire-fighting arsenal. This steam engine graced the small fire station in Tavistock Place. The town fire engine (this was the parish pump) which was then housed at the Free Library in Whimple Street, and Street Fire escapes were located at the Free Library and outside the Theatre Royal. Each Street Escape had a fireman who was given the title of Escape Foreman, whose sole job was to fetch the ladders to where they were required, and to assist with any necessary rescues.

The three towns still relied heavily upon the goodwill of the military, who would often attend incidents with their manual engines, accompanied by a large contingent of soldiers, sailors or marines.

Devonport was still without an organised fire brigade, and following the local water company installing new fire plugs to the water main in 1878, it was mooted that a fire brigade should be formed out of the police force, and that the men appointed to this duty should be paid extra.

This recommendation followed a period of practice, whereby the men appointed to bring the parish engine to the scene of fires in the borough were busy familiarising themselves with connecting the standpipes to the new plugs. Much speculation followed, as firefighting arrangements within the borough were very crude, as the men were not properly trained. If the police force and fire engines were placed upon the same footings as those in the Dockyard, the town would possess a well-organised corps of firemen, who would be so efficiently trained that they would be able to cope with any fire that might break out.

When the fire engines and reels were last taken out for practice in Marlborough Street and Princess Street, it was clearly visible to the spectators that several of the men, under Superintendent Lynn, of the Devonport Police, were quite new to this work. This was commented upon both by the Fire Brigade Committee and those interested in operations. Certainly no blame could be attached to Mr Lynn for the state of things. Mr Lynn had proved himself most energetic in bringing the men up to their work, but the drawback experienced by him was the constant teaching of new hands. If a fire were to break out at any time in Devonport, Mr Lynn could only depend upon available men, including both old and new. But if a certain body of policemen were trained as a fire brigade, they could be depended upon, instead of having a mixed body of constables, each telling his less experienced comrade what to do.

The inhabitants of the town could set their minds at rest to the fact that they already have a fire brigade behind the Dockyard wall who looked after their interests. Devonport still failed in their responsibilities and dragged their heels, and they still relied heavily upon the military fire engines and the Metropolitan Police Fire Brigade within the Dockyard, for a further ten years, as it was not until 1888 that they actually formed their own fire brigade.

Theatre Royal destroyed by fire

Shortly before eleven o'clock on the night of 13th June 1878, the dreaded shout of 'Fire' was heard in the centre of Plymouth. As in January 1863, smoke was seen ascending from the roof and through the upper windows of the Theatre Royal. The fire engines, this time, were quickly on the spot, and, with all possible speed, the windows fronting the Athenaeum and those overlooking George Place were broken, and jets of water were thrown into the building. The fire must have obtained a considerable hold, even at this early stage, as forever and anon a lurid light was observed creeping stealthily across the windows at the Athenaeum end, followed by tongues of flame.

Whenever observed, these points received the full force of the fire hose, and in the moment that followed was darkness, a circumstance which failed to evoke the sympathetic cheers of the large crowd which had assembled on the ground. It was believed, indeed, that but for a burst in one of the hoses, the fire would have been extinguished. Several minutes elapsed before the damaged hose was replaced. Unhappily those were precious moments, fraught with disastrous consequences.

In the meantime the fire was observed to be making sinister advances towards the main entrance to the building. Gleams of deep red light were seen playing fitfully and anon with steady vigour about the upper circle and gallery windows. The excited crowd raised loud shouts of warning, and though policemen, firemen and energetic citizens ran about with laudable alacrity, there was no water until the burst hose was replaced. About this time, the Street Fire Escape was trundled to the scene, and was extended against the building. Now extra hose was directed through the windows, a deluge of water ensued, and as the clock struck the hour of midnight, there was once more darkness across the windows. But this was only for a few moments.

Far back down the middle of the theatre, the fire was doing its own fell work, gathering volume, and collecting energies for one destructive spring. The fire triumphed: a tongue of flame shot upwards, illuminating the upper windows and forcing its way through the roof. From that moment, the building was doomed. Creeping stealthily yet surely towards the Royal Hotel end of the building, the fire gained complete mastery. Vast volumes of dark lurid smoke ascended from the centre of the roof of the building, throwing a myriad of sparks and lighting up the sky, bringing the smallest objects into striking relief.

At a quarter to one, a loud rumbling was heard, as the roof fell in with a crash, thus laying the fiery pit within completely open to the actions of the air. So bright was the light shed around, that all the houses in the neighbourhood of that ill-fated building were brought into relief. Looking from the middle of George Street and the Crescent, they were lit up. The bright light brought into striking relief the white stone, the windows aglow as if with a thousand lamps, and the trees toning down the picture until it resembled a sketch from a transformation scene.

Another remarkable feature was the extreme tranquillity of the scene. There was very little noise and practically no excitement. The people were too shocked by the calamity to utter a word. All that could be heard was the cracking of the fire-eaten fabric and the deep swing of the fire engines. By one o'clock, the fire had made such progress that the Royal Assembly Rooms were felt to be in jeopardy, and certainly there was justification for this fear, as it seemed as if the entire block was doomed. The thin, silver-like streams of water seemed totally inadequate to the work cut out for them. They fell with a faint hissing noise upon the parapet of the gleaming roof, and entered the fiery furnace through the fierce heat of the yawning windows, turning into steam, and nothing more. But thin and romantic looking as the sweeping jets of water seemed, in the face of the huge body of flame with which they were sent to cope, they were, in reality, potent enough. At this time, the firemen had warmed thoroughly to their work, the engines were in full play and the supply of water was unlimited. The energy of the firemen who directed the hoses and the unfailing body of water thrown upon the building from several independent sources of supply combined to conquer the fire.

About a quarter past one, it was clear that the fire was got under control, and the apprehended ignition of the Royal Hotel was happily averted. Despite the heroic efforts of the West of England brigade, the town brigade, two Royal Marine fire engines, the Stonehouse Fire Brigade, a contingent of men with their fire engine from the Naval Hospital, engines of the 25th Regiment and the Royal Artillery, accompanied by hundreds of soldiers, the building could not be saved. The entire theatre had been con-

Firemen of the Stonehouse Fire Brigade with their manual fire engine c.1890.

sumed: stage, scenery, dress circle, upper circle, gallery, dressing rooms and theatrical paraphernalia. All had been devoured by the fire fiend. There was nothing left now save a heap of smouldering wood, canvas and upholstery, lying at the bottom of a pit formed of four blank walls. This fire tested the resilience and courage of all who fought the fire. Entry into the burning building was restricted in the early stages due to the tremendous heat and the falling debris. Once again the torrid stench of the aftermath of another huge fire hung over Plymouth for several days.

Meeting of Stonehouse Fire Brigade

The following report was taken from the *Western Daily Mercury*, dated 6th November 1878. This report highlights the problems being encountered with the Stonehouse Fire Brigade.

> Last evening a meeting of the Stonehouse Fire Brigade was held at the St George's Hall, for the purpose of nominating new members.
>
> Mr Bone was voted to the chair, and in opening the proceedings, explained that the meeting was held for the purpose of nominating newcomers, in order to fill the vacancies which had occurred in the brigade. The names of the gentlemen were then proposed on motion of Mr Hell, seconded by Mr Goad: Messrs. Westlake, Penrose, C. Bincock, Rawlings, and Lear.
>
> Mr Thuell thought it most desirable that there should be a deputy captain, in order to call the brigade together, and put them through the necessary duties – (hear, hear). This was considered ought to be done at least once a month. He complained of Mr Taylor, the present captain of the brigade, and alleged that he did not attend to his office in a proper manner. The fire-escape, which they owned, was in a bad state of repair, and as such might lead to serious, if not fatal consequences, an examination should be made. It was not fair that the men comprising the brigade should endanger their lives, when steps could be taken beforehand. He would make a resolution to the effect, that the machinery be examined.
>
> Mr Lucas seconded the proposition.
>
> Mr Blight thought it not right to dictate to the local board. Would it not be advisable to simply recommend that an examination of the machinery be made? He suggested that the local board should be consulted as to providing a place where to keep the fire-escape.
>
> Mr Thuell: Is the machinery fit for use?
>
> Mr Blight said he would not undertake to give an answer to this question as an individual member of the board.
>
> Mr Thuell remarked that he had a strong objection to work with the machinery in its present condition. The ropes and iron-work were unsafe.
>
> Mr Walters agreed with the previous speaker as to the dilapidated condition of the fire-escape, and thought it expedient that it should be examined.
>
> Mr Thuell felt convinced that precautionary measures should be taken. It was no use when a fire occurred, to say that the machine was out of order. The escape should be examined previous to the place in which to keep it.
>
> Mr Blight thought the local board should merely receive the suggestion of the Fire Brigade.
>
> Mr Thuell considered the matter should be brought before the local board, as he had suggested.
>
> Mr Blight remarked that the local board was interested in the efficiency of the machinery as much as they were. It would have much greater weight with that authority, were the suggestion made, instead of passing a resolution on the subject.
>
> Mr Thuell intended to adhere to the resolution which he had proposed, and which had been duly seconded.

Mr Blight moved an amendment, the effect of which, was that they should ask the local board to give their serious consideration to the condition of the fire-escape, with a view of having it put in a thorough state of repair.

The amendment was carried.

Mr Hearn made a suggestion that the local board be asked to supply hose and buckets, also lights.

Mr Thuell: A penny lamp will do (laughter).

Mr Lucas: We want gas.

Mr Walters: We still have the electric light (laughter).

Mr Thuell: A couple of penny lights will do.

Mr Thuell thought it most desirable that a second officer should be appointed. In the absence of the captain, everyone was inclined to take the lead. They must be properly organised or the work could not be attended to in a proper manner. Who would be responsible?

The chairman remarked that the meeting could nominate a person as second officer, and the matter could then be brought before the local board. Another meeting of the brigade could be called.

Mr Hearn nominated Mr Lee as a candidate.

Mr Thuell was about to make some observations with respect to the negligence of Mr Taylor when he was called to order by the chairman.

Mr Lucas seconded the proposition with respect to the nomination of a second officer.

On the motion of Mr Hearn, it was seconded by Mr Blight, the meeting was adjourned until Tuesday evening.

Helmet Plate and tunic button of Stonehouse Fire Brigade 1875–1916.

Stonehouse Fire Brigade poses in front of their Shand Mason steam fire engine, c.1902. Chief Officer Frederick Thuell and his brother George Thuell, who was deputy, are in the centre of the picture.

Stonehouse Fire Brigade reorganised

The Volunteer Fire Brigade of East Stonehouse was reorganised in 1881 following criticism of the brigade after the recent fire in Newport Street. Mr Curtis reorganised the running of the brigade, and Mr William Walter Blight was made superintendent of the brigade, with Mr William Vosper as third officer. The fire engines and ancillary equipment were overhauled, and other new equipment was purchased. In 1893, the brigade moved into a new fire station adjoining the Town Hall. A year later, in 1894, Mr James Cornish Wills, a prominent local tradesman, presented the brigade with a brand new Shand Mason Double Vertical steam fire engine, together with 1,000 feet of new hose.

The Death of William Marshall

On February 28th 1882, Mr William Marshall, Solicitor, and Chief Officer of the West of England Insurance Company Fire Brigade, died at the age of sixty-six years. Mr Marshall was appointed Chief Fire Officer when the West of England brigade was formed back in 1838. Mr Marshall had served for forty-four years, and was one of the most respected and well-known figures within the realms of the fire brigades throughout the country. Mr Marshall was born in August 1815 and was the son of Mr Charles

The Crocker Brothers, Albert, Henry, and James, of the Stonehouse Fire Brigade. These men joined the Stonehouse brigade shortly after leaving the West of England Insurance Fire Brigade in 1891. The Crocker family once had six members serving in the West of England brigade. They were; Foreman John Swigg (J. T. Crocker's grandfather); William Crocker (J.T. Crocker's father); J.T.Crocker and his sons Albert, Henry, and James.

Fireman Albert Crocker of the Stonehouse Fire Brigade.

The West of England Insurance Company Fire Brigade showing off their new uniforms and brass helmets, which were issued to celebrate their jubilee in 1890. The ornate brass breast badge had been withdrawn at the change of uniform.

Marshall, of Plymouth. Since the death of his wife, in November 1878, his health had failed, and in March 1881, he went to Madeira to convalesce. He returned home the following month, but his health never recovered, and he subsequently died. During Mr Marshall's absence, Mr Brooks conducted the business and fire brigade matters with great ability.

The agency was taken over by Mr William Derry, and the fire station was relocated from its site in Cornwall Street, and moved to Station Road, off Union Street. Mr Charles James Brooks was appointed Superintendent of the brigade, and Mr William Crocker became the Foreman.

Firemen in those times tended to work well into their twilight years, unlike the modern day firemen, who, depending upon their rank, can only work within the brigade until they are sixty years of age, irrespective of how fit they are. Perhaps it was the fact that the volunteer firemen of old did not have a fire brigade pension scheme to subscribe into, to look after them and their families in their old age.

Between December 1882 and August 1885, the brigades of the three towns attended notable fires at Mr Almond's Cement Works, Cattedown; Presbyterian Church, Eldad Hill; Plymouth Market; Laira Bakery; Loughter Mills, Plympton; Gibbs Vitriol Works, Cattedown, and Plymouth Promenade Pier, to name but a few.

An interesting account, which is worthy of mention, concerns the non-appearance of the fire brigade at the Bakery fire at Laira, on 30th April 1885. The premises in which the fire occurred were a bakery, shop and dwelling house, owned by Mr William Bovey. The fire originated in the bakehouse and quickly spread to the roof. A neighbour ran to the junction railway box to raise the alarm, and the signalman telegraphed Plymouth to send a fire engine. Unfortunately, no engine was dispatched, and the bakery sustained very serious damage, despite the efforts of a bucket chain formed by the neighbours.

Much indignation was expressed by the people of Laira at the refusal to send out the fire engines. Mr Brooks, the agent of the West of England Office, visited the village early in the afternoon and explained that he considered it useless to send the engines, there being no water available. The people there said that there was enough water available from the wells to feed one fire engine. The building was by now in total ruins; Mr Brooks considered it hopeless to offer any assistance and he returned to Plymouth.

Members of Stonehouse Fire Brigade, Police and civic dignitaries outside the nicely decorated fire station and police station, to celebrate Queen Victoria's diamond jubilee, in June 1897.

Third Officer William Vosper, Superintendant William Blight and Fireman Henry Crocker, of the Stonehouse Fire Brigade in 1893.

December 1885 brought Plymouth a most disastrous fire, with an appalling loss of life. Much bravery, and acts of heroism were witnessed at the fire in Looe Street. This fire holds an unenviable record in that the high loss of life in a single house fire has never been surpassed, other than by enemy action during the blitz of Plymouth.

CHAPTER SEVEN

THE LOOE STREET DISASTER – PLYMOUTH'S WORST PEACETIME TRAGEDY

A FEARFUL CALAMITY visited Plymouth in the early hours of 13th December 1885, by which thirteen persons, many of them children, were hurried into eternity by that most awful of visitations, a fire in the dead of night. The loss of life makes the calamity one of the heaviest of the kind that had fallen upon the town of Plymouth since the tragedy on 9th March 1863, when a firework-maker named Lawrence and five other persons were burnt to death as a result of an explosion in a house in Stonehouse Lane. The terrible loss of 300 souls in September 1796, when the naval frigate *Amphion* exploded *en masse* whilst moored up in Hamoaze, is not included. Most of the victims died as a direct result of the terrible explosion, or were drowned whilst in an injured state, rather than actually dying from the fire.

The house, No. 3 Looe Street, was once the publishing office of the old *Plymouth Herald*. The premises, which were of substantial construction, had been converted into a double house, with central passage, the ground floor being occupied by shopkeepers, and the two upper floors let out in tenements. The premises in which the fire occurred was situated a few yards down the hill, near the Naval Bank and the Old Guildhall. Almost without exception, the houses were very old, and crowded with tenants. Families of seven or eight people occupied one or two rooms. Judging from the dilapidated condition of many of the buildings, a fire, once started among them, would have a good chance of sweeping through the whole district. Fortunately, the premises that burnt down were separated from the adjoining property by very stout walls, and there was no wind blowing. Altogether, the inhabitants of the ill-fated house numbered thirty-one. Mr Sprague, a butcher, owner of the premises, occupied the shop on the higher left-hand side of the passage and the room behind, with a bedroom on the first floor. His family consisted of a wife and two children. The lower shop, a general dealer's, was rented by a widow named Babbage, who also occupied two bedrooms with her lodger brother, a single man named Edmund Downing, a plasterer, and Mrs Kirby, sister to Downing. Mr and Mrs Davey and four children occupied the back apartments on the first floor.

Three families were located on the upper floor, A family named Foss occupied two of the front rooms. The husband, Edward Foss, had been employed for some years as a shipwright in Devonport Dockyard; the other members of the family were Mrs Foss, four girls named Lizzie, Minnie, Lily, and Florry, and three boys – William, Alfred and John. A Mrs Newcombe and her daughter Amy, a young child, occupied another room on the same floor, and two rooms behind were tenanted by a widow named Jane Bickford, her five children, and a lodger named W. H. Daniel. Mrs Bickford's children were Edward, aged twenty years; William, aged eighteen; Frank, aged fourteen; Frederick, aged eleven; and Alfred, aged nine.

Out of the thirty-one persons here enumerated, twelve were found dead after the fire was got under control. Foss's wife and all seven children were suffocated in their beds. The other victims were Frederick Bickford, Mrs Sprague, Mrs Kirby, and Downing, her brother. Foss himself had a narrow escape; he jumped from the top storey while the fire was raging furiously, and he sustained terrible injuries. Mr Sprague saved his two children, and was under the impression, until too late, that his wife had managed to escape. The Davey family was rescued by means of ladders, from the windows at the rear of the premises, and the Bickford family and the Newcombes were saved, with the exception of little Freddie Bickford. Sadly, he got separated from his family and was found in one of the front rooms.

The fire broke out shortly after one o'clock. A merchant seaman named Mahney, who was on his way home, observed a glimmer of light between the shutters of Mrs Babbage's shop, and immediately raised the alarm. He then commenced to tear down the shutters. Several neighbours were alerted by the shouts and ran to lend assistance. A man called George Ellery ran to the police station and raised the alarm. Inspector Farmer, who was on duty, rounded up his men, and taking their hose reel cart, they raced to the scene. By now the fire had got a good hold and flames were belching from every window. The parties of constables from the central station were quickly followed by the town fire brigade, under the command of Mr McKeer. The West of England brigade also arrived on the scene, and quickly got to work. Chief Constable Wreford arrived after a short time, and assumed control of the Police Force. He was assisted by Inspector Farmer and Sergeants Monkley, Prout, Redd, and Gay; the force being augmented as rapidly as the men could be brought to the spot.

Some of the occupants of the burning house were evidently aroused by the first alarm. Among these were Mr Foss, who occupied a part of the top storey with his wife and seven children. Before the arrival of the police, Foss was seen by people in the street getting out of the window of his bedroom. The unfortunate man was terribly distraught, and was hanging on to the window sill amidst smoke and flames, which were issuing from his bedroom. It was obvious that for any persons remaining in the apartment, their condition was a most desperate one. Foss quickly tired, lost his grip and fell, pitching on the cornice over the butchers shop, and rebounded onto the roadway, striking the ground headfirst. Mr Foss's shattered body was taken from the scene by his neighbours, and was later conveyed to the South Devon and East Cornwall Hospital, where he remained in a very serious condition.

In the meantime, Mr Sprague and some of the other occupants of the house, including the Daveys and Bickfords, had been aroused to a sense of their perilous position. Mr Sprague caught up his two children, and rushed with them to the back of the house, which at this time was freer from smoke than the parts nearer the original seat of the fire. The firemen and others expedited the escape of those residents who got to the rear of the house. A ladder was obtained, and by this means, Sprague and his children were rescued; sadly, Mrs Sprague was unable to make good her escape and she perished within the burning house. The Daveys all escaped by the back, as did the whole of the Bickford family, with one exception, the boy Frederick. Davey, Sprague, and others, worked bravely, and the two elder Bickford boys, Edward and William, were most heroic in their efforts to save others. Their bravery and heroic acts were worthy of much praise.

Fortunately, a long ladder had been left in the court by masons, who had been working on the property, and this undoubtedly proved to be the salvation of several lives. Edward Bickford, who was the first of his family to awake, went to the Newcombes' room and roused them. He also knocked at Foss's door and shouted, but could get no answer. There was no time to be lost, for the smoke was thickening, and the heat coming up the staircase was intense. Young Bickford got out of the window of his room, placed the ladder in a more convenient position, and one by one several of his brothers were got down to the court below. William Bickford, a lad of eighteen years, caught up little Amy Newcombe in his arms. Too frightened to wait for his turn at the ladder, he got out of the window with the child in his arms, and hung on to the window frame with one hand, grasping the girl with the other, until someone was ready to catch her.

Eventually he dropped his precious burden into the arms of his eldest brother. Bickford, senior, caught the child, but the force of its descent from a height of thirty feet, dashed him to the ground. The poor girl was badly hurt, but her injuries were not life threatening and she eventually recovered in the hospital. William Bickford made good his escape by jumping onto a pile of bed linen, which was placed below him; he escaped with minor injuries. Mrs Bickford was rescued by means of the ladder; little Freddie Bickford, a boy of eleven years, who seems to have slept in Mrs Newcombe's room, was missed in the confusion, and his body was later found by firemen on the landing.

Mrs Babbage was the only one of three persons occupying her portion of the house who escaped with her life. Mrs Kirby, who was sleeping downstairs with Mrs Babbage, was supposed to have been one of the first occupants to be aroused. She ran upstairs to call her brother, but was overcome by smoke before she could effect her purpose. Her corpse was eventually discovered near that of her brother; both were only slightly burnt.

The saddest case of all is the fate of the Foss family. Mrs Foss and her seven children were all found dead in the room from the window of which the distracted father had made such a desperate exit. The poor woman had got out of bed, and had apparently made some effort to help her little ones, but she was unable to do much before the smoke overcame her. Five of the children were found huddled together in one bed, all dreadfully charred.

The staircase leading to the room was destroyed by the fire, and the firemen had to remove the bodies by means of the fire escape, which was brought to the scene from the old Guildhall. It is interesting to note that this fire escape was brought to the scene within five minutes of the arrival of the first hose reel. No successful attempts were made to use the fire escape for the purpose of rescuing the residents, due to the consequence of the fierce headway which the fire had obtained. Everybody seemed to have been under the impression that all the occupants had left the premises before the fire had made much progress. Great efforts were made by the firemen to prevent the fire spreading to other properties, and the efforts to extinguish the flames were carried on with untiring persistence and energy, for an hour or more. It was not until Mr Sprague began to worry as to the whereabouts of his wife that the authorities suspected there was anyone left in the house.

The efforts to reduce the fire were renewed with redoubled vigour when the possibility of loss of life forced itself upon the minds of those present. Before three o'clock, Mr McKeer, with Mitchell and other firemen, forced their way into Mr Sprague's room, and the body of Mrs Sprague was found half under the bed. After the removal of her body, a search was made of the rest of the premises as quickly as possible, and gradually the fearful tale of victims mounted up. An entry of Foss's room was affected by means of the fire escape, and it was then, for the first time, that the terrible extent of the calamity became evident.

The heart-rending nature of the scene presented itself to the horrified gaze of the firemen. As already stated, the bodies of Mrs Kirby and Mr Downing were found in the bedroom of her brother, and that of the little boy, Freddie Bickford, was discovered on the landing. Mr Foss succumbed to his injuries later that day, bringing the total number of victims of that terrible fire to thirteen.

The usual signals for the military and navy to attend – the firing of guns, and the burning of rockets – were not given, because the flames, due to the low-lying position of the premises, could not be seen at Mount Wise, where the night signalman was on duty.

Both Edward and William Bickford, together with fireman W. Brock, of the Corporation Fire Brigade, were later awarded a cash sum and certificate from the Society for Protection of Life from Fire, for their brave deeds that night.

Superintendent McKeer's account

Mr J. McKeer, who resided at the head of Treville Street, only a short distance from Looe Street, and was the second in command of the Corporation Fire Brigade, made the following statement about the Looe Street tragedy:

> I was called at about 1.25 a.m. on Sunday morning, hurrying as fast as I could; I got to the scene of the conflagration six minutes afterwards. Then I found that the hose reel from the Guildhall had already been brought out, and was at work. The hose connected with the reel from the Harbour Avenue police station, was being laid out, as was the hose of

Artist impression of the horrific scenes during the terrible fire in Looe Street Plymouth, on December 14th 1885, where a total of thirteen lives were lost.

the Corporation Fire Brigade, whose office was situated at the Old Guildhall, or otherwise the Free Library, which is facing the top of Looe Street. The Fire Escape, which was under the superintendence of my foreman, Mr Marshall, and which was in perfect order on Wednesday last, when it was trialled in Whimple Street, followed him. Immediately on my arrival, in the absence of Mr Lethbridge, who would undoubtedly have been there but for illness, I took charge of the whole of the operations.

Flames were springing forth from both the butcher and grocer's shops, as also from the windows over. Indeed, so great was the heat, that one woman living in a house opposite, who was trying to escape with her children, had her arms frightfully blistered.

My first exclamation on getting to Looe Street, seeing as I did the man Foss being carried away injured, were: 'Are there any persons in the house,' I called these words, or words to that effect, out loudly several times, to the many people around, and received no answer in the affirmative, I concluded there were not. However, the fire escape was placed against one of the top windows, namely, that of the sleeping room of Mr Foss and family, and an effort was made by me and other men to enter, but it was unavailing, so intense was the heat, and so thick the smoke. A hose was taken up the escape, and men proceeded to pour water into Mrs Foss's room, without knowing that there were any bodies in it.

In fact, there were in the room the bodies of Mrs Foss and five of her children. The two other Foss children were lying in a room just off Mrs Foss's bedroom. By about two o'clock there was in all five streams of water being thrown on the burning mass. The reels were connected as follows: Central Police, the top of Buckwell Street; Harbour Avenue, the corner of Batter Street; the Corporation Fire Brigade, corner of Kinterbury Street; the West of England Fire Brigade, close by where the escape was stationed; and the Barbican police reel. Thus a splendid stream of water was being thrown, both from behind and in front, on the burning house. I am positive that when I arrived, there could be no living soul in the house.

When the fire had been nearly conquered, and it was thought that people had remained in the house, I had a ladder placed against Mr Sprague's window. This is the lower portion of the building, just over the grocer's shop. Mr Sprague had taken advantage of the alarm, and escaped with his two children, and it was his belief that his wife was following him. For some reason, probably being overcome with the dense smoke, she did not do this, and when Mitchell, another fireman, and I entered, we found her on the floor in her nightdress, partly under the bed. Her nightdress was singed, as was the bedding slightly. The body was brought down by means of the stairs, which were not very greatly burnt, on a stretcher, and then sent to the mortuary at the Central Police Station. When on a further search, it was found other bodies were still on the premises, it was suggested to me that we should not seek to remove them until daylight.

The inadvisability of this was evident, rugs were brought, and men sent into other rooms there, to collect the remains of the other persons who had been mostly suffocated to death. These remains were carried down on the shoulders of the men, by means of the fire escape, and then likewise, conveyed to the Guildhall. It was in the top room over the butcher's shop that Mr Foss and his family was sleeping. Mr Foss escaped from the burning house by jumping from the window. I cannot tell now whether he was living or dead, for he was conveyed to the hospital. Firemen subsequently came across the charred remains of his wife and five children. The woman who kept the grocer's shop was one of the first to be alarmed by the fire. At the back of the shop was her sitting room, and then behind that again, was the bedroom. It was here that the woman and another elderly person were sleeping. Mrs Babbage made good her escape by the back of the premises. The other woman, who went back, as she said to call someone, was overcome, and was not seen afterwards by her. Mrs Babbage had said that the fire must have originated in her shop, but pointed out that she entered it between 12 and 12.30 without any light, turning off the gas. Then everything seemed to be safe.

There were I have been told, upwards of thirty people in the house, and altogether twelve were suffocated or burnt to death. The house was a very old one, and on the premises were printed the old *Plymouth Herald*. It was astonishing how the house, which was mostly built of wood, the partitions of the room being composed of timber, had been burnt through. The flames and smoke must have gone up the stairs, and thus into the rooms, the doors of which must have been left open. I could not say for certain, but I believe there was no door at all to Foss's room, at least I saw none. Brock, a fireman of the brigade, who resides in Buckwell Street, his house coming right out at the back of the burning premises, was early alarmed by the screaming. He was quickly up and helped Sprague get his two children, who were taken over to Mr Rowe's in Buckwell Street, out of the building, and assisted Mitchell in getting out the bodies. As yet, I cannot account for the outbreak, but I believe it first broke out in the grocer's shop.

This was the worst fire known in Plymouth since the one at Lawrence's in Stonehouse Lane, where fireworks were being made for the celebration of the Prince of Wales's wedding, and then many persons were burnt to death. Inspector Farmer was on the scene before me, and he said he was called from the police station at 1.23 a.m. It was true his brigade, in consequence of illness and other causes, was numerically very weak. But still the police and the West of England men worked well, and there was no lack of help. Up to 9.15 a.m. at which time I left for an interval, all were busy, and even during my short absence, more water had to be thrown on the ruins.

I should add that during the progress of the conflagration, the partition wall not being built right up, fire was discovered raging in No. 2 Looe Street. Seeing this, I ordered two of the West of England and two of my own men, to get up through the top hatch and pour water upon it. This they soon did, and all fear the fire spreading was removed. I have been told that a sailor, on discovering the fire, immediately proceeded to pull down the shutters, and this served to fan the flames. This is often done, but is a very absurd thing. The manner in which the flames seemed to have plated about the room is remarkable, and could not have occurred in a modern built house. In rooms where there had been fire, there were many things entirely untouched. The clock in Mrs Babbage's room was still 'Going', being apparently unharmed.

The social side of firefighting

A fireman's life is not only a tragic one; there were occasions when a jolly social get-together was as good as any modern day counselling! For a considerable period, the greatest unanimity has existed between the members of the West of England and the East Stonehouse Fire Brigades, bodies of men whose value has so often been demonstrated when their services have been called into requisition. In the summer of 1886, for the purpose of further cementing the bonds of friendship, and also for individual enjoyment, an excursion was organised to Leg o'Mutton Corner near the Rock, on the moors.

The West of England brigade (twelve in number) commanded by Mr C. J. Brooks, hitched up their horses, whilst that of East Stonehouse (twelve men and two torch boys) commanded by the second Captain W. W. Blight, gathered up their men and were ready for the off. The West of England men proceeded with their engine, which was drawn by four greys, whilst the Stonehouse brigade were conveyed in a well appointed four-in-hand carriage from the establishment of Mr E. Sloggett, of Stonehouse.

Upon their arrival on the moor, the men from the respective brigades took part in various competitions to demonstrate their skills. The outdoor sports being over, a move was made for the Bullers Arms, where much merriment and toasting was undertaken. The men arrived back in Plymouth at a very late hour, all in a happy mood. Social gatherings and public dinners between the fire brigades of the three towns were often undertaken and served to promote good relations and comradeship between the officers and men of each brigade.

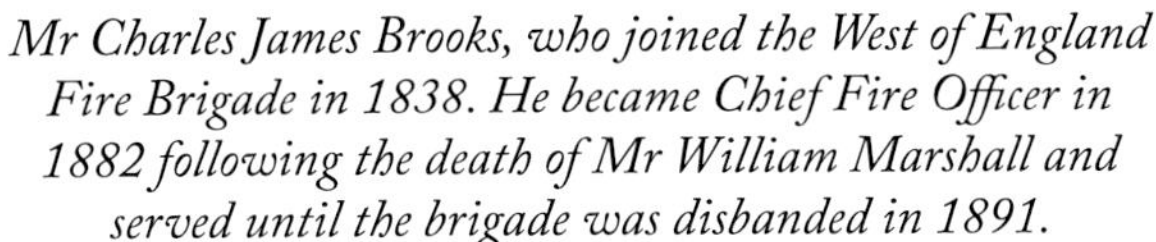

Mr Charles James Brooks, who joined the West of England Fire Brigade in 1838. He became Chief Fire Officer in 1882 following the death of Mr William Marshall and served until the brigade was disbanded in 1891.

Edward Philp, of the West of England Insurance Fire Brigade, in 1889.

Chief of Plymouth Fire Brigade retires

Another milestone in the history of fire brigades within the three towns was reached in September 1886, when Mr Walter Lethbridge, Superintendent of the Plymouth Borough Fire Brigade, tendered his resignation to the Watch Committee of the town council. Mr Lethbridge reported that he was prepared to carry on until a suitable replacement could be appointed, and he thanked the committee for all their help over the last twenty-three years. The brigade was now under the superintendence of Chief Constable Wreford, as the brigade was transferred to the police. One of the inspectors was to act as his deputy and drill instructor. The services of Mr McKeer (as third officer), and some of the old brigade were retained.

Mr Lethbridge was appointed as head of the town brigade on 11th August 1863, and his resignation, twenty-three years later, came as a shock to the men of his brigade. Mr Lethbridge's health was not good, and that, together with the fact that he was becoming increasingly disillusioned with the town council, who appeared to be indifferent to the recommendations which he put forward following the tragedy at Looe Street, just before Christmas the previous year, no doubt influenced his decision.

Before Mr Lethbridge's appointment, there existed some friction between the Mayor and the military Commander-in-Chief of the Western District, concerning the control of persons employed in extinguishing a fire, which occurred in a manufactory at Coxside. Inasmuch as the town had mainly to rely on, in case of fire, military and naval aid, it was not surprising that there should be a disposition to ignore the civil authority. The upshot of the difference of opinion was that the Council resolved to call a fire brigade into existence. At that time, the only means for saving life and property from fire, beyond that at the command of the naval and military authorities, consisted of an engine and brigade belonging to the County Fire Office, which the town assisted to support, and the West of England Insurance Office made similar provision.

Upon the appointment of Mr Lethbridge, the Corporation acquired the fire extinguishing appliances of the disbanded County Fire Office, consisting of two or three old hand manual engines, which were worked by seven or eight firemen. After a short time, much needed improvements were made. A Shand Mason thirty-man manual engine was bought, and later six hose-reel carts supplemented this. The reels were stationed at the following places: Harbour Avenue, Barbican, Octagon Police Station, Guildhall fire station and the workhouse. Two patent fire escapes and ladders were added to the original plant; one was at the Guildhall and the other at Alton Terrace, off Tavistock Road. For many years, the Corporation Fire Brigade consisted of nine men and three officers, and at the time of Mr Lethbridge's resignation, there were thirteen men and three officers.

From the above information, it was gathered that the actual material at the disposal of Mr Lethbridge had not been increased to any considerable extent since his appointment as superintendent. It must be said that the Plymouth Corporation Fire Brigade, albeit one of the most cheaply worked of Corporation departments, had attained a state of efficiency, unsurpassed by that of any other town of similar size. It is astonishing indeed that so much should have been accomplished with so little means.

A steam fire engine was the principal instrument used in the majority of large towns like Plymouth, and its initial cost would not amount to less than £600 or £700. It is obvious that the expenditure incurred by the Corporation of Plymouth had been far less than that which would have been necessitated, had the Fire Brigade Department been controlled by less able and economical hands. There were some other matters requiring almost equal attention, and these were mentioned in Mr Lethbridge's report to the committee soon after the terrible disaster in Looe Street. Some of the recommendations were adopted, but much remained shelved. Mr Lethbridge made some comments in his report as to the necessity of better all-round provision against fire. He submitted to his committee the question of whether the time had not arrived when the town should have such appliances and brigade as would render it comparatively independent of outside assistance, which the Council has no power to command. He pointed out that should the committee deem it advisable to adopt this suggestion, it would be necessary that the brigade should have increased accommodation provided at the Old Guildhall station. Far better, would have been that a new station should be erected at the Western end of the municipal offices.

Mr Lethbridge asked for a steam fire engine and an addition to the brigade of seven firemen, one engineer, and another officer. The total strength would then amount to twenty firemen, one engineer, one engine and housekeeper, two call boys and three officers. As a result of the recommendations of Mr Lethbridge, in January 1886 the Council sanctioned the expenditure of £258 for fire appliances. Some improvement was promised towards telephonic communication between the various stations and the central police station. Provision of an electric alarm bell to the foreman of escapes and also to the residences of a number of selected firemen was considered.

Within a week of Mr Lethbridge submitting his written resignation, he fell ill, and Mr John McKeer, a trunk maker and fancy goods dealer, of Treville Street, took command of the brigade in his absence. Mr McKeer was in command of the Corporation Fire Brigade at a serious fire in Frankfort Square at the beginning of October, whereby a gas leak ignited and caused extensive damage to a store, prematurely roasting fifty fowls and two cats. Sadly, Walter Lethbridge did not recover from his illness, and he died towards the end of 1886.

CHAPTER EIGHT

DARING RESCUES AND OTHER TRAGEDIES

ON THE MORNING of November 24th 1886, a serious fire, by which one life was lost and at least forty others endangered, broke out in a large dwelling house in Cobourg Street. The house, a double fronted one, was used as the Devon and Cornwall Blind Institute before the residents moved to the new premises at the top of North Hill. The fire furnished important evidence of the defective appliances used by the Corporation Fire Brigade, compounding Lethbridge's report.

The house was three stories high and contained in all twenty-four rooms, which were occupied by ten different families, numbering in all, twenty adults and forty-four children. Luckily, the fire did not break out in the middle of the night, as surely a more dreadful calamity would have taken place had it done so.

The house construction offered a splendid run for any fire that might occur, as did most of the old properties in Plymouth at that time. In order to understand the remarkably narrow escapes which occurred, it is necessary to give a little description of the building. As stated above, it was a double fronted house, and the front rooms on either side of the doorway were converted into shops. Mr Reuben, grocer and confectioner, occupied the one on the right; that on the left was occupied by Mr Evans, a general dealer and greengrocer. There were two rooms at the back of each shop. Mr Reuben did not live at the house, but he occupied one room behind his shop as a sort of rest room during the day.

The small room at the back was used by Mr Evans as a lumber room, in which he stored features, old clothes, washing trays, and other spare articles. Right underneath this lumber room was a bakehouse, fitted with a baker's oven, the property of Mr Reuben. The oven was embedded in three layers of bricks. Above this were the rafters, which supported the lumber-room, where the fire originated. Between the lumber-room and the two rooms at the back ran a lofty staircase with a big stairwell. A plumber named Welch, his wife and six children occupied the rooms on either side of the staircase. On the first landing, the two tenement rooms were occupied by William Woods, a pensioner, his wife, and four children. J. Woods, a tailor, with his wife and five children rented the two rooms on the same landing, one of which was immediately over the lumber-room.

A plasterer named Turner, his wife and six children, and a baker named Edmonds, with a wife and six children tenanted the remaining five rooms on this landing. On the second landing, a third storey, there were seven rooms. It was in one of these in which the prostrate bodies of a woman named Issacs, wife of a dockyardsman, and two of her children were found. Mrs Issacs, who lived apart from her husband, rented the first two rooms on the right. She had five children living with her, and her brother-in-law, Henry Issacs, who was employed in the Dockyard, as a lodger. Four of the children, Clara, ten years old; Alfred, seven; Maud, five; and Blanch, three, slept with their mother, whilst the eldest boy, Frederick, twelve years old, slept with his uncle. A railway labourer named Perdon, with his wife and seven children, occupied one of the rooms. A back room was occupied by Edward Cotton, gardener, his wife and five children.

There was no sign or smell of fire when all the occupants retired for the night. Shortly after half-past five in the morning, W. Woods got out of bed as usual, and he heard the breaking of glass. When he opened the door, there was a considerable amount of smoke, with little flame, issuing from the lumber room window. Taking his children, he rushed into the street with only their nightclothes on; his wife followed in her nightdress. Mr Woods returned to his room to gather up what clothes he could and took them to his frightened family. He went back to the room for the second time, and found two children; he did not know to which family they belonged. They were running about crying piteously for their mother and family, he picked them up and took them into the street. Woods then re-entered, and endeavoured to climb the staircase, but was driven back by dense smoke and flames, which were issuing with some power. Mr Issacs, upon opening his door, found the staircase smoke-logged. He too raised the alarm, and in a few minutes the children of the different families and the parents were running about half-naked in a state of panic.

The smoke was so overpowering, and the screams of the women and children were heartrending. The husbands, so dense was the smoke, could not distinguish their own wives and children from the others, and clutching to the first that came to hand, made an attempt to get down the staircase. They were driven back by the smoke and heat. They rushed to the windows of the top front rooms, breaking them in order to admit air and to vent the choking smoke. Outside the top windows of the house was a cornice, barely a foot wide, and finding no assistance at hand, the occupants of the top rooms, with their children, got out on this cornice; this action obviously saved many lives.

The alarm of fire was spread far and wide, and within a short space of time, many willing and ready hands were on the spot doing what they could to render assistance. Some helped to rescue the children as they were passed out of the window, whilst the neighbours offered the stricken families a temporary resting place. The fire escape and hose reel were brought from the Harbour Avenue station in charge of PCs Setters, Farmer, Prowse and Slowman. The Corporation reel in charge of Mr McKeer, the Superintendent, was next to arrive. Reels from the Octagon Police Station, in charge of Sergeant Rodd, PCs Kingston, Monkley and Venton, and the West of England reel, in charge of Mr Brooks and Mr Crocker, followed later. All the reels were soon connected to the fire plugs, whilst the fire escape was placed against the building, and one woman and two children were rescued by firemen who carried them down.

A thrilling scene occurred, in which a young plumber, Mr P. Whitfield, was the principal hero. Whitfield arrived at half past five, went into the passage with a policeman and saw the flames at the back of Reuben's shop. He tried to go upstairs, but was forced back by flames and smoke. Then, in the company of a man named William Rich, he went to the back premises and got a ladder for the purpose of rescuing the people who were standing on the cornice. The cornice was only eleven inches wide, was sloping, and about thirty feet from the ground.

Finding the ladder too short to reach the cornice, Whitfield and Rich mounted the roof of Mr Start's house, drew up the ladder and planted it against the house in which the fire was burning. The ladder now reached to within a foot or two of the cornice. Whitfield and Rich helped several people to get down the ladder, among them Mr and Mrs Perdon. When Mr Perdon had been rescued, he began shouting, 'For God's sake, save my boy.' He told Whitfield that the boy was in the first room on the side near the ladder. Whitfield went up, walked the cornice and got in the window of the room indicated. He searched the room, despite choking smoke and flames, but found it to be empty. He then found his way into the adjoining room, and after a moment or two, stumbled against something, which proved to be Mrs Issacs and the boy Perdon, who were laying side-by-side, unconscious. He tried to rouse Mrs Issacs, but she was too far gone. At this moment, another man got in at the window, and with his help Whitfield got the insensible woman out of the window and put her into the hands of policemen, who had by this time raised a ladder. Having thus secured the safety of Mrs Issacs, Whitfield pluckily went back to the room, seized the child and brought him out.

The policemen's ladder being encumbered by the men who were trying to carry off Mrs Issacs, he was unable to use it. Nothing was left but to walk along the cornice with the child in his arms, a very perilous business, seeing that the ledge was not only narrow, but also very slippery, and there was no projection of any kind to hold on to. Standing with his back to the wall, Whitfield, amidst the excitement of the spectators, slowly made his way along the cornice, and at length, safely brought the boy down a ladder planted at the other end of the house. Whitfield was almost exhausted when he reached the ground; the spectators loudly cheered his gallant conduct.

During the early progress of the fire, one of the Corporation firemen, named Newton, entered the first floor and handed out a woman and four children to PC Tucker. Another Corporation fireman named Brooks also entered the house. Getting in via the top window, he set about rescuing several of the residents. Policemen, firemen and members of the public made dramatic entries into the burning house and emerged with children in their arms. The rescues from the upper floors were severely hampered by the state of some of the escape ladders. The town authorities were criticised for the condition of some of their equipment. Sergeant Warne of the borough police mounted one of the escape ladders in order to rescue people from upper rooms, when it broke in half, and he fell heavily to the ground, injuring himself.

Inspector Hill, also of the borough police, had the promptitude to send for medical help during the early stages of the fire, and within a short time, surgeons Mr W. Square and Mr J. May were on the spot and attended to the suffering. The fire was all but out after about half an hour of the first police reel to have arrived on the scene. The little girl, Maud Issacs, who was five years old, was found to be dead, whilst her poor mother was badly burned about the face and arms. The rest of the Issac children were all suffering the effects of smoke inhalation, and were put to bed in the house of Mr John Hifley, a local chemist. At the coroner's inquest, following the fire, much praise was heaped upon those who performed gallantly; their names were forwarded to the authorities for special mention.

Huge conflagration in Frankfort Square

Great commotion was caused in the three towns on the night of 6th January 1887 – the news was spreading that a large fire was raging in the centre of Plymouth. The inhabitants, however, did not require the signal guns that were fired to warn them of the fact, for the skies were lit with a lurid glow, and to all who were out of doors, the fact that an immense conflagration was raging in Plymouth was very evident. The fire had broken out in a building known as the Old Barracks in Frankfort Square. The building was the property of Mrs J. Walter Wilson (the wife of the town clerk). Mr Isaac Watts, of the Globe Hotel, rented the two lower floors for the purposes of a stable. The top two upper flats were held by Mr Cole, basket maker. Whilst the alarm was being raised, the neighbours managed to rescue eighteen horses from the stables.

The police reel was first to arrive and they set into the hydrant at the corner of Frankfort and Russell Streets, but by the time the first jet was played upon the burning premises, the fire had secured such a hold that it was evident to everyone that the building was doomed. The pressure from the mains was so poor that the jet could not reach the roof and therefore was ineffective. While the Police were busy in Frankfort Square, the West of England brigade had arrived, and was doing good service, having connected at the corner of Westwell Street and Russell Street, where a good supply was obtained.

Other reels were brought to the scene from the Octagon and Barbican, and were quickly set into other hydrants. The Stonehouse Fire Brigade appeared on the scene with all haste, and using the appliance of the West of England were in a position to fix onto the Plymouth hydrants. Naval and military detachments were arriving at intervals. The immensely powerful steam engine (the Sutherland) from Devonport Dockyard came up ready for any contingency. The building had been blazing up to an alarming degree, the flames being seen for many miles around, with the result that a mob of great magnitude had assembled. The arrival of assistance was greeted with applause.

The fire was observed between 10 p.m. and 10.45 p.m. by the men on duty at Mount Wise Signalling Station, who at once informed the Naval Commander-in-Chief, Admiral Augustus Phillamore. He immediately gave the necessary orders, and the harbour station was communicated with. The usual guns were fired from the battery at Mount Wise. A party of the Steam Reserve, including forty-five men of the Royal Adelaide, was marched into Plymouth with buckets, grappling irons, etc. On their way in, they raised the alarm at the Raglan Barracks, and a picket of the Royal Irish Regiment, which was stationed there, proceeded to the scene of the fire. Other military personnel to respond were 250 men of the 2nd battalion of the South Staffordshire Regiment, based at the Citadel, many of them being armed. A detachment of Royal Marines from Stonehouse was also dispatched with their fire engine.

As soon as the troops and sailors were assembled in the vicinity of the fire, cordons were drawn. These were to keep the enormous crowds of people who had assembled out of the way of the police and the fire brigades of the three towns, who were engaged in the task of suppressing the outbreak. The fire was within a square, completely hidden from the main streets, and only discernible by the flames shooting high above the houses that enclosed it.

The police and military struggled to maintain their cordon against the excited crowds. Numerous outbreaks of violence broke out, and there was a lot of stone-throwing going on. Whilst the fire was still raging, ugly scenes were being enacted on the outskirts of the crowd, resulting from collisions between the police and military on one hand and the spectators on the other. The government steam fire engine was protected from the pressure of the mob by a line of soldiers with muskets in hand. Several arrests were made; this led to a general melee, in which soldiers, police, and civilians were indiscriminately mixed up.

The police used their batons freely, while some of the soldiers used their muskets with much violence. A series of ugly rushes kept the street in a tumult for a quarter of an hour or so. Every now and then, the military chased groups of young men and scattered them amid the shouts of the onlookers. The mob retaliated by closing in on the soldiers, who happened to be separated from their comrades in the confusion. The soldiers hit out savagely at some of the mob, several of which received bad injuries by soldiers wildly brandishing their weapons.

The firemen, unaware as to the disturbances going on, did good work to stop the fire spreading, and the fire was got under control in the early hours. At three a.m., another alarm of fire was raised. The sound of whistles blown in two or three quarters, together with shouts of 'Fire' called the attention of the police and others who were still on duty in Russell Street. Leaving a few men in charge of the smouldering ruins, the available force made for the direction of Looe Street where a fierce fire was raging. The fire had broken out in a large malt house, belonging to Messrs Pitts and King, in lower Stillman Street. There was much commotion in the area, as there was a considerable body of fire within the five-storey building.

The neighbourhood was thickly populated, being in the heart of the oldest part of Plymouth, and many people ran into the streets with just their night clothes on; women and children were huddled together barefoot in Batter Street.

The West of England brigade, the Stonehouse Fire Brigade, and several police reels were soon on the spot, and the fire escape from the Old Guildhall was brought down. The fire was under control within an hour, and there were no signs of the disturbances that occurred earlier in Frankfort Square.

Improvements to the town fire brigade

The Plymouth Corporation Fire Brigade was reorganised early in January 1887, and part of the police force was incorporated with them. Superintendent Wreford made the following remarks during a speech at a celebratory dinner attended by the borough police and fire brigade at Routley's Farley Hotel early in January. He stated that there was adverse criticism regarding the amalgamation of the police and fire Brigade, but he failed to see the reason for it. They really still had the old brigade with twenty trained men of the police force, ten of these always being ready to attend fires. Besides that, every member of the force would be trained as a fireman, and further, they had the telephone connecting them with eight different places in the borough. He was convinced they would at least be able to extinguish fires as well, if not better than hitherto.

Presentations following Cobourg Street fire

On 31st January 1887, the Mayor (Mr W. H. Algar) was called upon to carry out a task, which was most pleasing. It was that of handing to several men, who were particularly conspicuous by acts of daring at the Cobourg Street fire. Certain awards were to be made by the Royal Society for the Protection of Life from Fire. The Mayor was accompanied by the following local dignitaries: Captain Inskip, RN; Mr T. Brook, borough magistrate; Mr W. Derry, agent to the West of England Insurance Company; Chief Constable Wreford, Detective Inspector J. Hill, and Mr McKeer (Superintendent, Deputy Superintendent, and Inspector respectively of the Corporation Fire Brigade); Mr C. J. Brooks (Superintendent of the West of England Fire Brigade), and W. W. Blight and Captain W. H. Vosper (Stonehouse Fire Brigade). In addition, there were in attendance many men belonging to the several brigades, all appearing in their uniforms.

After addressing all the recipients, and giving a narrative of the brave acts, the following men were presented with awards: Mr Peter Whitfield was awarded a silver medal and £5; Corporation Fireman William Brock, a certificate plus £5; Police Constable John Tucker, a certificate plus £2; Mr William Rich, a certificate plus £3; Charles Hellyar, a certificate plus £2; Edwin Catton, a certificate plus £2; William Woods, a certificate plus £1.

A special award was also presented to Mr C. J. Brooks, of the West of England Fire Brigade, by the Royal Society for the Protection of Life from Fire, in recognition of outstanding service in connection with the suppression of fires in this district since he joined the brigade back in 1867. Mr Brooks not only attended fires within the three towns, but in places so wide apart as Cargreen in Cornwall, to Brent. This numbered no less than 400 occasions, and during the preceding ten years, he had practically the sole direction of the company's brigade. On the occasions of the numerous fires which occurred in Plymouth in December 1885, and especially the calamitous fire in Looe Street, Mr Brooks was the head of his brigade. He was among the first to enter and explore the ruins, and to discover the awful loss of life that occurred on that occasion.

The directors of the Royal Society, at that time, passed a special resolution thanking Mr Brooks and his Plymouth brigade for the efficient manner in which they always carried out the duties entrusted to them. They expressed their entire satisfaction with the management of the brigade. Mr Brooks having been present on all the occasions when special services were rendered in saving life from fire, had always taken a prominent part in bringing the various cases before the Royal Society for the Protection of Life from Fire. His services in this direction were especially valuable at the recent Cobourg Street fire, when an unusually large number of acts of bravery had to be investigated and laid before the society. All these circumstances led the society to desire that a testimonial from the London society be publicly presented to him. Mr Brooks was by many years the oldest official connected with the fire establishments in Plymouth.

Mr Wreford takes command of Plymouth Fire Brigade

A significant event took place in Plymouth in January 1887: Chief Constable Wreford was put in charge of the newly reorganised fire brigade. The Corporation Fire Brigade was amalgamated with the Police Firemen. This amalgamation meant that some policemen could resume their police duties. This arrangement worked reasonably well until 1891, when the whole of the police force took on the responsibility of firefighting in Plymouth. The police and police firemen did not prove to be as harmonious as had been first envisaged, and it proved to be a strain upon the force. Much bad feeling between the fire bobbies and the regular police was evident throughout their existence, and the problem was not remedied until after the war had finished.

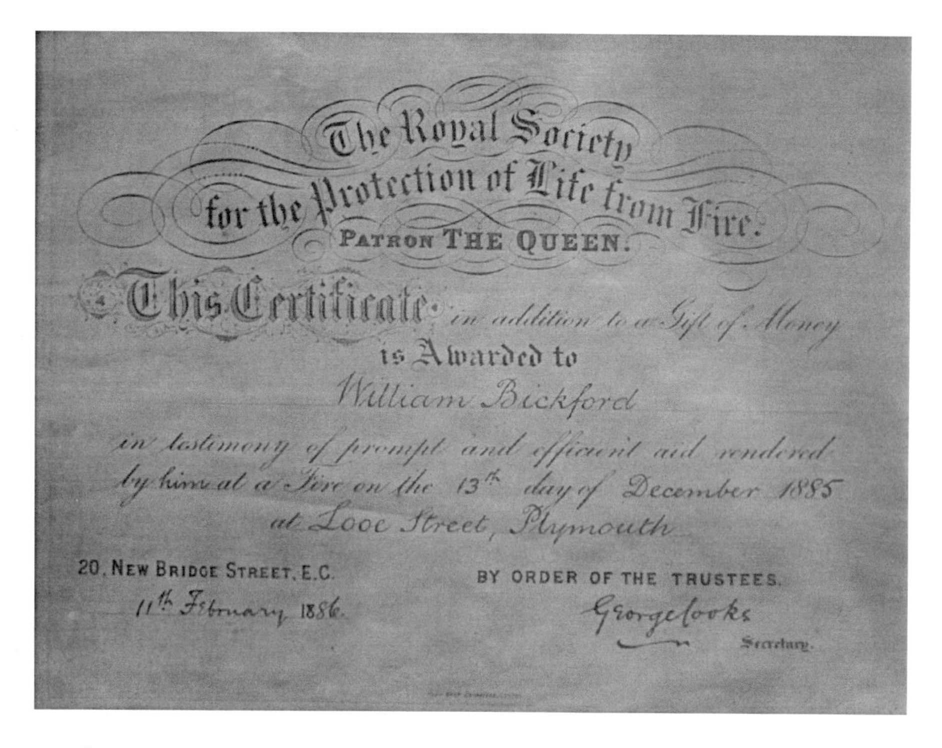

The Royal Society
for the Protection of Life from Fire.
PATRON THE QUEEN.

This Certificate in addition to a Gift of Money
is Awarded to
William Bickford
in testimony of prompt and efficient aid rendered
by him at a Fire on the 13th day of December 1885
at Looe Street, Plymouth

20, NEW BRIDGE STREET, E.C.
11th February 1886.

BY ORDER OF THE TRUSTEES.
George Cooke
Secretary.

Bravery certificate awarded to William Bickford by the Royal Society for the Protection of Life from Fire, for his actions at the Looe Street tragedy in December 1885.

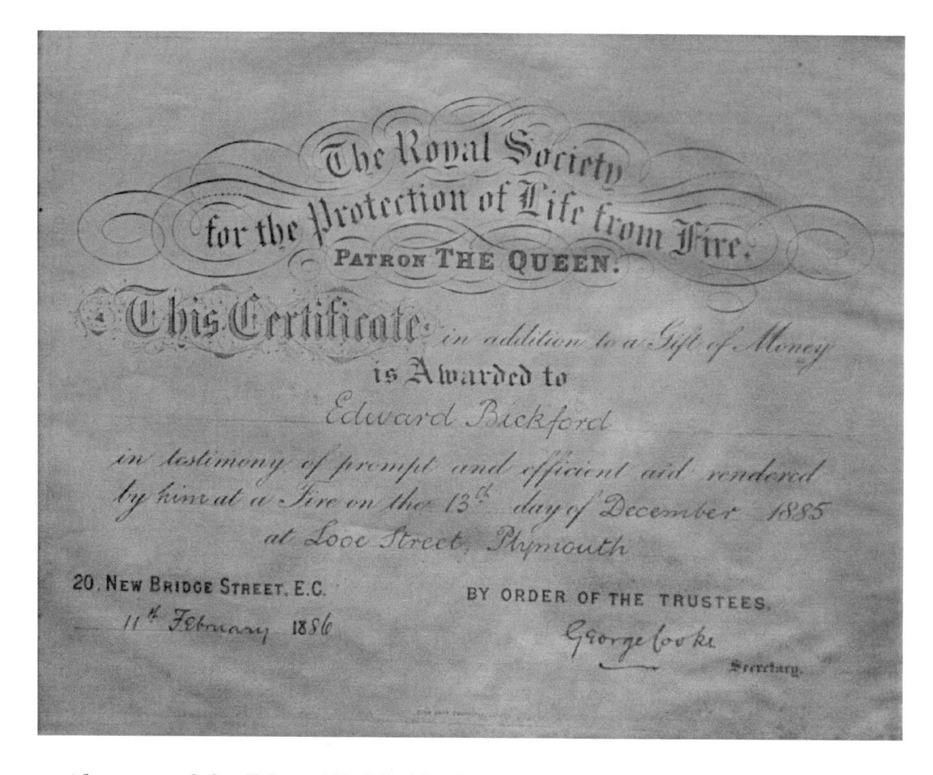

The Royal Society
for the Protection of Life from Fire.
PATRON THE QUEEN.

This Certificate in addition to a Gift of Money
is Awarded to
Edward Bickford
in testimony of prompt and efficient aid rendered
by him at a Fire on the 13th day of December 1885
at Looe Street, Plymouth

20, NEW BRIDGE STREET, E.C.
11th February 1886

BY ORDER OF THE TRUSTEES.
George Cooke
Secretary.

Bravery certificate awarded to Edward Bickford by the Royal Society for the Protection of Life from Fire, for his actions at the Looe Street tragedy in December 1885.

Fire at the old Frankfort Barracks

The old Frankfort Barracks, situated on ground adjoining Russell Street, was once again the scene of a huge fire. This time, the fire occurred on 8th August 1887, seven months after the big fire there in January. The fire occurred in the early evening, and upon the arrival of Mr F. Wreford (Chief Constable), and firemen, with hose-reels from various police stations, it was found that the water mains were dry. The representative from the water company was found, and sent off to the reservoir to turn on the water.

The West of England brigade, with Mr Charles Brooks in command, was soon on the scene, as was Mr John McKeer, with the Corporation engine. All the hoses were connected, and everything was ready for operations, but without water, all the fire appliances possessed by the town were useless. The firemen were standing about like dummies, whilst waiting for the supply to reach them.

The entire building was a mass of flames, and by the time a water supply was available, it was too late to prevent widespread destruction. Three horses, in the lower stables, were burnt to death, and others were badly scorched. Once again, the fire was fought with the assistance of the military with their engines, and a large detachment of soldiers, to prevent scenes of disorder that occurred back in January of that year.

Great alarm at Kinterbury Street fire

The year of 1887 was a particularly busy time for the respective fire brigades of the three towns, who attended several large fires within the district. It was just over a week since the brigades were tested in Frankfort Square, when once again, on 17th August, another large fire was reported to be raging in Plymouth. The fire occurred in the early hours of the morning in Gibben's aerated water manufactory, in Kinterbury Street. This flimsy structure was given over to the flames whilst the cries were being raised and the reels were rattling up from the police station. The building was soon well alight and in less than five minutes all that remained of Gibben's manufactory was a crashing, gruesome mass of ruins. As soon as the circumstances permitted, the police, under the command of Superintendent Wreford, were placed at various points. Before 2.30 a.m., the burning mass seemed to be flaring with a force suddenly subdued. In the meantime, all unsuspected, the flames had eaten their way into Watt's rag stores, an immense building at the rear, in which, of course, were a vast quantity of inflammable materials. By the time the various engines had arrived, the fire was burning simultaneously from all corners of the roof.

The scene was one of growing excitement; Kinterbury Street was one of the narrowest streets in Plymouth. The houses in it were very old, ill-constructed, and for the most part, considerably overcrowded. The routes from it, moreover, led to courts and alleys, in which there were dwellings of the same character. From these places, the people swarmed up, men, women, and children, shouting, crying, and frightened, with scarcely any clothing upon them, all carrying articles of furniture that they prized the most. They were soon reassured that the fire was blazing away in a direction that was not likely to immediately affect them.

By 2.50 a.m., the flames obtained entire control of Watt's stores, and were leaping and curling into the air in grand and terrible proportions, casting the whole area in a majestic light. The various brigades in attendance appeared to be having difficulty in connecting the hoses, and at one stage, it was feared that the whole area would fall prey to the conflagration. The authorities were doing their level best and every minute reinforcements were arriving. The guns could be heard firing from the Citadel. Detachments of soldiers and sailors soon arrived at the double, taking command of all the approaches. They made a way clear through the considerable crowd that had assembled.

The steam fire engine from the Keyham Yard, driven by a pair of horses, which stood flecked with foam and wet with perspiration, took up its position in Bedford Street, and hoses were stretched through Old Town Street.

The first among the military to arrive on the scene was a party of the South Staffordshire Regiment, with standpipe. With commendable alacrity, they got two hoses laid in Old Town Street, and both were carried through the passage of a house to the back of the building. With these hoses, the Staffordshire men did most valuable work. Corporal Taylor, of that regiment, was seriously injured, when a roof on which he was standing, collapsed, hurling him to the ground. He was rushed off to hospital.

By about 3.30 a.m., through the combined exertions of the police brigade, under the Chief Constable (Mr F. Wreford); Inspector J. Hill, and Mr McKeer; the West of England Brigade, with their engine, under Mr C. J. Brooks; and the Stonehouse Fire Brigade, under Captains W. W. Blight and W. Vosper, the fire was got under control. A detachment of Metropolitan Police arrived from the Dockyard with their Sutherland steam engine, but it was not used.

As stated earlier, 1887 was a busy time for our fire brigades, and on 10th December, the fiery fiend visited Plymouth once again. Had it not been for the united efforts of the police, the West of England and Stonehouse Fire Brigades, together with a large contingent of the military authorities, it would have proved to be one of the most disastrous fires to have occurred in the borough for some time.

The fire broke out in the early evening in a large store occupied by Messrs Walters and Son, forage merchants, in Exeter Street. The building had a shop frontage in Exeter Street, and extended right back to North Quay. The upper floor was soon well alight, but the hose- reels and fire brigades were speedily on the scene. Once the hoses were connected to the fire plugs, it was found that the mains pressure was poor, and the jets were unable to reach the upper floors.

The indignation of the public can be better imagined than described, and it was only when the West of England and Stonehouse Brigades occupied their positions on the top of Kiley's mission hall next door, that any appreciable volume of water could be made to play upon the flames. Within a quarter of an hour of the discovery of the outbreak, the roof was one mass of fire, and a little later, it fell in with an almighty crash, the flames shooting up to a tremendous height. The falling of the roof seemed to have the effect of igniting the flammable material stowed in Messrs. Walter's store, and the fire then extended the whole length of the building. By this time, nearly all the engines and hoses were at work, but the immense quantity of water thrown on the burning mass produced little effect, and attention was then diverted to protecting other buildings.

The fire broke out at 9.45 p.m., and by about 10.30 p.m., the following men and engines were on the spot and working furiously: The West of England Brigade, with their hose reel; The Stonehouse Brigade, with their hose reel and hand cart; police hose reels from the Central police station; Avenue station; and Old Guildhall. The Royal Engineers and the Royal Irish came from the Citadel with their engine, as did more of the Royal Irish Regiment from Millbay Barracks, with their engine. By about midnight, the fire was got under control, and the men and brigades began to scale down their operations.

Even though there was an inexhaustible supply of water within the harbour, it was of little use, as most of the appliances at the scene were hose reels, which were connected directly to the water mains. As more and more plugs were opened up, the pressure dropped accordingly. In a debrief following the fire, it was commented that a fire of that magnitude, close to a large open water supply, it would have been more beneficial to have more engines on the scene rather than hose reels. A good supply could have been drawn from the open water, therefore leaving the reels solely to the water main.

CHAPTER NINE

IMPROVEMENTS TO FIREFIGHTING ARRANGEMENTS

IN EARLY JANUARY 1888, the Watch Committee of Plymouth Town Council received a communication from the Western Insurance Company, who had recently set up business in Plymouth. They were generously offering the town a gift of a brand new powerful Merryweather steam fire engine. There can be no doubt that another steam engine would have been an invaluable addition to the stock of fire-extinguishing appliances at the command of the municipal authorities. However, before a definite decision could be made and they could accept this kind offer, the question of water supply, housing, maintenance and management, were all to be gone into. These were carefully and properly investigated by a sub-committee, consisting of practical men well qualified to form an opinion on various points.

The chief problem to be overcome was the connection with the water supply. The engine which was offered, was one of Messrs Merryweather's largest, known as their Metropolitan No. 1, which had a pumping capacity of 350 gallons per minute. It was wondered whether the water mains of Plymouth were large enough to deliver a sufficient amount to keep the engine at work. Of course, in the event of a fire occurring within a short distance of the Barbican or Sutton Harbour, an unlimited supply of seawater would be obtained. The steamer on offer was capable of supplying itself from such a source through a quarter mile length of hose, without seriously impairing its throwing power. The sea water would be available within a tolerably large area, leaving the town's mains for the manual engines.

It was envisaged that considerable expenditure would be required to utilise the steamer in the manner indicated, but that was not an insurmountable obstacle. The directors of the Western Insurance Company were willing to supply 1,000 feet of hose also. Letters were sent to various businesses in Plymouth asking if they would sponsor two good horses to pull the engine. This done, the only expenditure falling upon the Council was the keep and care of the animals. After much deliberation, the Council agreed to the kind offer, and a meeting was set up to discuss the arrangements and presentation celebrations.

The date agreed for the presentation was the last day of February 1888, and invites were sent far and wide to various fire brigades and dignitaries. The Guildhall Square, in which the ceremony took place was packed with townsfolk, all very excited as they awaited the arrival of the steam fire engine. The Mayor (Ald. Waring) and the rest of the Corporation assembled in the council chambers, awaiting the procession to leave the stables of the Globe Hotel and make its way to Guildhall Square.

Four different fire brigades were invited to partake in various competition drills for cash prizes, as part of the celebrations. They were: The East Stonehouse Fire Brigade, under Superintendent Blight and Captain Vosper, with two hose carts and eighteen men; the West of England Fire Brigade (Newton

Branch), under Captain Chudleigh, with engine, and hose carts, and five men; the Newton Abbot Fire Brigade under Captain Dobell, with hose carts and five men; and the Falmouth Fire Brigade, with their engine, appliances, and eighteen men, under Lieut. Williams and secretary Rogerson.

An elaborate handbill produced by the Western Assurance Company to announce a banquet in celebration of presenting the borough of Plymouth with a steam fire engine in February 1888.

THE

WESTERN INSURANCE COMPANY,

Limited, of PLYMOUTH.

MARINE. FIRE.

CAPITAL---£100,000.

DIRECTORS:

Councillor A. PEROSSI (Treeby & Co.), The Exchange, and of Stella House, Citadel Rd., Plymouth, *Chairman.*
W. H. YEO, Mount Pleasant, Plymouth.
A. HENDERSON (A. Henderson & Co.), Nottingham Place, Plymouth.
E. FREEMAN, Mutley Avenue, Plymouth, *Managing Director.*
Major W. WALFORD, Thorn Park, Plymouth, *Secretary.*

BANKERS:

BATTEN, CARNE & CARNE, The Plymouth and Penzance Bank.
(London Agents—The London and Westminster Bank, Limited, Lothbury, E.C.)

SOLICITORS:

GREENAWAY & SON, Frankfort Street, Plymouth.

AUDITOR:

D. DERRY HUBBARD, Accountant, Courtenay Street, Plymouth.
S. LEONARD, Branch Manager, Constantinople.

MARINE DEPARTMENT.

Managers—TREEBY & CO., The Exchange, Plymouth.
Assessor—W. JENKINS (Surveyor to the American Record and "Registro Italiano.")

FIRE DEPARTMENT.

London Office—1 and 2, Poultry Chambers, Poultry, London, E.C.—A. Absell, Manager.
Manchester Office—26, King Street, Manchester—Blackall & Co., Managers.
Glasgow Office—Central Buildings, 12, Waterloo Street, Glasgow—W. Thomson, Manager.

Notice.—Agents have been appointed in many of the leading British and Foreign Commercial Centres and the Directors invite Applications from Gentlemen of good standing, desirous of being appointed in the Districts where the Company is at present unrepresented.

Head Office:

VICTORIA CHAMBERS, WHIMPLE STREET, PLYMOUTH

Printed for the Proprietors by MERRITT & HATCHER (and Published by ARTHUR DALE), 2, Grocers' Hall Court, Poultry, E.C.

Advertising sign for the short-lived Western Insurance Company.

The procession was headed by the band of the Prince of Wales's Rifle Volunteers. Among the dignitaries who accompanied the steam fire engine was Mr J. Compton Merryweather and some members of his employ from London, and Mr Achilles Perossi, Chairman of the Western Insurance Company. The official handing over was carried out with much pomp and ceremony, and the steamer was officially christened The Western. It was then fired up, and jets were thrown over the roof of the Guildhall. The fire brigade drills commenced, and were examined by three Captains of the London Auxiliary Fire Brigade. They were all found to be extremely efficient, and the prize money was divided equally among them.

The ceremony lasted for a considerable time and was thoroughly enjoyed by the citizens of the three towns, who flocked in their thousands to witness the event. The day was concluded with a civic reception and dinner in the Guildhall for all the invited dignitaries, where many speeches and much merriment were undertaken.

The presentation of a Merryweather steam fire engine to Plymouth by the Western Assurance Company in February 1888; this picture was taken in Guildhall square, and was witnessed by hundreds of townsfolk.

The Western Insurance Company had a very short affair with Plymouth, as they ceased trading during the following year, when their chairman, Mr Perossi, absconded following allegations of fraud. A sizable reward was put out for his arrest. He was subsequently arrested in a foreign country and returned to England, where he was put on trial, found guilty, and sentenced to seven years' imprisonment. As regards the Merryweather steam engine (The Western), it transpired at a meeting of the Council, at a later date, that the Corporation were perfectly willing to hand over the engine on an order being received from the Court of Chancery. As trustees for the inhabitants of Plymouth, the Corporation felt themselves bound to keep within the lines of legal formality. They were prepared to cordially support an application to the Court for the transfer of the engine to the trustees of the estate. It transpired that the borough was to keep the engine within their arsenal for the protection of the people of Plymouth.

It would appear that the embarrassment and stigma associated with the shamed Western Insurance Company caused the Plymouth Corporation to distance themselves from them. At a later date, the Western steam fire engine was re-liveried, and the initial brass plaque removed; it was later re-christened The Plymouth. In February 1928, the Plymouth was eventually sold to Messrs Willoughby Brothers Ltd. of Millbay Docks, presumably for breaking up.

The Western earns its spurs

The steam fire engine passed its first test with honours, as on 6th July 1888, a large fire occurred in a three-storey china warehouse in Old Town Street. Had it not been for the powerful jets of water produced by it, the damage would have undoubtedly been much worse than it was. Mr Payne occupied the premises, which consisted of a shop with a large warehouse at the back. Smoke was seen issuing from the upper windows at about 8 p.m., and before the arrival of the police hose-reel, a fierce volume of fire had possessed the top two floors. More police reels and men, together with the West of England brigade, were soon on the spot, but their work was seriously hampered by lack of pressure in the mains.

Deputy Superintendent Henry Hill, who was at the scene, ordered the Western to be made ready and brought to the fireground. Mr McKeer, the engineer of the borough brigade, got steam up, and supervised the pump until the arrival of Mr Cole, the engine man. Within eight minutes of its arrival, two hoses were taken through the side door and up over the stairs, and two powerful jets of water blasted into the inferno with telling results. Meanwhile, good work was being carried out at the rear of the premises. The military fire engine from the Citadel was feeding a jet at the head of a builder's ladder, which played into the heart of the fire. A large contingent of the Royal Irish Regiment worked the fire engine, and others distinguished themselves by their energetic conduct.

There was no wind, and the column of fire and smoke, which ascended straight into the air just after the outbreak, signalled far and near that a big conflagration was in progress. Consequently, excited crowds soon thronged the streets in all directions, making it very difficult for members of the military to get to the scene. The roof and walls gradually fell in, and after a few hours the fire posed no further threat of spread, and their bugler recalled the military. They made up their equipment and returned to their respective barracks, and the fire was left to the Police Fire Brigade to completely extinguish.

Devonport Volunteer Fire Brigade

Previous to 1888, there was no organised body of actual firemen to deal with fires in the borough of Devonport. The Devonport Police Force used to turn out with an old manual pump and hose reel, but they were not properly trained in firefighting. The borough relied heavily upon the military engines, and the Metropolitan Police Fire Brigade in the Royal Dockyard. It was generally understood that if a fire occurred within the district, the property of the War Office and other departments would be in danger, due to the close proximity of the town to the Dockyard and military establishments within the borough.

Consequently, the Dockyard and military engines, together with large bodies of men to work them, would come to the assistance of the local authorities. Despite years of speculation and recommendations as to Devonport forming its own fire brigade, nothing was done until early 1888. Following a conference, it was decided to appoint Mr John Burns, the borough Engineer and Surveyor, as Chief Officer, and he was instructed to form the fire brigade. Subsequently, a brigade was eventually formed, with a Second Officer and twenty firemen. The new brigade was kitted out with smart uniforms, leather boots, axes, and brass helmets, just like their neighbouring firemen colleagues at Stonehouse.

The brigade originally operated with two manual fire engines and hose-reels, but in August 1900 they were to have a powerful steam fire engine. This steam fire engine was a Merryweather Greenwich Gem and was the pride of all the inhabitants of Devonport and surrounding towns. It was christened 'Annie' by the then Mayoress, Mrs Annie Hornbook, at a ceremony in 1900.

Chief Officer John Burns of the Devonport Fire Brigade 1888–1916.

Devonport Fire Brigade outside Ker Street Guildhall, with their competition drill certificates in 1907.

Merryweather London Pattern horse-drawn manual fire engine. This type of manual fire engine was supplied to Devonport Fire Brigade.

A serious fire broke out in a second-hand clothes shop in Queen Street, Devonport, on 15th April 1889. Strangely, the borough police and the Dockyard police attended with their reels, and after a concerted effort between the police forces, the fire was got under control. Mr Burns, the newly appointed chief of the borough fire brigade was at the scene, but he decided that the services of his men were not required. It should be borne in mind that the newly appointed firemen were not actually 'on duty' at a station, as were the police, and perhaps it was more expedient to use the latter, rather than send messengers around the borough to round up the firemen from their respective houses.

Mr Superintendent Burns, in his report of the Devonport Fire Brigade for 1890, stated that the members of the brigade continued to perform their duties to his entire satisfaction. The brigade, during the past year, had been called together for fifteen drills, and a member of the brigade had been on duty at the Central station for at least four hours each night. During the past year, eighteen fires had been reported, fifteen of which had occurred in the borough, and the remaining three outside the district. The brigade received calls for sixteen of these fires, but fortunately, none of them was of such serious character as to call for special mention. A new fire escape had been provided, and was located at the Central station.

The following regulations, in respect to fires in the County Borough of Devonport, are taken from the three towns' almanac of 1891:

Fires

1. On the occurrence of a Fire, the Constable nearest to the spot will give immediate alarm, and will, as expeditiously as possible, either in person or through another constable, convey the information

Helmet Plate and tunic button image of Devonport Fire Brigade 1888–1916.

to the nearest of the following: The Police Station, Guildhall; New Passage Hill lock-up; Dockyard Gates; Keyham Dockyard Gates; Main Guard; Water Company's Offices; the residence of the Superintendent of the fire brigade, 2 Valletort Road, and call the nearest firemen within the limits of his beat, and return directly to his beat.

2. Constables at a distance from the fire are on no account to leave beats, unless ordered.

3. The Superintendent or Senior Officer on duty at the police station, will immediately send notice to the Mayor, or to the Magistrate acting in his absence, to the Superintendent of the fire brigade and firemen, the turncock's, The manager of the Town Engines, and the agents to the West of England Fire Insurance Office.

4. On the arrival of the Military, Naval, or other hose reels and engines on the ground, the Officer of the Municipal Authority in charge, (who is to be in uniform) will place himself in immediate communications with the Officers or other persons in command. No engines will be sent from the Devonport Dockyard or Keyham Dockyard except in writing, signed by the Officer of the Municipal Authority in charge, who will be Superintendent of the Borough Fire Brigade, or in his absence the Deputy Superintendent.

5. If the fire is outside the boundary of the Cornwall Railway, hose-reels and engines will not be sent, except on the requisition in writing, of the Officer of the Municipal Corporation in charge.

6. In the case of fire in any of the Government establishments, the Municipal Authority will render all the assistance in their power.

7. The direction of the hose-reels, fire engines, and the general arrangements for extinguishing, or arresting the progress of the fire, will be under the direction of the Officer of the Municipal Authority in charge, who will act in communications with the Mayor or Magistrate present.

8. The Officer of the Municipal Authority in charge, will indicate to the Officer or other person in charge of the Military or Naval hose-reels, and engines attending the fire, the position in which such hose-reels and engines can be placed so as to afford the most effectual assistance.

9. For this purpose, the Officer of the Municipal Authority in charge, will be careful to address himself to the Officer or other person in command, and is, on no account, to give any order or direction to Soldiers or others acting under their own Officers.

10. The Superintendent, or other Officer in charge of the Police, will, in like manner, address himself solely to the Military Officer, who may be present in command of an armed party. In reference to the arrangements for keeping the ground clear, or taking other steps for maintaining order and preserving property.

11. The Superintendent of Police, and the men under his direction, will be careful to observe, and report to the Mayor or Magistrate, any interference or improper conduct on the part of any person towards the Military, or others affording assistance at fires. To identify offenders, they may be afterwards dealt with as the case may require.

As stated earlier, Devonport was in the need for a fire engine with much more capability than the manual engines they possessed. After much deliberation, it was decided to purchase a new steam fire engine, to serve the borough of Devonport. An order was placed with Merryweather and Sons in London in 1900 for a Greenwich Gem pattern steam fire engine.

Merryweather Greenwich Gem steam fire engine, bought for the borough of Devonport in 1900. © Ron Henderson

Devonport Fire Brigade, with their steam fire engine and manual engine, in Ker Street in 1904.

Soon after its arrival in Devonport, a date was earmarked for its christening, public tests and displays. On August 30th in the Glebe Field, Devonport, the new engine commenced her trials. Nearly all the aldermen and councillors were present, and among those who took part were Captain Pett, of the Exeter Fire Brigade; Captain W. H. Vosper (chairman of the South-Western District of the National Fire Brigades Union), attached to the Devonport Fire Brigade; Messrs. Thuell and Blight, of the Stonehouse Fire Brigade; Mr J. D. Sowerby, Chief Constable and Chief Fire Officer of Plymouth Fire Brigade; Mr J. Matthews, Chief Constable of Devonport; Mr Duncan, Governor of Plymouth Prison; and Mr H. Francis, Chief Engineer of the Devonport Water Company. The new engine, drawn by a pair of horses, was driven onto the field at 2.45 p.m., the fire brigade being under the charge of Superintendent J. F. Burns and his deputy Superintendent Edwards. Earlier in the day, the engine had been tested outside the Guildhall in Ker Street, in the presence of the Fire Brigade Committee. A jet of water damped the Corporation flag flying on the Column, which was 140 feet high.

The Greenwich Gem was decorated with flowers in the front and back. Over the fire box was a bottle of champagne, suspended in red, white and blue ribbons. Alderman Whitby, who was chairman of the Fire Brigade Committee, called upon the Mayoress (Mrs Annie Hornbrook) to perform the christening ceremony. The Mayoress was led forward by the town clerk (Mr A. B. Pilling), and the bottle of champagne was smashed against the fire box, Mrs Hornbrook saying, 'Annie, may you ever be ready at duty's call.' The stoker immediately lit the fire and within minutes steam was up, the gauge registering a pressure of 120lbs. The display concluded by four half-inch jets sending streams of water over a building 100 feet high. After all the tests were complete, everyone returned to the town hall for a reception.

Fireman George Marshall Boaden, of the Stonehouse Fire Brigade.

Willoughby's Foundry fire

Plymouth was thrown into a state of great alarm shortly before midnight on 21st May 1890, when a large fire broke out at Messrs Willoughby's Foundry in Rendle Street. Police on their beat in Manor Street discovered the fire, and they raced to the Octagon station to raise the alarm. Sergeant Yabsley and a party of constables responded immediately with their hose-reel. The foundry was situated in one of the most crowded districts of Plymouth, the dwelling houses surrounding it being thickly tenanted.

The flames were leaping high into the night sky, illuminating the entire area with a lurid light. Nearby were large stables, containing several horses, but the prompt arrival of other fire brigades enabled the animals to be removed to a place of safety before they could be harmed. Within a relatively short space of time, the police brigade, under Chief Constable Wreford, Mr McKeer, and Inspector Henry Hill; the West of England brigade; the Stonehouse brigade and the Devonport brigade, in the charge of Messrs Brooks, Blight, and Burns respectively, all arrived with commendable promptitude, and immediately got to work. Several powerful jets of water were soon playing upon the fire.

Other fire pumps which were quickly brought to the scene were: the Royal Naval Hospital engine, in charge of Inspector Wonnell and a party of Metropolitan policemen; a detachment of the Dorset Regiment with their engine, commanded by Captain Goddard; an armed party, together with a company of men, bringing an engine of the Plymouth Division RMLI, under Captains Johnson and Hadley, with a contingent of men and their engine, from the Royal Naval Barracks. Due to the valiant efforts of all the brigades, who worked untiringly, the fire was contained to Willoughby's foundry, which unfortunately, was completely gutted.

Exciting rescue of children

Soon after nine o'clock on the evening of 1st June 1891, the north of Plymouth was illuminated by a large fire. The premises were No. 13 Mutley Plain, which was the corner house of Marina Place, occupied as a draper's shop and dwelling house by Mr J. R. Hill. The ground floor at the corner was the shop where the fire was believed to have originated. Mr Hill, the occupier, was away on a business trip at Princetown. At the time of the outbreak, there were on the premises only Mrs Hill, her servant maid, and two young children. Neither Mrs Hill nor the servant seemed to have been aware that the shop was on fire until the smoke and flames came up the staircase and into the living apartments. They rushed into the street and raised the alarm of fire, leaving the two little children asleep in the bedrooms. Mr Frank Ellis, of a firm of auctioneers and surveyors, who had chambers over the Wiltshire and Dorset Bank, happened to be passing at that time, and Mrs Hill rushed to him begging for him to save her children.

At once he ran into the house and up the stairs to the top storey (the second floor), thinking the nursery was there. He went into every room, but was unable to locate the children. He tried to descend, but was beaten back by dense volumes of smoke coming up the staircase. He was, therefore, obliged himself to go to one of the back windows and call for help. After about a quarter of an hour, Thomas Park, a plasterer, of Ebrington Street, and some other men brought a ladder and placed it on the tenement, and by this means Mr Ellis descended unharmed.

In the meantime, Police Constables Hutchins and Palmer, who were on duty on Mutley Plain, had come up at the cry of 'Fire'. There was a fire station at Marina Place, and Hutchins immediately ran there and telephoned to the Central station, and afterwards got out the Mutley hose-reel. Palmer broke into the side door of the house and managed to get upstairs to a room where he found a baby in bed, which he rescued and brought it to its mother. Some volunteer helpers had also, in the meantime, found the other child, and also restored that to Mrs Hill who, poor woman, was in a terrible state of panic.

Thanks to the telephone call, other hose-reels were soon on the spot, and were got to work as quickly as possible. The Mutley reel was first connected with the main opposite Seaton Terrace, where there was a good pressure of water, but unfortunately, the crowd had by that time caught onto the reel, and by their pressure, snapped the standpipe right off. This caused a much regrettable delay of several minutes before another standpipe could be fixed and the hose connected to it. Other reels were soon on the spot: these included reels from the workhouse, the Central station, Vinegar Hill, Union Street (late West of England) and the reel of the Stonehouse Fire Brigade, as well as the fire escape from Alton Terrace. The water supply was good, and several jets were playing upon the building. By this time however, the fire had penetrated the roof, and, fanned by a stiff breeze, was blazing up with a great fierceness, illuminating the entire neighbourhood.

A strong gusty wind was blowing from the south-west, which, fortunately, carried the fire away from the adjoining shops and across the opening of Marina Place. Great efforts were of course first made to prevent the fire from spreading beyond the house in which it broke out, and these united efforts proved successful. The fire was got under control by eleven o'clock.

The operations of the firemen were under the direction of Inspector Henry Hill, and after the first mishap with the standpipe, everything worked smoothly and satisfactorily. Among those who were present to render assistance were Mr C. J. Brooks, Superintendent of the late West of England brigade; Mr G. D. Bellamy, the borough engineer, and his assistants; and the police under Inspector Wood. The assistance of the military and Royal Marines was offered, but not considered necessary.

Fire during the Great Blizzard of 1891

Devonport had enjoyed a long immunity from fires of a serious nature, but unhappily, this was broken during the Great Blizzard of 1891. The fire, which broke out at about eight o'clock at night on 8th March, originated at No. 4 Wingfield Villas, in the higher part of Stoke. The premises were the residence of Mr J. Venning, the town clerk, and his wife, but fortunately they were away in London on business, and the house was being looked after by the servants. The scared servants fled the house, and the locality was very quiet due to the bad weather which prevailed. Once the alarm was raised, the news soon spread, and it was not long before the news was conveyed to the house of Mr Burns, Superintendent of the Devonport Fire Brigade, and his deputy, Mr Dennis, who respectively lived at No.s 1 and 2 Valletort Road, Stoke. Mr Burns was not at home, having gone to Devonport, but Mr Dennis, with great promptitude, took the hose which was kept at the Superintendent's house in case of need, and proceeded to the scene. Mr Dennis attached the hose to a hydrant opposite the house, and began playing a jet upon the premises; meanwhile Mrs Burns telephoned the Central Police Station, who immediately dispatched a hose reel.

Notwithstanding the blinding snow and cold piercing wind, the police soon arrived on the spot, set into another hydrant, and attacked the fire. The fire had a good hold on No. 4 and fire was now threatening No. 3. Very little was salvaged from Mr Venning's house, but a large amount of furniture and silver plate was removed from No. 3. By now, the fire, which lit up the neighbourhood, could be seen from different places in the three towns.

Shortly after nine o'clock, two companies of the Kings Own Scottish Borderers, with some men of the Welsh Regiment, and a company of the Royal Artillery, arrived on the spot and rendered valuable help to the police. They were charged with looking after the furniture and keeping the roads clear for those occupied in subduing the flames. Soon afterwards, the West of England Fire Brigade put in an appearance, and connected to a hydrant and began to play on No. 3. By this time, a fire was burning in the servants' quarters. Mr Venning's house was beyond saving, as it was completely gutted.

The firemen, soldiers, and police, worked remarkably well considering the sub-zero temperature, falling snow, and the biting wind, which was blowing at hurricane force, creating blizzard conditions. Once the fires were got under control, the military were returned to their respective barracks, and the crowd soon dispersed, and headed for the warmth of their homes. The neighbours looked after the servants from the two houses until the owners returned.

The West of England Insurance Company Fire Brigade disbands

Numerous fire insurance companies throughout the country have maintained fire brigades, the first being in 1680. Some lasted only a few years, while others flourished for many years before they handed the responsibility of firefighting over to the local authorities. The West of England Insurance Company, in line with other insurance companies, decided that it was only right that the fire protection of Plymouth, and other towns and cities, should be in the hands of the local councils, and not a private company. They made the decision to disband their fire brigade at Plymouth. They also brought to an end other fire brigades which they maintained in various parts of the country.

The West of England Fire Brigade had operated in Plymouth since 1838; they established themselves in Cornwall Street, with Mr William Marshall as their superintendent. Following his death in 1882, the brigade moved to new premises in Station Road (Union Street), and appointed Mr Charles James Brooks as his successor. The brigade attended their last fire on 11th April, and ceased to operate as a fire brigade on 28th April 1891.

Their powerful manual fire engine, and the whole of their plant at the Union Street station, including the station itself, was presented to the Plymouth Corporation Fire Brigade. Mr Brooks decided it was time to retire, and he duly hung up his boots! Several other members of the disbanded fire brigade joined the Plymouth Borough Fire Brigade.

It would not be right to close the chapter on the West of England Insurance Company without applauding the achievements of their fire brigade over their fifty-three year existence. It is true to say that, the West of England maintained fire brigades in other parts of the country; their head office was in Exeter, where they maintained a good fire brigade of national acclaim.

The West of England at Exeter disbanded their brigade there in 1888 following a public outcry for a regular fire brigade following the terrible Theatre Royal fire in September 1887, where 188 souls perished. It is also well documented that their brigade at Plymouth was among one of the most proficient and admired fire brigades in the country.

The West of England, under the leadership of William Marshall, 1838–1882, and Charles James Brooks, 1882–1891, set the standard that others sought to achieve. The inhabitants of the three towns owed them a huge debt of gratitude for the professional way in which they performed at the hundreds of fires they attended during their existence. When the West of England Fire Brigade was first formed, the population in Plymouth Borough was about 34,000. It is interesting to note that the last insurance fire brigade to disband in this country was the Norwich Union, which ceased to operate as a fire brigade in Worcester in 1929.

Front view of the leather fire helmet for fireman No. 8 of the West of England Insurance Company Fire Brigade c.1860.

CHAPTER TEN

PLYMOUTH BECOMES A POLICE FIRE BRIGADE

WITH THE DEMISE of the West of England Fire Brigade, it was evident to the city leaders that Plymouth was in need of a much larger and better organised fire brigade to protect the growing population of Plymouth. The population within the three towns was growing at a steady rate, and by 1889, the combined population was 137,664. Following a meeting between the Corporation and the police, it was deemed necessary to hand over complete control of the Fire Brigade to the police, rather than form a new fire brigade. Chief Constable Frederick Wreford was to be in charge of the fire brigade. Plymouth ran their fire brigade as a branch of the police force, rather than as an independent fire brigade; this arrangement often created clashes of interest among the force. History was to show that police-run fire brigades were fraught with problems, and these problems were highlighted in the war years.

The West of England Insurance Company donated all their fire extinguishing equipment and their fire station to the reorganised brigade. A number of firemen from the West of England also joined the new fire brigade. Within a few months, they had all handed back their uniforms and resigned. They were: William Crocker, and his three sons James, Henry, and Albert Crocker, Edward Philp, Samuel Hodge, John Phillips, and William Walland. One can only speculate as to why all the former West of England men resigned. Perhaps there was bad feeling amongst the policemen, who had to do both fire and police duties, and were subject to different discipline regulations than their civilian counterparts. The sons of William Crocker, Henry, James, and Albert, then joined the Stonehouse Volunteer Fire Brigade, where they served with distinction, until the brigade disbanded in 1916. The Crocker family had, at one time, six members of the family all serving the West of England Fire Brigade, they were: Foreman J. Swigg, (J. T. Crocker's grandfather), William Crocker, (J. T. Crocker's father), J. T. Crocker, and his sons Albert, Henry, and James.

Police Firemen re-organised

Due to the fact of losing an important fire brigade, it became vital that the police addressed the short-comings with some urgency. The entire police force was now trained as police/firemen. Training and drills were undertaken on a regular basis. The fact that the police force in Plymouth shared the responsibilities of policing and dealing with outbreaks of fire within the town put a strain on loyalties, as the fire brigade appeared to be very much second best. The practice of the police force also running the fire brigade worked reasonably well in some cities throughout the country, but it would be fair to say that the arrangements in Plymouth were not ideal. The Police Chief, Mr Wreford, took over responsibility for the Corporation Fire Brigade back in 1886/7, and according to the stores report book, an entry for November 1892 showed they were then in possession of the following plant:

Central Station

- One steam fire engine complete with 600ft of canvas hose and three lengths of feeder hose. This was the fire engine donated by the Western Insurance Company in 1888
- One combination ladder complete with 300 ft of canvas hose
- One hand manual pump with 1100 ft of canvas hose
- One large telescopic escape 27 ft–62 ft with canvas shute
- One small telescopic escape, 27ft–53ft, kept at Guildhall Square
- One fly ladder
- One ladder cart with seven lengths of scaling ladders

Hoe Station

- One hose-reel complete with 300ft of canvas hose

Station Road

- One ladder cart with seven lengths of scaling ladders, 300 ft of canvas hose, and two torches

Octagon Station

- One hose-reel complete with 300 ft of canvas hose
- One hand manual pump
- One ladder cart with seven lengths of scaling ladders and two ordinary ladders, one hanging at back of station, the other in the house with ladder cart in Granby Lane

Oxford Street Station

- One hose-reel complete with 300 ft of canvas hose

Mutley Station

- One hose-reel complete with 400 ft of canvas hose
- One escape fly ladder kept at North Hill

Workhouse

- One hose-reel complete with 300 ft of canvas hose

Providence Street Station

- One hose-reel complete with 300 ft of canvas hose
- One ladder cart with seven lengths of scaling ladders

Avenue Station

- One hose-reel complete with 300 ft of canvas hose
- One manual hand pump and one ordinary ladder of twenty-two rounds, hanging in the Avenue

Barbican Station

- One hose-reel complete with 300 ft of canvas hose

Old Guildhall

- One Currick ladder complete with 300 ft of canvas hose
- Two manual fire engines, one fitted out with 500 ft of canvas hose and four lengths of leather hose, one canvas tank and branch pipes with suction complete
- The second pump is not completely kitted out, but both are in good condition

Theatre Royal

- Five lengths of canvas hose, permanently fixed to hydrants, three at back of the stage, one ordinary ladder fixed to a frame with wheels in Athenaeum Place, and one without wheels, hanging against the wall

There was no mention as to the whereabouts of the Torrent steam fire engine which was gifted to Plymouth by the Liverpool and London and Globe Insurance Fire Brigade when they disbanded in 1876. It was known to have been stationed at the old fire station off Tavistock Place. I can only surmise that it either fell into disrepair or was sold off as surplus to requirements, but this I find hard to believe.

Chief Constable Wreford retires

On March 30th 1892, Chief Constable Frederick Wreford retired from the force. He served the borough of Plymouth for many years, as both Chief Constable, and Superintendent of the Fire Brigade. He died five days prior to his being placed on the superannuation list, viz, 25th April of the same year, and was succeeded as Chief Constable and Chief of the Fire Brigade. The newly appointed Chief Constable was Joseph Davidson Sowerby, who, before his appointment, was a senior police officer with Leeds Police Force. Leeds was also a police/fire brigade, so no doubt Mr Sowerby had a great deal of experience in that field. The Plymouth brigade was said to be amongst the smartest and most efficient in the West. It now consisted of one chief, one deputy, one inspector, one sergeant and twenty-one members of the police, one inspector and four men of the old brigade, total thirty. The appliances included one steam fire engine, two manual engines, nine hose-reels, six ladder carts, seven escapes, and a large quantity of hose. Joseph Sowerby remained as Chief Constable and Superintendent of the Police Fire Brigade from his appointment in 1892, until he retired in 1917.

Fire at Fox, Eliott, and Co

Just before Christmas 1893, a fire broke out in a timber yard belonging to Messrs Fox, Eliott, and Co, in Richmond Walk, Stonehouse. A member of the Stonehouse constabulary, who was on patrol in Edgecumbe Street, which was opposite the Stonehouse Pool, discovered the fire. He ran across the bridge and into Richmond Walk, where he alerted the gatekeeper to the fire. He then reached the building and found that there was a mass of fire inside one of the buildings, in which was located the sawpit. He immediately raced off to call out the Stonehouse Fire Brigade. In the meantime, PC Palmer of the Devonport Police Force, who was patrolling the western end of Richmond Walk, also saw the fire. Together with a bargeman, they alerted the caretaker and his family, who were asleep in a house at the end of the yard. Within a short space of time, Devonport Fire Brigade, under Superintendent Burns and Deputy Supt Dennis; Stonehouse Fire Brigade, under Supt Blight and Mr Vosper, and the police, with a hose-reel from the Octagon, were soon on the spot. They were hampered by the fact that the nearest hydrant was some considerable distance away. The 4th Rifle Brigade was also quickly on the scene with their engine, and together with the police, they worked on the sides of the timber stacks. Supt Burns of the Devonport brigade called for the assistance of the Metropolitan Police from the Dockyard, with their powerful steam fire engine, and they duly arrived two hours after the fire was discovered.

By the sharing of hoses, the firemen eventually prevented the fire from spreading, and with the Dockyard engine pumping from the sea, they were able to supply several good streams of water onto the fire. By the united efforts of the Stonehouse brigade, the police and the 4th Rifle Brigade, the caretaker's cottage and several stacks of timber on the south side of the wharf were saved.

First steam fire engine for Stonehouse

Stonehouse Volunteer Fire Brigade, which had a new fire station built in 1893, was again involved in much ceremony in January 1894, when a well known local tradesman and member of the East Stonehouse Local Board, Mr Jas. C. Wills, Esq., presented the township with a brand new Shand Mason Double Vertical steam fire engine. Steam fire engines were the way forward, as the old manual fire engines were less efficient and required a large number of men to pump them. Some brigades throughout the country, on having steam fire engines, renamed their brigades to Steam Fire Brigades, just to impress their less well-off neighbouring fire brigades, who still had the old manual engines.

Stonehouse Fire Brigade poses in front of their fire station in 1902. Chief Officer Frederick Thuell and his brother George Thuell, who was his deputy, are in the centre of the picture.

Devonport, not to be outdone, also took delivery of a steam fire engine at the later date of 1900, which was christened Unity; hence, the fire brigades of the three towns then had a powerful steam fire engine in their arsenal, which was a significant step forward in the development of the fire brigades of the area.

It is interesting to note that in 1914, the government passed the Defence of the Realm Act, known as DORA, which meant that items could be seized to aid the war in France. Stonehouse's manual fire pump was seized, and reportedly taken to France to be used as a pumping engine. An article by 'Citizen' in the *Western Evening Herald* in September 1939, commented that it may appear incredible, but the fact remains that the engine was never paid for, nor even returned.

With Stonehouse now settling in with their new steamer, Devonport's Chief Officer, Mr John Burns, presented his annual report for the year ending 1894. This was his 6th annual report since the formation of the brigade in 1888. No fires had occurred within the borough of Devonport during the last twelve months ending December 12th 1894, with the exception of those within the Dockyard, at which the assistance of the brigade was offered and respectfully declined. During the year, a new Merryweather Manual engine was purchased, and this, with the extra hydrants fixed in the vicinity of the new streets laid out, gave additional means of dealing with outbreaks in those districts which may have required further protection against fires. The Superintendent suggested for the committee to consider some means of more promptly notifying the brigade of the outbreak of fire. Some delays have necessarily occurred in sending a messenger to the central station, but by adopting a system of street fire alarms, and also a magnet electric circuit, the situation would be dramatically improved.

Huge fire at Tuckett's Jam Factory

The new steam engine belonging to Stonehouse Fire Brigade was given its first real test at a large fire which broke out at Mr Tuckett's Jam Factory shortly after half past five in the evening, in November 1894. The factory situated in Millbay Road employed about fifty women, who were at work when the alarm of fire was raised. The entire workforce, with the exception of two, in a state of great panic, made good their escapes before the exit was cut off. Bessie Hooper, one of those left behind, jumped over the burning stairs without injury, and reached a place of safety. Nellie Down was unable to follow her example, and made her way to a window, where she attracted the attention of the neighbours. A blanket was held out as a makeshift jumping sheet, and the girl jumped from the window into it. It was not strong enough and she hit the ground with considerable force, sustaining serious injuries. She was carried into a house in Bishops Place where a doctor attended her; he then arranged for her to be taken to hospital. In the meantime, soldiers from the Millbay Barracks opposite turned out with their manual fire engine, and assistance came from the borough fire brigade, and the military from the Citadel and Raglan Barracks, with their manual fire engines.

The fire had by now assumed such proportions that it was impossible to approach the buildings from the main road, and the firemen, soldiers, and police, had to work under the greatest difficulties. A north-westerly breeze prevailed at the time, and fanned the flames towards the main portion of the buildings. The fire had originated on the second floor above the offices. Within a quarter of an hour, the whole of the block, extending parallel with Millbay Road, was in a blaze, and the flames soon advanced on the jam factory, situated at the rear. A large body of men, under the command of Chief Constable Sowerby, worked with a will, and water was poured on the burning pile from every direction.

The Stonehouse engine drew its supply from the basin in the Great Western Docks, on the opposite side of the road, and the other engines, with the exception of the Dockyard engine, were at work in other directions. The Corporation steamer took up its position at the main entrance to Millbay Barracks, and speedily got to work, as did the whole of the Corporation reels. Chief Constable Sowerby had supreme direction, being assisted by Mr McKeer, and Inspectors Wood, Wyatt, Dart and Warne. Devonport Fire Brigade, with their reels, in charge of Superintendent Burns and Mr Dennis, came in, and the whole of the Regiments in garrison supplied fire parties, with manual engines. When the brigades were all at work, no less than fifteen hoses were playing upon the building. It was soon seen, however, that the whole of the buildings belonging to Messrs Tuckett were doomed, and the firemen devoted their attention to preventing the flames from spreading to adjoining properties.

For nearly two hours the fire continued its devastating course, and everything that was combustible had been consumed. So great had been the reflection from the flames, that it could be seen for miles, and hundreds of persons soon thronged every approach to the scene of the catastrophe. Unfortunately, there was some delay at first, owing to the lack of water, due to insufficient pressure, and the fact that the water main in Millbay Road was too small. In addition to the fire parties, the military authorities also sent armed detachments to assist the borough police in keeping the dense crowds in check.

A fireman named Arthur Sharpe, of the Stonehouse Fire Brigade, who was at work on the ground floor of the building, was rendered unconscious, when a large piece of iron pipe fell from above and struck him on the head. He was taken to the South Devon and East Cornwall Hospital, where he remained insensible for a couple of days. The fire was got under control by 9.30 p.m. and the services of the military engines were dispensed with. The civic engines continued working until after one o'clock, and it was late the next morning that the fire was declared out.

Merryweather Greenwich pattern Curricle Fire Escape. This one-man operated escape and tool cart extended to 40 feet. Plymouth had two of these ladders within their arsenal.

Victoria Factory gutted by fire

One of the most disastrous fires in the annuls of the West, surpassing in magnitude and destructive force even the recent conflagration at Messrs Tuckett's factory, occurred at the Victoria Factory, Phoenix Street, Stonehouse, on 10th February 1895. The factory was in the occupation of Messrs Lancaster and Co., wholesale clothiers, and resulted in the complete destruction of the extensive range of buildings occupying almost the whole of the eastern side of the street. It was discovered a few minutes before seven o'clock, by two porters, whose duty it was to light the fires and prepare the rooms for the workforce, who were due to arrive at eight o'clock. The fire spread with appalling rapidity. Within a quarter of an hour, the entire block was ablaze from end to end. High tongues of flame leapt across the narrow roadway and scorched the houses opposite. In less than an hour, the roofs had fallen in and the whole place was gutted, with only bare walls left standing.

A neighbour alerted the police to the fire: within a few minutes, a reel from the Octagon station arrived on the scene, and commenced play at the rear of the building at the Union Street end. In quick succession, the Stonehouse Fire Brigade, with their steam fire engine; reels from the Union Street, Hoe, and Central police stations; the Metropolitan Police Fire Brigade and steam engine, and the Devonport Fire Brigade, followed them. The Plymouth contingent commenced operations from the Union Street points of vantage, chiefly directing their attack from the north-east corner.

The building was now well alight, with flames leaping from every window on each storey. The Metropolitan and Stonehouse steam engines were located in the Great Western Docks, where they were able to command an unlimited supply of water from the inner basin. Devonport Fire Brigade were not so fortunate. To their great mortification, they found that their standpipes did not fit the Stonehouse hydrants. With plenty of water in the mains, they were compelled to stand like idle spectators for a quarter of an hour, losing most valuable time, while messengers were obtaining standpipes of the proper size.

The two steamers in the Docks rendered splendid service, each discharging several powerful jets of water on the burning building, simultaneously from different points. The leather hose, weakened by frost, was unable to sustain such pressures, as every now and then, a section would burst, and the engine supplying it had to be knocked off while the damaged length was changed. Within half an hour of its discovery, the massive block of buildings had become a roaring furnace. Phoenix Street was impassable, and the situation was grave and perilous in the extreme. The shops and dwellings immediately facing the burning factory were in imminent danger of igniting.

The wind kept changing direction, which caused chaos, as it was feared the whole neighbourhood would become involved. The men of the Stonehouse Fire Brigade worked with extreme courage, as they stood in fierce heat directing their hoses on the cottages in Phoenix Place, in an endeavour to save them from the same fate as the factory. Three shops and a tenement house were partially destroyed as far as the frontage was concerned. Several elderly residents were rescued from their homes as the fire threatened them. They were placed in the care of neighbours, who were residing at a safe distance from the conflagration. The fronts and roofs of a further six cottages were severely damaged, while the Phoenix Tavern got away with a good scorching.

While the fire was at its height, hundreds of soldiers and sailors were arriving on the scene with various manual engines. Also on the fireground was the Plymouth brigade, under the command of Chief Constable J. Sowerby and Inspector Woods; The Stonehouse brigade, under the command of Supt W. W. Blight, Captain Vosper, Lieutenant Thuell, and Sub-Lieutenant E. Blight; the Devonport brigade, captained by Supt J. Burns; and the Metropolitan brigade, under Supt E. Smith, and Inspectors Stoope, Kellock and Morland. The factory was completely destroyed within an hour, and Phoenix Street presented a dismal and distressing appearance.

Dense smoke from the smouldering embers filled the air, water was as plentiful as during a flood, and ashes, copings, and debris of every description, littered the whole street. A plenteous flow of water, however, was still maintained in all directions, and it was four o'clock in the afternoon that the steamers ceased their pumping operations.

The Victoria Factory was a desolate scene of havoc and ruin. It was erected in 1862, with a further wing being added in 1867. The building, which was originally a foundry, was destroyed by fire in 1868, only the walls remaining standing. The building was rebuilt, and in 1890, it was enlarged, and Mr Edward Lancaster, needing more commodious premises for his rapidly growing business, leased the entire block from Messrs Pickford and Co.. The building had a frontage 400 feet long, consisted of three floors, and was forty feet wide. Within a week of the fire, over one hundred persons were re-employed again, as cutters at Messrs Dampney's store. A relief fund was set up to assist the remaining 213 employees, who were put out of work due to the devastating fire.

It is interesting to note that, prior to the end of the Second World War, there was no standardisation of equipment, couplings, threads types, etc., and there were often difficulties when different fire brigades came together. The City of Plymouth Fire Brigade carried special adaptors, to enable their standpipes to be connected to Stonehouse and Devonport hydrants, just in case they came across non-standard hydrant outlets. British Standard 750 was introduced just after the war, to ensure that all hydrants conformed to the same specifications. Plymouth eventually dispensed with the adaptors in the early 1960s.

The death of Fireman John Wood

The remains of the oldest fireman in the three towns, Mr John Wood, formally of the West of England Insurance Company Fire Brigade were buried with full honours on February 20th 1895. The members of the Plymouth Fire Brigade and Police Force, under the direction of the Chief Constable (Mr J. D. Sowerby); Supt. Gasking, Inspectors Wood and Wyatt; Mr John McKeer and several famous old West of England firemen; Devonport Fire Brigade, and Stonehouse Fire Brigade, were also well represented.

The deceased was one of the first firemen of the West of England brigade when it first established itself in Plymouth in 1838, occupying the position of branchman. He narrowly escaped death during the numerous conflagrations at which he had been present, especially in the Great Fire of Devonport Dockyard in 1840, when a portion of wall fell on him. He had done splendid work in saving many lives during his forty-two years' service, having retired in 1880. John Wood was a noted poet within the fire brigade, and his work was read throughout the country.

A practice among all fire brigades throughout the country was their annual dinner, where presentations and plaudits were conducted with much ceremony. On one such occasion, in January 1896, Ex Inspector Wood, formally of Devonport, was presented with suitable retirement presents, and votes of thanks for his fire brigade duties, from, not only his own officers, but also from neighbouring brigades.

The three towns enjoyed a couple of years in which no big fires occurred, but in November 1897, the Beer Creek Oil Company, in Newport Street, Stonehouse, was totally destroyed by fire. The vessel *Canterbury Belle* lying alongside the quay nearby, had her masts scorched and mainsail burnt, due to the radiated heat. The Stonehouse and Devonport Fire Brigades dealt with the outbreak.

Just before Christmas, 1898, the new Palace Theatre, in Union Street, was badly damaged by a fire, which started about half past midnight. The stage area was totally destroyed, and the auditorium badly damaged, but the combined efforts of the Plymouth and Stonehouse Fire Brigades extinguished the blaze within a couple of hours. It is sad to think, that about sixty years later, the theatre was ruined by lack of support, and closed down as effectively as if the fire had destroyed it.

Fire destroys sweet factory

Almost twelve months to the day, another huge fire occurred in Plymouth, when a fire broke out in a sweet factory owned by Messrs Bull and Co, shortly after nine o'clock at night. The factory was about 200 yards from the last big fire, which occurred at the Palace Theatre. The whole area was lit with a lurid glow as the fire leapt through the roof of the building. Dense clouds of smoke and sparks enveloped the area between Octagon Street and Flora Cottages, which were situated in a narrow thoroughfare at the rear of Union Street. The neighbours were in a state of panic, as their houses were quite close to the burning factory.

Within a short time, the police fire reels came from all directions, the hoses were promptly connected, and a copious supply of water was forthcoming. Those directing the operations quickly realised that the services of their steamer would be required, and a message was sent for it. In the meantime, the Stonehouse Fire Brigade appeared on the scene with their engine, and steam was quickly raised in Octagon Street. Within a quarter of an hour from the time of the alarm, the combined efforts of the two brigades were being directed to the subduing of the flames.

The fire was attacked from all sides, but its hold on the building was considerable, and for some time the flames seemed to increase rather than diminish. The upper half of Mr Bull's factory resembled a furnace, the roof having collapsed, and the flames leapt high into the air. The firemen used ladders to gain vantage points on neighbouring roofs, and from these points, hundreds of gallons of water were being continuously thrown onto the fire. Only the tremendous courage and resilience shown by the firemen prevented the blaze from spreading to adjoining properties.

The whole of the Plymouth Police Fire Brigade was present at the fire, under the direction of Chief Constable Sowerby and Inspector Wyatt, who had additional assistance of about thirty-five beat constables. A huge crowd had assembled, effectively arresting traffic in the thoroughfare. The upturned faces were illuminated by the intense glare, which together with the bank of cloud caused by dense smoke hovering over the centre of the conflagration presented a striking picture.

Helmet badge of the Police Fire Brigade (Borough & City) 1881–1948.

CHAPTER ELEVEN

THE NEW CENTURY BRINGS CHANGES

Royal visit to Stonehouse

THE KING AND Queen visited the borough of Stonehouse on 7th March 1902, and Captain Blight decided to form a large guard of honour, comprising firemen from brigades within the area. Brigades from Exeter, Torquay, Ilfracombe, Penzance, St Austell, Liskeard, Truro, Newton Abbot, Dawlish, Marazion, Bodmin, Camborne, Falmouth, Penryn and Redruth sent contingents of fire officers and firemen. They assembled with the Stonehouse Fire Brigade at Plymouth. Under the command of Captain Thomas (Penryn), they were marched to the Stonehouse Town Hall, where they were entertained at lunch by the chairman of the Fire Brigade Committee. At three o'clock they re-assembled, and were marched to their respective stations along the route, Captain Blight of Stonehouse and Superintendent Pett from Exeter superintending the affair. They all remained on duty until the royal party had passed, and they returned to the Town Hall for tea, before being dismissed.

New fire chief for Stonehouse

The new century also brought new changes for East Stonehouse Volunteer Fire Brigade in 1902. Following a meeting, the Stonehouse local board appointed Mr Frederick William Thuell as the Chief Officer, attracting a salary of £25 per year, with his brother George Thuell as Second Officer. Both these men were already serving officers in the brigade, and were members of the local board. The former Chief Officer, Supt. W. W. Blight and his deputy Captain W. Vosper retired from the brigade.

Both these newly appointed officers commanded the brigade until it was disbanded, along with Devonport, in 1916. During Mr Blight's office as Chief Officer, he was very active in the formation of the National Fire Brigades Union. Devonport were also members of the National Fire Brigades Union, and along with Stonehouse, they entered numerous drill competitions organised by the Union. The two brigades won many prizes between them, as they pitted their skills against brigades from all over the South-West.

Stonehouse Fire Brigade, under their new command, rendered good assistance with their steamer at a severe fire in Devonshire Lane, at the rear of Union Street, on 1st June of that year. As well as the Stonehouse Brigade, there were several police reels, and their steam fire engine The Plymouth (previously called the Western), all under the command of the Chief Constable, who was in overall charge of operations.

The Western Morning News
Fire Brigade.

Captain G. T. Light (later E. Croft), Lieutenants J. Taylor & E. C. Northcott, Engineer W. Broadley.
Members of Brigade :- R. V. Atwill, E. Anstis, B. Broadley, J. Bradford, C. E. Crook, A. Finnimore, J. Langdon, T. Reed, J. Shires, E. Tunstall, W. Upton.

Objects :- The brigade to be trained in the use of all Fire Appliances for the protection of the premises, and if necessary, the surrounding properties.

Rules

The Brigade to consist of a Captain, two lieutenants, (one employed during the day and the other by night), an Engineer, and representatives from each department.

The Captain to take full control of the Brigade.

The drills to take place monthly, on days appointed by the officers, and also emergency drills.

The names of the members attending drills to be recorded in a book kept for the purpose.

In the event of a fire occurring, the Captain and officers to be summoned immediately and notification to be sent to the manager (Mr E. Croft).

THE FIRST PERSON ON DISCOVERING A FIRE TO IMMEDIATELY SOUND THE ALARM. The members of the brigade in the department in which the fire occurs to get to work. The remaining members to assemble at the timekeepers office to take orders from the officer-in-charge.

NOTE No water to be turned on at a drill without permission of a manager.

July 1902

Rules of the Western Morning News Private Fire Brigade, July 1902.

The Western Morning News Company forms a fire brigade

The newspaper offices of the *Western Morning News* formed a private fire brigade in 1902 under the leadership of Capt. G. T. Light. He soon retired to take up a new job elsewhere. He was superseded by Capt. Bellamy, who had a great deal of experience of firefighting in the Straits Settlements, under government control. The chief officer was Mr Ernest Croft, the manager of the newspaper, with Messrs E. C. Northcott and J. Taylor as lieutenants, and Mr W. Broadley as engineer. The other firemen in the brigade were: Sergeant Finnemore, Firemen Bradford, Cheek, Chinn, Langdon, Tunstall, Anstis, Opic, Smith, Reed, Martin, Elliot and Austin.

Like similar business organisations throughout the country, the *Western Morning News* Fire Brigade was formed primarily to protect their premises against an outbreak of fire. For many years, there had been on the premises of the firm a number of hydrants, with hose and other appliances, necessary to deal with an outbreak in any part of the building. There was a great drawback, however, with this arrangement, in that only a few members of the staff had any knowledge of how the appliances should be worked, and of drills, there were none.

Mr Croft set to work with the support of the directors to provide a thoroughly trained brigade. Twenty members of the staff offered their services, and the brigade was promptly formed. This was the only private fire brigade to be in existence within the three towns, contrary to what might be documented elsewhere. So enthusiastic were the brigade under its inspiring leadership, that it sought opportunities to practise with both the Stonehouse and Devonport Fire Brigades. Impressed by the keenness displayed, the directors of the company purchased additional lengths of hose, standpipes, and other equipment, including a hose cart, which was fully equipped, with a view to participating in any outside work where the services of the men could be used.

Chief Fire Officer Bellamy and Second Officer Croft of the Western Morning News Private Fire Brigade c.1903.

At first, the Plymouth brigade seemed rather to discourage the well-meant offers of cooperation, but later, the *Western Morning News* Fire Brigade, who always first reported to the officer-in-charge, were welcomed at big fires. They were given a definite stand for operations, including the fires at Risdon's Flour Mills, the Grand Hotel and many others.

Members of the *Western Morning News* Fire Brigade met at Genoni's Café Royal, George Street Plymouth, on October 30th the following year, as the occasion was their annual dinner. Annual dinners were very commonplace in the pre-war years, to make presentations and other plaudits to members of the brigade and leading civic dignitaries. In the absence of the Mayor of Plymouth (Mr A. Edmund Spender), who was confined to his bed with influenza, Chief Officer H. F. Bellamy (W.M.N.F.B.) was in the chair. After an excellent dinner and the loyal toast, the Chief Constable of Plymouth (Mr J. D. Sowerby) handed the Spender Shield and medallions to the winning team at the annual competition. In the course of his remarks he stated that the *Western Morning News* Fire Brigade would be given every opportunity of assisting the Plymouth Brigade, and if there was a necessity that assistance would be returned. The Plymouth Watch Committee were just now considering the advisability of enlarging the Plymouth station to twice its present size, and tenders had already been obtained for the supply of a larger motor fire engine. If that was purchased, their means of fighting fires would be double what it had been in the past. The horsed engine could not compare with the one worked by motor power.

The newspaper brigade, who was affiliated to the National Fire Brigades Union, took part in several competitions organised by the Western Division of the Fire Brigades Union. They won first prize in the four man manual event at Torquay, and a second prize at Plymouth. At the annual event mentioned above, which created a good deal of enthusiasm, was the competition for the Spender Shield; the winning team being the recipients of silver medals as mementos. Many of the older members of the brigade received the National Fire Brigades Union's long service medal. The men wore leather helmets, the officers, those of brass, and each helmet had a large badge with the initials WMNFB. The whole organisation had full uniforms, fireman's boots, hatchets, etc; in fact, the brigade was fully equipped. It was disbanded in 1921 when the new proprietors acquired the *Western Daily Mercury* and *Western Evening Herald*, and removed to new offices in Frankfort Street, (now called George Street).

With modern firefighting equipment, it was thought to be practically a fireproof building, and it did indeed survive the ravishes of war, and the great fires that burnt all around it. They were a merry band and it was a pity when the brigade ended. Captain Burns of Devonport Fire Brigade took a deep interest in their welfare, and the practical help of Sergeant Crocker, of the Stonehouse Fire Brigade was long

Long service medal awarded to Fireman S. E. Martin of the Western Morning News Private Fire Brigade in 1912. This medal was given to members of the National Fire Brigades Union, of which this brigade was affiliated. The NFBU was formed in 1887 and changed its title to National Fire Brigades Association in 1919, as not to confuse people with the Fire Brigades Union, which was a political organisation.

The obverse of the NFBU medal.

remembered. The newspaper offices have since re-located to much larger and modern premises to the north of the city, but the old building frontage still remains today in New George Street.

Brendon's Printing Works in flames

The Plymouth brigade was subject to much criticism following a huge fire at West Hoe in May 1902. The fire broke out shortly after noon in the premises of Messrs W. Brendon and Sons, Printing Works. The flames rapidly obtained a strong hold on the premises. The building was noticeable for its fine appearance and substantial character. Its walls consisted of limestone, faced with brick. Indeed, had it not been for this, coupled with the untiring exertions of the fire brigades, the whole block would probably have been destroyed.

The fire originated in the lift-well, which was built of wood, and ran from the basement to the third floor. The flames rushed up the lift-shaft, which resembled a furnace, and the topmost storey was soon ablaze. The alarm was raised at the Central police station at 12.45 p.m. A fresh, south-westerly wind was blowing at that time, and the flames spread rapidly, unaffected by the drizzling rain. As Mr Sowerby arrived at the scene, the roof fell in, and the reels from several stations were soon got to work at different points.

The steam fire engine (The Plymouth) was dispatched at the same time as the reels. Unfortunately, it had to be hauled by twelve burly police officers, as the fire brigade was not supplied with horses which could be harnessed to the engine without delay. Consequently, the men had to draw it to the scene themselves if no time was to be lost. When the engine, under the direction of Inspector Wyatt, was being drawn into Princess Square, it was attached, by means of a rope, to an electric tramcar proceeding in the direction of the Theatre Royal.

The firemen were guiding it by holding a pole, which in ordinary cases, would be between the horses, when the rope tightened, the front wheels of the engine skidded on the tram rails, and two constables were thrown violently against a tramcar moving in the opposite direction; both were badly injured. The steamer eventually arrived on the fireground amid much jeering, their lateness being very much criticised by the crowds of onlookers. The Stonehouse Fire Brigade arrived and set up operations in the Great Western Docks, where a jet was got to work. The flames were now roaring out of every window of the upper floors, and any hope of saving the building was soon forgotten.

The firemen worked tremendously hard and were commended for their efforts. The fire was eventually got under control late into the evening, and jets were kept playing upon the smouldering mass throughout the night. All that remained of that lovely building were the huge walls, which were in a dangerous state, and it was feared that they could collapse. The crowds were moved to a safe distance. About 300 people were put out of work due to the fire.

The fire brigades of the three towns also attended fires at the Bywater Engineering Works at Millbay in March, and at Houndiscombe Farm, Mutley, which was destroyed, on May 7th. Devonport Fire Brigade was by now in possession of a Merryweather steam fire engine. This machine was under the command of Mr Edwards, and it performed with distinction at the Bywater Engineering works fire.

The Spooner's fire

The year of 1902 was proving to be a very busy year for the fire brigades of the three towns, and once again, on the night of 14th June, Plymouth was the scene of another huge and destructive blaze. The building attacked was the extensive block belonging to Messrs Spooner, the well known drapers and furnishers, fronting in Bedford Street and Old Town Street. The fire broke out about 8.25 p.m. and spread with such amazing rapidity, that within a couple of minutes, great flames were to be seen bursting through the lower windows facing St. Andrew's Church, and also those facing Old Town Street. Luckily, the fire broke out at closing time, and the shop was almost empty of customers. Trying as the circumstances were, the chiefs of departments kept their self-possession, and under their direction, every single member of the large staff made a safe exit from the doomed building.

The alarm reached the Central fire station at 8.28 p.m.. Immediately, a couple of detectives and a few constables rushed to the scene with a combination reel. The steam engine speedily followed, and within a short space of time jets of water began playing on the flames. It was evident to the hundreds of onlookers from the outset, that no power on earth could save the building, so rapid was the progress of the conflagration. Within a quarter of an hour from the discovery of the fire, the huge block of buildings was ablaze from roof to basement. Meanwhile, fire brigades arrived from Stonehouse and Devonport, followed by a large contingent of the military and navy personnel, with their engines.

Aftermath of the huge fire which destroyed the Spooners building in 1902; firemen can be seen damping down, and corporation workers are trying to repair the tram cables.

Plymouth alone provided over 100 firemen, and as many as twenty-one jets were playing on the burning building. Chief Constable Sowerby commanded the whole of the operations, and three-quarters of the entire police force were at work there. It soon became obvious to Mr Sowerby that it was impossible to save the Spooner's building, and he directed his efforts to prevent the spread of fire. Thanks to the devoted services of the firemen, he was successful. It was a long, hard, and trying fight to save Chubb's Hotel, but eventually the flames advancing in this direction were beaten back. The hotel roof caught fire, and the woodwork of the windows looking south on every one of the seven stories was scorched and charred; however, the fabric of the building was unharmed. Considerable damage was, of course, done by water, and a little by fire. This was the norm in the days before hand-controlled branches, but overall the preservation of the hotel from the flames was a feather in the cap of the united fire brigades.

A vast multitude of spectators was attracted to the scene, and most remained there from the moment of the outbreak well into the night to witness the spectacle. All business in Plymouth was practically suspended. Another effect of the fire was the stoppage of the electric cars on the corporation tramways. All traffic through Old Town Street was stopped, and it was several days before the through service of the trams was resumed. Considerable inconvenience was caused to business premises and dwelling houses in the town, by the absence of the electric light. A whole circuit was cut off through the effect of the fire. Communications were thrown into chaos, as a great pole, belonging to the National Telephone Company, bearing more than 200 lines, came crashing down in the early stages of the fire.

Everyone flocked to the neighbourhood of the fire, and thousands came in from Devonport and Stonehouse. The east end of the Guildhall Square, Basket Street, Old Town Street, Whimple Street, St Andrews Street, Treville Street, East Street, and Market Place, were thronged by as dense a crowd as had ever been seen in Plymouth. Great sheets of flame darted out of every window and through the roof with a kind of exultant fury, illuminating the sky all round. The sight was indeed one to be remembered, of that vast menacing fiery furnace, on which was concentrated the gaze of ten thousand upturned faces. The sounds of the stertorous breathing of the fire engines, the hoarse shouts of the firemen, the splash of water streaming into the building from a score of jets, the crashing of glass and the thud of collapsing walls and roofs all captured the enormity of the situation.

The morning after the huge fire that destroyed Messrs Spooner and Co in 1902.

It would apparently be impossible for a fire of any importance to occur in the three towns without the various brigades concerned in the work of extinction coming in for an amount of severe criticism. Unfortunately, there may have been good grounds for this in times past, and it was a custom to blame the firemen, or the poverty of the fire appliances. That the present conflagration should pass without some similar structure was perhaps too much to hope for. There probably has never occurred in the West, a fire of large dimensions in connection with which there should be less adverse criticism. The whole of the firemen engaged acted promptly, courageously and skilfully, and more importantly, the appliances answered the demands made upon them. No fire brigade in existence in those days could have prevented the spread of flames, and the fact that the fire was restrained to the destroyed area was only due to the splendid energies of the firemen employed there.

Plymouth's first self-propelled steamer

Following the criticism for the time it took for the steam fire engine to reach the fire at Brendon's Printing Works, and the need for better fire apparatus, Plymouth Fire Brigade took delivery of a brand new Merryweather self-propelled steam fire engine, known as a Fire King. This fire engine was revolutionary, as the need for horses or men to haul it to the fire was gone. Plymouth and its surrounding area have a rather hilly terrain which caused huge problems in either hauling the engines to the fire, or for the horses pulling the engine. The horses were known to have lost their footing on the steep hills. Once steam was raised, which was as quick as six minutes, the Fire King was fully self-propelled, and would reach speeds

Plymouth Police Firemen with the Merryweather Fire King self-propelled steam fire engine, which was purchased in 1902. This engine was capable of speeds of up to 20 mph on level ground, and was excellent at climbing steep hills in and around Plymouth. Note the sailor type hats worn by the firemen, the name ribbon on the cap read 'Fire Police', not to be confused with the Fire Police of 1823.

of up to twenty mph on level ground, and could also climb a steep gradient at a steady ten m.p.h. The front wheels were steered via a steering wheel located in the centre at the front of the fire engine, and the large rear wheels were driven by a large sprocket and drive chain arrangement.

The new steam fire engine made its debut on 5th July 1902 at a serious fire in the Greenbank area of Plymouth. A large fire had broken out at the Plymouth Workhouse in the early hours of the morning. It was discovered by the master of the establishment, who at once raised the alarm and began evacuating the inmates to other buildings in Clifton Place. The upper floors of the building were well alight, which in turn, spread to the roof, and by the time the fire brigade arrived, the roof had crashed in. The brigade's new motor fire engine performed admirably, and supplied two good jets, which were taken into the building, via the ground floor offices. Not long after the Plymouth brigade arrived, the Stonehouse Fire Brigade also arrived, and was soon at work. None of the inmates, of whom some were elderly, were injured, and the fire was eventually extinguished during the morning.

Risdon Flour Mill destroyed

As previously stated, the year of 1902 saw some large fires occur within Plymouth. Once again, on 25th November, Plymouth was the scene of a large and devastating fire. The fire broke out in the early hours and resulted in the total destruction of Messrs J. and R. Risdon's Flour Mill in West Hoe Road. The buildings adjoined extensive warehouses and other business premises adjacent to Millbay Docks, and were the centre of a busy hive of industry.

The alarm reached the Central police station at 2.23 a.m. via a message telephoned from the *Western Morning News* office, to which a young lad had carried the news of the fire. Two reels, with hose, were immediately dispatched to the scene from the nearest fire stations, and got to work pending the arrival of the steam engine. A contingent of the newly organised *Western Morning News* Fire Brigade, under the command of Engineer Broadley, in full uniform, and with hose and other appliances, reached the spot about the same time, and rendered valuable assistance in fighting the flames. The three-storey building was well alight, the flames leaping out of every window and bursting through the roof, illuminating the entire neighbourhood and presenting a spectacle at once majestic and alarming.

Under the charge of Inspector Tucker, the new motor fire engine arrived at 2.35 a.m. and immediately got to work. Four hoses were connected with the engine, and the water tank having been rigged up, the engine was working at 2.40 a.m. Further fire appliances were brought from the Octagon police station and the Hoe station. It was apparent that nothing could save the mill. The material it contained was mostly of a dry and inflammable nature, and the flames shot up to a tremendous height.

So brilliant was the light that people at the extreme ends of Devonport and Plymouth were attracted to the fire. It was almost three o'clock when the steam fire engine of East Stonehouse, under the supervision of Superintendent Thuell, and a large number of firemen of the township arrived at the mill. They placed themselves under the direction of Chief Constable Sowerby. By this time, hundreds of neighbours had rushed from their homes, and were greatly alarmed at the immensity of the fire. So fierce was the heat that people who were viewing the conflagration from the windows at the rear of Garden Crescent had to shut the windows and beat a retreat.

There was nothing that could save the chief portion of the mill, and the fire brigade then directed special attention to saving adjoining properties. The fire was got under control at 4.30 a.m. When the flames had subsided, the extent of the havoc caused could be realised. Little remained of the interior of the mill and only the huge outer walls remained. The Stonehouse brigade played on the building from a pontoon in the Great Western Docks. Chief Constable Sowerby expressed his acknowledgements of the services rendered by the *Western Morning News* Fire Brigade, who remained on the scene until the fire was finally extinguished. The newspaper fire brigade never had a fire engine of any sort, but they did have a fully equipped hose cart, which they hauled to every fire.

Trials at St Budeaux to allay fears

On July 4th 1902, a very interesting trial of the Devonport steam fire engine, and other fire extinguishing appliances, took place in the open space adjoining the railway station at St Budeaux (this site was later Westcott's coal yard in St Budeaux square). The inhabitants of St Budeaux were very concerned at the lack of fire cover should a fire occur in the area, and this show of fire brigade strength was brought about by putting their concerns to the local councillor, who arranged this demonstration to quell their concerns. Mr John Burns, chief of Devonport Fire Brigade, along with his deputy and all the firemen, made their way to St Budeaux with the steam fire engine and a manual engine. Several drills were carried out using all the appliances there, and proved to be very effective in throwing jets of water 100 feet high, fifty feet higher than any of the buildings in St Budeaux at that time.

It had been pointed out by several inhabitants of St Budeaux, that the Devonport fittings were being used, and not those of St Budeaux. Three men of the brigade were then dispatched for the hose-reel, which was kept at St Budeaux. This was connected to a hydrant, and threw a stream of water through two lengths of hose within three minutes. This demonstrated that the appliances kept at St Budeaux were quite sufficient to cope with any fire that might occur in the district. The trial showed the advantage of the manual engine over the hydrant pressure, and the great advantage of the steam, over both. Unification of standards of hose and hydrant fittings was not dealt with until after the 1947 Fire Services Act, and indeed there were still several types in use in the older parts of Plymouth up until the 1960s.

Huge fire in the Great Western Docks

The Great Western Docks in Plymouth were the scene of a very extensive and alarming conflagration during the early hours of 26th January 1903. Buildings and property belonging to the Bickle Engineering Company, and Messrs Jewson's Timber Merchants, who both had businesses in the western end of the dock, beneath the Longroom, were destroyed.

When the fire brigades from the three towns arrived, the huge corrugated iron roofed sheds were burning fiercely, and several large stacks of timber were alight. All attempts to obtain water from the mains were quickly abandoned, as the fittings on the government-pattern hydrants were alien to the standpipes of the brigades of the three towns. Luckily, the tide was high, and there was an inexhaustible supply of seawater available, to which the firemen dropped their suction hoses, and began playing jets upon the burning piles. The Dockyard tug *Industrious*, with floats, entered the dock, tied up alongside the West wharf and began pumping. The tug had an appreciable effect, and together with all the fire brigades, there were thirteen jets at work. Parties of Royal Artillerymen, Royal Engineers, The North Lancashire Regiment and the Royal Warwick Regiment made an appearance within half an hour. Strong detachments of seamen from the ships in the dock, and from the RN Barracks, also came to assist. The Bluejackets brought with them some manual fire engines, buckets and grapplers.

One of the Stonehouse firemen, Mr A. Coombs, had a nasty accident while positioning the steamer for operation. He was caught between the steamer and a truck, breaking his arm quite badly; he was taken to the Royal Albert Hospital, where his arm was reset.

The heat and smoke being generated was intense, and at one stage, there was about half an acre of the docks alight. Huge crowds, who were alerted by signalling guns being fired from ships in the Hamoaze, lined the Longroom and other vantage points to view the conflagration. Despite the miserable weather, they remained until the fire was got under control.

The huge wooden sheds, with corrugated iron roofs, came crashing to the ground, and the whole of the western end of the docks was emitting a lurid glow, which could be seen for miles around. Several ships in the dock had to be taken to safer moorings, as some suffered severe scorching, and there was a very good chance that they would become involved. Soon after 12.30 a.m., the machinery, moulding, and pattern shops belonging to the Bickle Engineering Company, came crashing down amid a myriad of sparks. Soon afterwards, Mr Jewson's premises collapsed in the same manner.

Soldiers and sailors worked amid choking smoke, in pulling down the huge stacks of timber to save them from the same fate as numerous other stacks. By about 1.30 a.m., the fire was got under control, and the large contingent of marines, soldiers, and seamen were withdrawn, leaving the firemen of Plymouth, Devonport and Stonehouse to continue playing jets upon the burning piles. Throughout the course of the fire, policemen from Stonehouse and Plymouth kept the hundreds of spectators in check, and there was good order throughout.

The cold light of the morning arrived, and combined with the stench of the fire, created a bleak and sinister picture of the immense loss which occurred during the night. By mid-morning, the blackened faces of the exhausted firemen could clearly be seen as they made their ways back to their respective fire stations, the fire having been finally extinguished. This fire was the last incident attended by Inspector Wyatt of the Police Fire Brigade. He retired from the force in April, after twenty-six years service to the police and fire brigade.

Fireman George Stone of the Devonport Fire Brigade.

London fireman in court

At Devonport on 28th September 1904, Edwin Martin, a London fireman and a native of Devonport, was charged with damaging a fire escape to the extent of £10, the property of the Devonport Corporation. Henry Edwards, deputy superintendent of the Devonport Fire Brigade, stated that on Saturday evening he found that the fire escape, which was stationed outside the Guildhall, had the extending ladders broken in five pieces, rendering them perfectly useless; the escape cost £50.

A witness stated that she saw Martin go into the Guildhall enclosure and draw the ladders of the fire escape up. When the ladders were fully extended, the escape overturned, knocking Martin's hat off, and falling across the railings. The ladders were smashed, and Martin picked up the pieces and put them in the enclosure. Martin did not run away, and the witness informed the police that there were no children by the escape. Sergeant Moore said Martin, on being asked what business he had in the Guildhall enclosure, replied, 'I am a fireman and belong to London, the children were about the machine and I came in and took charge.' Asked about the damage to the escape, he said, 'The children must have done it.' The witness told him he did not think children could get the ladders up. When confronted with the statement of the witness, Martin said the ladders were up and he was letting them down for safety, when the escape toppled over. Martin had been drinking, but knew perfectly well what he was about. The prisoner, Martin, consented to the case being adjourned until September 30th to enable enquiries to be made, and bail in two sureties of £10 each was allowed. On the re-hearing, the charge was withdrawn, on payment of the amount of the damage. I can only imagine that this London fireman, worse for wear, was showing off his ability with the escape when the inevitable happened.

The death of Mr Henry Edwards and other headlines

The following statement appeared in the Devonport newspaper on 20th August 1906:

> 'Many friends will learn with deep regret with the death of Mr H. Edwards, aged fifty-two years, a fire officer of Devonport Fire Brigade. The deceased had an apoplectic fit the previous Wednesday, from which he never recovered. Mr Edwards served the Royal Navy as a chief petty officer, and retired on pension some sixteen years ago. Mr Edwards had been one of the assistant sanitary inspectors of the borough for about fifteen years, and had also been a member of the fire brigade from about the year 1893. He took such deep interest in the working of the brigade, that in September 1896, he was designated Assistant Deputy-Superintendent, and shortly afterwards, on the resignation of the Deputy Superintendent Mr Wyatt, he was appointed to fill that position. He left behind a Widow and one son.'

Fireman Arthur Gilbert, Devonport Fire Brigade. He began his life in the brigade as a call boy. He was born in 1888 (the year when the brigade formed), and he died in 1966.

Newspaper headlines 'Paupers in Peril' appeared in the *London Weekly Dispatch*, in July 1907. It described how a fire involving the top storey of a Plymouth workhouse on the 5th July made it necessary for the fire brigade to evacuate some 250 men and women, many old and feeble, from the burning building. The Chief Constable thanked the *Western Morning News* Fire Brigade for their valuable assistance in rescuing the inmates, and for their part in extinguishing the fire. Reading the accounts of this and other early fires, one is impressed by the efficient work carried out without the aid of modern motor fire appliances, breathing apparatus, and other aids to speed extinction.

Manchester pattern leather fire helmet, as used by the Plymouth Police Fire Brigade throughout their existence.

In the early part of the twentieth century, 1908 to be exact, one particular fire at the Sugar Refinery in Mill Street resulted in the complete devastation of the premises, and the fire brigades were reported to have performed admirably. Improvements within the different brigades continued, and an entry in the Police Fire Brigade stores book for June 1906 shows the strength of the Plymouth Borough Police Fire Brigade as follows:

> J. D. Sowerby, (Superintendent); J. Tucker, (Deputy Supt.); Sergeants T. Stevens, T. Monksley, W. Body; Constables J. Somers, A. Harmer, J. Voysey, W. Collings, C. Willcocks, W. Bennett, J. Mann, J. Beer, W. Thomas, J. Chapman, S. Denley, G. Cook, W. Cuffs, T. Allen, H. Snow, H. Knight, J. Paley, J. Stoneman, S. Voisey, C. Lea, C. Bonshow, D. Damerell, C. Bartlett, W. Baghole, S. G. Palmer, H. Clarke, J. Westlake, J. Down, T. Byrues.

The stores book also showed that in 1909, two Shand Mason manual fire engines were sold back to the makers. This was a common practice between numerous fire brigades and the manufacturers at that time, very much like the modern practice of 'trading in' your old vehicle for a newer one.

Plymouth Police Fire Brigade c.1916. The firemen wore leather Manchester pattern fire helmets, unlike the former Devonport and Stonehouse Fire Brigades, who wore brass helmets.

The annual report of the Chief Constable of Plymouth (Mr J. D. Sowerby) for the year 1906, stated that the fire brigade had been called thirty-eight times, when the steamer and other appliances were used. This did not include chimney fires and fires of a small character. The year had been singularly free from serious fires, and damage to property had been comparatively small. Nearly half the members of the fire brigade were connected at their homes, with the Central Station, by electric bells, and this proved of great convenience. The steam of the motor engine was kept up at night and day at a pressure of 30lbs to the square inch, so that in the event of a call, full steam could be procured in less than fifty-five seconds. A new police and fire station had been opened during the year at Prince Rock, and was, very shortly, equipped with a combination escape and reel, and other necessary appliances. A second police and fire station was nearing completion near the Hyde Park Hotel, Mutley. This was to be similarly equipped, and covered the Peverell and Compton districts. An ambulance was also placed at each of these stations.

Between 1906 and 1908, the following plant was reported at the following locations:

Central Police Station

- One Merryweather Motor Fire Engine (Fire King) containing 1,200 ft of canvas hose, three standpipes, four branchpipes, three 'T' keys, three tightening spanners, one canvas dam
- One Merryweather Steam Fire Engine (formerly known as the Western but now retitled The Plymouth, containing 900 ft of canvas hose, two standpipes, four branchpipes, two 'T' keys, two tightening spanners, one dam, and four leak clips

Chief Constable/Fire Officer Joseph Sowerby 1892–1917.

- One thirty-seven foot combination fire escape, containing 300 ft of canvas hose, one standpipe, one branchpipe, one 'T' key, two spanners, one hand pump, one jumping sheet
- One forty-two foot combination escape
- One fifty-three foot fire escape

Hoe Police Station

- One forty-four foot fire escape
- One hose-reel and 300 ft of canvas hose, one standpipe, one branchpipe, one 'T' key and spanners

Station Road Fire Station, (Union Street)

- One Curricle combination fire escape, containing 300 ft of canvas hose, one standpipe, one branchpipe, one 'T' key, one tightening spanner, one Iron splice, two leak clips, one piece of rope, one bucket, and one connection for Stonehouse hydrants

Octagon Police Station

- One hose-reel with 300 ft of canvas hose, one standpipe, one branchpipe, one 'T' key, two spanners, one axe, one bucket, one splice, two leak clips, one piece of rope, one connection for Stonehouse hydrants, one jumping sheet, and one new fifteen foot ladder

Oxford Place Station

- One hose-reel with 300 ft of canvas hose, one standpipe, one branchpipe, one 'T' key, one spanner, one axe, one lamp, one iron splice, one leak clip, one bucket, one piece of rope

Providence Street Police Station

- One thirty-five ft combination fire escape containing 300 ft of canvas hose, one standpipe, one branchpipe, one 'T' key, two tightening spanners, one lamp, one bucket, one iron splice, two leak clips, one Jumping sheet, and one fifteen-foot ladder

Mutley Police Station

- One hose-reel with 300 ft of canvas hose, one standpipe, one branchpipe, one 'T' key, two tightening spanners, one axe, one lamp, one bucket, one iron splice, two leak clips
- In 1907 the Police and Fire Station was equipped with a new Merryweather combination fire escape, containing 300 ft of canvas hose and one new ambulance

Mannamead Fire Station (late local board offices), Compton Lane end

- One hose-reel with 300 ft of canvas hose, one standpipe, one branchpipe, one 'T' key, two tightening spanners, one leak clip, and one piece of rope

Laira Police and Fire Station

- One hose cart containing seven scaling ladders which would work to a height of about thirty-five feet. 300 ft of canvas hose, with all the necessary appliances
- In 1925, a combination fire-escape replaced the hose cart

Workhouse Fire Station

- One hose-reel with 300 ft of canvas hose, one standpipe, one branchpipe, one 'T' key, one tightening spanner, one leak clip
- In 1908, the above reel was transferred to Lipson Road with additional gear. The hose, etc., at the workhouse was then kept in a box ready for immediate use

Harbour Avenue Police Station

- One hose-reel with 300 ft of canvas hose, and all necessary appliances, one hand pump, one fifteen-foot ladder, one twelve-foot ladder, one eighteen-foot ladder

The Barbican Police Station

- One hose-reel with 300 ft of canvas hose, and all necessary appliances

Theatre Royal

- 200 ft of canvas hose, with four branchpipes, in different parts of the theatre, ready for immediate use

Infectious Diseases Hospital (Mount Gould)

- About 170 ft of canvas hose

Elliot Road, (Off Embankment Road Police Station)

- One Shand Mason manual fire engine (sold in 1909), four lengths of canvas hose, one branchpipe, one 'T' key, two tightening spanners, one old dam, and five lengths of old suction
- The manual fire engine was replaced with a new Merryweather combination fire-escape

Lipson Road Reel House

- Situated just above Woodside, under Freedom Park, containing the reel transferred from the workhouse, with 300 ft of canvas hose, and all necessary appliances

Chief Constable/Fire Officer Joseph Sowerby (Crossed legs), who served Plymouth from 1892 until 1917; the officer to his left was Inspector J. Hill.

CHAPTER TWELVE

TIMBER YARD FIRES AND OTHER EVENTS

ONCE AGAIN, IN September 1910, the Great Western Docks at Plymouth was the scene of a huge and serious conflagration. Strangely enough, the same owners of property suffered in the same way as they did seven years previously, in 1903. The outbreak occurred at the timber yard of Mr E. W. Jewson.

Several factors made the outbreak more than usually dangerous. The yard, with a sawmill at one end of it, was situated on West Wharf, and was well stocked with timber. Once the flames obtained a grip of these huge baulks, and the lighter planks, the task of subduing them was a tremendously formidable one. The fire ate up the timber at an amazing pace, and when the fire brigades arrived, the heat was almost too great for the men to work within an effective distance.

Surrounded by a working-class community, with many dockworkers among the residents, the blaze quickly attracted a large assemblage of men. They were not slow to set to work to take all the precautions that could be taken, and all moveable property was removed from the close proximity. One of the chief concerns of those engaged was the danger presented by the Royal Marines' powder magazine, which was situated just outside the dock boundary. The glare of the fire lit up the night sky, and could be seen for miles around. From all quarters of the three towns, men, women and children hurried in the drenching rain, and their rapid arrival at the different entrances to the Docks presented severe difficulties.

Along Durnford Street and Millbay Road, the excited people rushed, until the pressure on the gates was dangerous to the would-be spectators. This presented a serious handicap to the firemen, and those co-operating with them. Indeed, the officials were caught in a cleft stick, between firemen with their appliances desiring to enter, and the public, anxious to rush the gates, but they were only partially thrown back. The difficulty was eventually overcome, though many hundreds eluded the vigilance of the officers at the gates, and gained a close view of the blaze.

The alarm was given at about 10.15 p.m. to the Stonehouse Fire Brigade, who promptly turned out, under the command of Captain F. W. Thuell. They were quickly followed by the Plymouth Fire Brigade, with their Fire King self-propelled steam fire engine, under Inspector Tucker. By that time, many of the Marines were already at work. Within minutes, the Devonport Fire Brigade arrived, and the united fire brigades quickly got their hoses out, and huge volumes of seawater were pumped from the basin and projected onto the blazing woodpile.

Constable James Stoneman of the Police Fire Brigade c.1912. He was stationed at Laira Police Fire Station. This building is still there today and has been in use as a library since 1925.

In addition to the Marines, who rushed to lend a hand, about 150 men, commanded by Commodore R. E. Wemyes, arrived from the RN Barracks with their manual fire engine. It was a wonderful scene of animation, such as had not been seen for a long time at a Plymouth fire. There were hundreds of soldiers and sailors on duty, many of the former being armed with their rifles, with which they overawed the invading crowd. The men of the Leinster and Staffordshire regiments, who were stationed at Raglan Barracks, were brought to the docks to assist in dismantling huge piles of timber.

The Metropolitan Police steam engine (The Sutherland), and other Dockyard steam fire engines, were also pressed into service. Plymouth and Stonehouse policemen were kept busy, and there appeared to be no lack of helpers, naval, military, and civilian.

A most regrettable incident was caused during the chaotic scenes at the gates, Captain Burns, of the Devonport Fire Brigade, who made his way to the fire in his motor car, was refused admittance by the hard-pressed officials on gate duty, notwithstanding the fact that he was wearing his uniform. Mr Burns had no option but to make his way to another gate, where entry was permitted, this resulted in his lateness in reaching his men and supervising them.

The hundreds of spectators who managed to gain entry into the docks were kept at bay by the troops, who, with fixed bayonets, managed to maintain a safe distance between themselves and the hard working firemen. The fire raged with alarming intensity, and despite the fact that no breeze was blowing, the flames licked their way towards the high party wall of the barracks, throwing out an overwhelming heat.

At one time, matters looked most serious, for on the other side of the wall were ranged the stables, forage sheds, etc., of the barracks, and the buildings appeared to be in imminent danger. However, the men in the barracks procured hoses, which they attached to the hydrants, and were able to throw five jets on the burning mass, averting the danger. Large sheds and other buildings in the docks were so badly weakened by the fire that they came crashing to the ground. Towards midnight, the gaps in the mass of blazing timber showed how great had been the efforts of the workers in trying to create firebreaks. The basin was full of charred timbers, which had been thrown into the water by the Marines and Bluejackets.

At one o'clock, the firemen had succeeded in checking the spread of the flames. Their task, however, was far from being complete. There were still large fires burning in the centre of the docks, and they were left to burn themselves out. The surrounding land and water was not as visibly illuminated as it had been an hour or so earlier, yet for some considerable distance away the buildings, shipping, and crowds were clearly silhouetted.

From midnight onwards, there had been a gradual thinning out of the ranks of people thickly clustered beyond the military barriers, though thousands remained. No accidents were reported, but for a long time the press of the crowd had been tremendous. Occasionally, there were ugly rushes, as false alarms were raised, and here tact, as well as force, was needful. Remarkably, over 2,000 persons, made up of firemen, policemen, soldiers, marines, and sailors, were engaged in extinguishing the vast fire.

Timber yards seemed to be where the resources of the fire brigades were stretched in times of fire, and once again in December 1913 an outbreak of fire was discovered at the timber yard belonging to Messrs Fox, Elliot, and Company, in Richmond Walk. The fire was discovered about one o'clock in the morning by the foreman of the yard, Mr Bird, who lived in a cottage adjoining the yard.

Assistance was summoned, and within a short time, a large posse of police, together with the Devonport Fire Brigade, arrived on the scene. Three companies of the Middlesex Regiment, with their fire engine, and a company of marines, were also quickly on the scene. Other corps in the garrison also sent detachments, and there were about 1,500 soldiers and sailors assisting at the fire. The whole of the premises, covering about one and a half acres, including 2,000 standards of timber, each containing about 165 cubic feet of wood, were by now a mass of flames. The firemen and helpers were powerless to stop them.

The firm of Hancock's, who occupied an area of wasteland beside the timber yard for their pleasure fair, also suffered quite badly. The fire had ignited a couple of their roundabouts, as well as a scenic railway.

The aftermath of the fire which partly destroyed the pleasure fair at Stonehouse in 1913.

Members of the Hancock family who owned a pleasure fair at Stonehouse. They lost a lot of roundabouts and a scenic railway to fire in 1913. The fire originated in the timber merchants of Fox, Eliot and Company, and spread to waste ground, where the fairground folk lived in their caravans.

There was quite a big colony of caravan folk dwelling at the fairground site, and they were soon panicked by the extent of the fire. The menfolk, assisted by soldiers, worked furiously in removing their belongings to a place of safety. The women, dressed in their nightclothes and wrapped in blankets, were hurrying with the children to a safe location, where they could only stare in disbelief at the spectacle which developed before them.

The flames burnt furiously, and the glow in the dark sky could be seen from many miles away. The fire was completely out of control, but the firemen, ably assisted by the soldiers, poured huge volumes of water upon the flames. Other helpers sought to check the advance of the fire by throwing the burning baulks of timber into Stonehouse Pool. Other fire engines were arriving at the double, and were hauled across Ha'penny Bridge by the soldiers who brought them, and were sited as close to the water's edge as was practical.

Meanwhile the Devonport Fire Brigade, under Captain Burns and Second Officer Dart, and the Stonehouse Fire Brigade, under Chief Officer Thuell and Second Officer Thuell, were at work. The latter directed their attention chiefly to preventing the flames, which had by this time reached a tremendous height, from spreading to the buildings on the other side of the water, which at that point was not more than eight yards wide. Thousands of planks were thrown into the water, soldiers embarking in small boats and pulling them out into midstream, so as to free the congestion at the quayside. The bluejackets mounted a roof of a neighbouring building, and played water streams onto the stacks of timber.

Merryweather Hatfield pump escape, bought for Devonport Fire Brigade in 1914. The engine was a four-cylinder Merryweather-Aster 60 B.H.P. The escape was a sliding carriage design, which could reach up to 45 feet. This motor fire engine was christened 'Unity', and complements the Merryweather Greenwich Gem steam fire engine, which was bought for Devonport in 1900.

Just before four o'clock, the Metropolitan Police engine from Devonport Dockyard arrived, under the control of Sergeant Broad. They performed some useful work at the north end of the fire, in conjunction with the Marines' engine. The numerous firefighters were augmented by a government tug, and by a large body of bluejackets from the Naval Barracks. The spread of the fire was now checked, and the main body of fire was allowed to burn itself out. Damping down operations continued well into the next day.

Motor fire engine for Devonport

Whilst improvements were made to the plant of the fire brigades of the three towns from time to time, it was the arrival of the first motor-driven fire engine to the Devonport Fire Brigade which caused much excitement throughout the borough. The engine, which was trialled in September 1914, was a Merryweather Hatfield pump escape, with an Aster 60 BHP engine. A forty-five foot escape ladder with sliding carriage was included. This fine fire engine, together with the Merryweather Greenwich Gem steam fire engine, which was delivered in 1900, afforded greater protection to the inhabitants of Devonport.

The christening and trials of the new engine took place on Saturday 5th September in front of a large gathering at the front of the Guildhall in Ker Street. Those present included Councillor G. A. Daymond (Chairman of the Fire Committee); Councillors W. George; A. Weakford; W. J. Smith; W. Watson; C. H. Healy; W. Welsford; J. Moon; T. P. Trehlohan; S. Perkins; W. J. Olver; J. Hellens; T. Jane; T. A. Clarke; W. H. Jackson; First Officer J. F. Burns and Second Officer Dart, Devonport Fire Brigade; J. D. Sowerby,

Chief Constable of Plymouth; J. H. Wiltshire, Chairman of Torpoint District Council; Captain Pett, Exeter Fire Brigade and Chairman of the South Western District NFBU; Captain F. W. Thuell, Stonehouse Fire Brigade; Captain Bellamy, Western Morning News Fire Brigade; Mr E Smith, Deputy Mayor of Saltash; Chief Officer Mace, Saltash Fire Brigade; and Chief Officer Wodehouse, Torpoint Fire Brigade.

Various trials were proceeded with to demonstrate the capacity of the engine; two jets reached the top of the Devonport Column, which is 190 feet high. The escape was then tested, and one of the firemen rescued a person from the top floor of the municipal building. An interesting and important part of the ceremony was the speed trials and hill climbing tests. For this purpose, the engine was run over from Devonport to St Budeaux, Crownhill and Plymouth. Members of the Corporation and representatives of the fire brigades accompanied the engine and had an exciting experience.

On arriving at the Guildhall Square, Plymouth, the company was met by the Mayor (Mr T. Baker), who welcomed the Devonport party. Mr G. Daymond made a few remarks. He said they were pleased to meet at the Guildhall Square that afternoon. He believed some of them would presently be representing the larger borough. He went on to say, that on their first visit to Plymouth, as members of the Corporation, they had not come empty-handed.

The fire brigades of the three towns had always worked in harmony, and had always been willing to render each other every possible assistance. Referring to the misunderstanding with regard to the fire at Fox, Elliott, and Co. in Richmond Walk, the speaker said the only reason why they did not seek the help of the Plymouth brigade on that occasion, was because such ample assistance from the Government and Stonehouse firemen was more than adequate, and that if the brigade had come out, there would have been no room. Mr Daymond added that they had bought an up-to-date fire engine and appliances, which would not be for the exclusive use of Devonport, but for the benefit of the forthcoming larger borough. The new fire engine was christened Unity, as they hoped it would benefit the whole community.

Amalgamation of the three towns creates changes

A significant milestone in the history of Plymouth finally established itself on 1st November 1914. The boroughs of East Stonehouse and Devonport were absorbed into the now larger borough of Plymouth, under local government provisional order confirmation No. 18 dated Saturday May 2nd 1914, and a local act (5 and 6 Geo V ch.clxxxiii), which received royal assent on Monday August 10th 1914. Plymouth Borough Council held its last meeting on Thursday October 29th 1914 and amalgamation took place from November 1st. The term 'three towns' was then locked into history, but there is still evidence around today where the use of that terminology still exists, long after the amalgamation was brought about.

The respective fire brigades were not disbanded at that time. It wasn't until 1916 that the Plymouth Watch Committee approved the reorganisation of the Police Fire Brigade on the following lines: The voluntary fire brigades in the Devonport and East Stonehouse areas to be disbanded on the 31st March, and a new Police Brigade for the new larger borough, consisting of one chief officer (who at that time was the chief constable), one superintendent, two divisional officers (one for Devonport and one for Stonehouse) and sixty-one men. The two sections were to be at Catherine Street, Plymouth, and Devonport Guildhall, Ker Street. The remainder of the men in the police force to be instructed in fire-escape and hose drill. Competitive examinations were held by the sub-committee for the posts of superintendent and divisional officers. The examination for superintendent was confined to inspectors, and that for divisional officers to inspectors and sergeants. Deputy Supt Rogers performed the duties of superintendent pending the examination for the post. The service of Engineer H. O. May was retained in the Devonport Division. The houses of all members of the brigade living in the vicinity of the Devonport Division fire centre were connected with electric bells, similar to those at the central fire station. The general question of street alarms was deferred. The Merryweather pump escape, which was new to Devonport in 1914, was repainted into Plymouth livery and remained at the Devonport fire station in Ker Street.

The Chief Constable reported that connecting pieces had been provided which would enable the necessary connection to be made with the two sizes of hydrant existing within the borough, as they were

Group photograph of the Plymouth Police Fire Brigade in front of the Guildhall in 1915. The appliances are the Merryweather self-propelled steamer and the Merryweather pump escape; the escape ladder is slipped and is being used at the rear of the picture.

Plymouth police firemen show off the Merryweather Hatfield pump escape c.1925. This appliance was like the one bought for Devonport Fire Brigade in 1914. This appliance was Plymouth's first motorised pump which was purchased in 1917.

proved to be efficient. This would obviate the heavy cost of replacing a large number of hydrants; the report was duly approved. There was no standardisation of equipment among the hundreds of fire brigades throughout the country at that time, and it wasn't until the Fire Services Act 1947 came into being that this problem was addressed. The City of Plymouth Fire Brigade carried special adaptors on their fire appliances up until the 1960s, as there were still several old pattern hydrants in the older parts of the city.

Devonport Fire Brigade with their new fire engine in 1914.

Chief Constable Sowerby retires

Mr Joseph Davidson Sowerby retired in 1917, having served Plymouth for twenty-five years, both as Chief Constable and Chief Fire Officer. Mr Sowerby, previous to his appointment here (incidentally, he was the first in Plymouth to hold the rank of chief constable), was chief clerk of the Leeds Police Force. His advancement in that large city was little short of phenomenal – constable at seventeen years old, sergeant twelve months later, inspector at twenty years old, and Chief Inspector at twenty-one.

At this period, his youth only prevented him applying for the Chief Constableship of Liverpool. In 1892, vacancies occurred in two towns, Worcester and Plymouth; Sowerby applied for both. He lost Worcester by one vote, but was interviewed at Plymouth, where he was successful, he was twenty-nine years old. Mr Sowerby will take his place in local history among the foremost of our public servants, who gave their best in the interests of this city and its people. Sadly he was in failing health, and did not survive long after being relieved of the cares and worries of his office. Mr Herbert Sanders became the next chief constable of the Borough Police Force.

Mr Sanders soon learned that it was not an ideal situation for a policeman to wear two helmets, viz, police and fire. Whenever a policeman was required to do fire duties, this of course, weakened the strength of the policemen on the streets, as it was a case of rob Peter to pay Paul. There were about sixty police-run fire brigades around the country at this time. Some coped rather well, whilst others, like Plymouth, were struggling to provide a good service to the ever-growing population and expanding area.

There was also a certain amount of resentment within the force; the policemen doing full-time firemen duties were paid an annual retainer, which was additional to their wages.

Plymouth made great improvements to the fire apparatus during the period from about 1914 through to the 1920s. There were motorised pumps at both Catherine Street in Plymouth, and Ker Street in Devonport. These pumps were Merryweather motor pump escapes, and were bought in 1917. It was common practice in the early days to name fire engines, and Plymouth christened the Devonport-based pump the Tamar, and the Catherine Street-based pump, The Plym. These fire engines were Merryweather appliances with reciprocating pumps. The Merryweather pump escape, originally bought for Plymouth in 1917 at a cost of £1,452 was then located in Catherine Street, Plymouth. In the same year, two old manual fire engines, which had done sterling service prior to the motor age, were sold off to the War Office for £195.

The Merryweather Fire King self-propelled steamer, and other older fire appliances, were all replaced at various times. The steam fire engines from Stonehouse and Devonport were either sold off or scrapped.

1931 Dennis Big 6 Pump Escape (JY 956). © Ron Henderson

The age of steam power was at an end with the now much improved internal combustion engines. Incidentally, the powerful Sutherland steam fire engine, which was bought for the Dockyard back in 1863, was eventually retired in 1905. It was gifted to the Merryweather museum at Greenwich, where it remained until 1924, and it was then presented to the Science Museum in London, where it remains to this day at the former RAF Hospital at Wroughton. The two Merryweather pump escapes served Plymouth well. The Tamar was scrapped following an accident in 1932, whilst the Plym was scrapped in 1962.

Apart from the two main stations in Plymouth and Devonport, the police had fire apparatus located throughout the city, at the sub-police stations or police boxes. Many of these sites contained hose reel carts, which were laden with hose, standpipes, and other useful tools, which were hauled by hand, to wherever they were needed.

In November 1892, the stores book of the Police Fire Brigade showed the following locations of fire fighting appliances within the borough as follows: Central station (Catherine Street), Hoe station, Station Road (Union Street), Octagon station, Oxford Street station, Mutley station, Workhouse, Providence Street, Avenue station, Barbican station, Old Guildhall and Theatre Royal.

After the amalgamation of the three towns in 1914, and into the 1920s, the police extended their fire appliances to the following locations throughout Plymouth: Central Police Station, Hoe Police Station, Station Road Police Station, Octagon Police Station, Oxford Place Station, Providence Street Police Station, Mutley Police Station, Mannamead Fire Station, Laira Police Station, Workhouse Fire Station,

Harbour Avenue Police Station, Barbican Police Station, Theatre Royal, Infectious Diseases Hospital (Mount Gould), Elliot Road, Lipson Road Reel House, Compton Tram Depot, Elphinstone Flats Reel House, Ker Street Fire Station, Morice Town Station, Melville Road, Warleigh Avenue, Camels Head Station, Johnston Terrace Police Box, St Budeaux (Lower), St Budeaux (Higher), Pennycross Co-op Bakery, Cattedown Wharves and St Levens Road Police Box.

The former fire station at Laira, which has been in use as a library since 1925.

Plymouth gains city status

Plymouth Borough had increased enormously in area and population since the mid-1800s, hence the need for the police to place appliances at strategic points throughout the city. The status of a city was conferred on Plymouth in 1928, and the old borough police were renamed the City of Plymouth Police Force.

Improvements to the motor appliances continued throughout the 1920s and 1930s. In 1931, Plymouths first turntable ladder, (JY 937), was purchased from Merryweather and Sons; this appliance had a seventy-foot wooden and metal trussed ladder. Plymouth now had the ability to deal with high level rescues, and to fight fires from a much loftier position than ever before. Prior to the arrival of the turntable ladder, two Dennis Hatfield pumps were purchased in 1930. Their registrations were DR 7553 and DR 7555, and they were located at Ker Street Devonport, and Catherine Street Plymouth; both appliances were sold off in 1951.

1931 Merryweather turntable ladder with wooden ladders and steel trusses. © *Ron Henderson*

Dennis Big 6 Pump Escape (JY 956) at Greenbank in 1937.

No regular firemen and ongoing problems

The Plymouth Police Fire Brigade came in for much criticism, and at times they were really stretched for available manpower at larger fires. The practice of the military aiding fire fighting, as in the early days, had finished long ago. The question of the police force having to provide two essential services was often brought up in discussions.

In an edition of the *Western Morning News* for March 19th 1931, there were serious concerns expressed as to the effectiveness of the Police Fire Brigade in Plymouth. The report mentioned that the personnel of the fire brigade was composed of thirty-two police auxiliary firemen, of which the Chief Constable (Mr A. K. Wilson) was Chief Officer. 'There are no regular firemen in the accepted sense,' commented Mr Wilson, although several members of the force were employed whole-time on fire duty. By arrangement with the Home Office, the sum of £1,163 per annum was contributed to the police account. This amount represented the pay and pension liability, etc., of four constables, to be employed whole-time on fire duty. Four men were, of course, wholly inadequate, and one Inspector (who acts as Superintendent of the fire brigade), one sergeant and six constables were set aside for fire duty.

There were three constables allocated to Devonport, and three to Plymouth. This number was required so that a driver would be available at each station by day and night. The constables at the central station also acted as drivers of the police vehicles when required.

During the previous year, the brigade received 137 calls to fires, of which four were false alarms. The Chief Constable reported that two of the fire engines required a complete overhaul, and further appliances were required before the brigade could be regarded as being adequately equipped. A number of urgently needed appliances were purchased during the year, and in so doing, the money allocated for the purchase of new uniforms had to be used.

The personnel of the brigade, from a fire fighting point of view, could not be improved upon, and few fire brigade authorities commanded the services of such a capable officer as the Superintendent (Mr Jim Mead), or such a loyal staff. In 1916, the strength of the brigade was sixty-five, but that number then dwindled to thirty-two, the diminution in numbers being entirely due to lack of accommodation. It was not possible to obtain houses, or even rooms, near enough to the two fire stations, to be included in the alarm circuit.

The strength of thirty-two was in some measure illusory, and the effective strength available on receipt of most calls of fire was limited to seventeen, the number of men whose houses were connected to the alarm circuit. Even that number was not constant, because some of the men were always either engaged elsewhere on police duty, or were off duty. It frequently happened that when an engine departed from the central station, there was no fireman available to leave in charge of the station, to drive the second engine, should it be requisitioned.

To put the matter briefly, in order to obtain a reasonably efficient crew to man an engine, the officers of the brigade were dependent, on practically all occasions, upon the loyalty of the men, who either purposely remained at home, when off duty, or frequented the fire station during the greater part of their waking hours.

Fire Superintendent William Mead, with his wife and daughter, in 1931. Mr Mead was in charge of the Police Fire Brigade in Plymouth and his son Francis (Jim) was also a fireman, having joined in 1938. Jim Mead left Plymouth on promotion in the 1960s, and he served at Bristol, Belfast and London.

Dennis motor pump, delivered to Plymouth in 1931. Personnel are from L to R: George Weeks, Bobby Steer, Joe Gerretty, Jack Brown, Phil Parsons (Driver), William Mead (O.I.C.). Standing rear of the ladder are Constables Francis, Westlake and Stevens.

The report also explained that the duty of inspection of all licensed places of public entertainment was to be carried out by the fire brigade staff. Some idea of the magnitude of the task is gained when it is remembered that there were six theatres, fourteen cinematograph theatres, and 108 premises licensed for public music, singing, and dancing. A further task imposed on the brigade, was that of inspecting and maintaining the fire appliances in all Corporation premises, but as at that time constituted, it was impossible to adequately perform these duties.

This report gave some cause for alarm, but, 'I should fail in my duty as Chief Officer to your brigade, if I did not place the facts before you,' concluded Mr Wilson. The problem of housing, and living accommodation, for police firemen was not isolated to just 1931. Very little progress ensued over the next few years, as once again, in May 1938, it was reported in the *Sunday Independent*, that there was a housing crisis in Devonport. The problem had arisen over the provision of living accommodation for firemen at Devonport, near the Ker Street fire station. Though stated as not a serious matter, it was a very important one, and the Watch Committee were seeking a way to make the Devonport division more efficient than it was, with firemen living rather considerable distances away.

There was only one permanent fireman at Devonport, the other five or six members of the brigade also acting as policemen, and when they were off duty, they were called in case of fire by means of bells in their own homes. These homes, however, were not as near to the station as they ought to be. The Watch Committee had asked the Housing Committee for a site in the vicinity of Ker Street, to enable the necessary accommodation to be provided. The reply, however, was not helpful, as there were no available sites.

It was not suggested that there had been any serious delays in getting to Devonport fires, but it was felt that in case of a serious outbreak, the minutes that might be saved through firemen living close to the station might be invaluable. Alderman W. J. Modley, the chairman of the Watch Committee, was reported as saying that he might be compelled to build the accommodation close to the station. The only accommodation they had built was at Greenbank, which was very close to the fire station, and that was to accommodate the firemen after the Catherine Street station was closed and the police moved to the Greenbank area of the city.

Fire Superintendent William Mead, Chief Constable/Fire Officer A. K. Wilson and Superintendent Lee.

Serious mutiny and fire at Dartmoor Prison

The Plymouth Police and Fire Brigade were called into action on January 24th 1932, after reports of a serious riot and fires at the prison at Princetown on Dartmoor. The trouble at Dartmoor Prison was not unexpected, as trouble had been brewing the day prior to the riot, and the governor of the prison had permission from the Home Office to call upon Plymouth if the situation got out of hand. On the morning of the 24th, the riot commenced, and the Governor's office was set on fire and several sets of keys were now in the hands of the inmates. At about 10 a.m., the Plymouth Police had a call from the prison. The Chief Constable (Mr A. K. Wilson) and Chief Superintendent Lee put their pre arranged plans into effect, and with very little delay, between thirty and forty men were sent to the prison in fast vehicles, arriving about 10.50 a.m. When the police arrived, the rioting convicts were out in the yard, threatening and calling upon the officers to 'come and get it'. Because the Governor's whereabouts was unknown at that time, it was thought his life might be in danger. Therefore, the police stormed the rioters, and a mighty struggle ensued. Many convicts felt the full weight of the trusty truncheons, and within a very short space of time, many were lying about injured, following the police charge. Not all the prisoners took part in the riot. There were 480 inmates at the prison, and between 200 and 300 took part in the riot. The riot was broken up within ten minutes, and order was restored within half an hour. Between sixty and seventy prisoners were treated at the prison hospital, some with head wounds, and others suffering from buckshot injuries from the warders' rifles.

The fire brigade from Plymouth speedily attended. Under the supervision of Superintendent Mead, the men got to work in extinguishing the flames. The whole centre block and the tower were destroyed, including the Governor's office and all the records.

Chief Constable A. K. Wilson resigned in 1932. He was replaced by W. C. Johnson, who served as chief constable until 1936. Mr G. S. Lowe took the reins from 1936 until 1941, when the National Fire Service was formed.

Scene of the aftermath of the devastating riot and fire at Dartmoor Prison in January 1932.

Four lives lost in city blaze

Four lives were lost and three persons were injured in a fire which broke out in King Gardens, Plymouth, in April 1934. The fire started in a front room on the lower ground floor, and gained a good hold before it was discovered shortly before 2 a.m. It is believed that the thick smoke overcame some of the family while they were still asleep, and two of them burned to death in their beds. A neighbour called the fire brigade, who arrived in a good time. The firemen immediately donned breathing apparatus and entered the building in order to carry out rescues. In the meantime, Inspector Lee and Police Constable Croft made a desperate attempt to reach Mr James Henry Ferguson, a resident of the house. When they did so, they found that he was already dead.

Inspector Lee was overcome and collapsed unconscious. The police constable was also badly affected, but still managed to drag his colleague to a place of safety outside. Most of the property was badly damaged in the fire. The four dead were: Mr James Henry Ferguson, aged seventy-eight; Miss Eva M. Ferguson, aged fifty-four; Mrs Irene Symons, aged thirty-eight, and Esme Thelma Symons, aged six, daughter of Mrs Symons. The injured were Mr Albert S. Symons, aged forty, husband of Mrs Symons; Ivor Symons, aged ten, his son, and Police Inspector Lee.

Brass helmet plate of the Police Fire Brigade.

Firemen outside the Guildhall in 1932, the appliances are, from L to R: 1931 Merryweather turntable ladder (JY 937); 1932 Dennis pump escape (JY 956); 1930 Dennis Hatfield pump (DR 7555).

The opening of Greenbank Fire Station

The need for bigger and better facilities to house the police force and the fire brigade was addressed in 1935. The cramped and dated accommodation at Catherine Street had outlived its purpose, and the police moved to the site of the old prison at Greenbank. The official opening ceremony of the fire station and police headquarters took place on Thursday 28th February, when Mr A. L. Dixon, assistant Under-Secretary for the Home Department, officiated.

At the opening of Greenbank fire station in 1935 the Chief Constable, William Johnson, leads the parade through the lines of policemen, some of whom are firemen. Among the dignitaries present was Mr. A. L. Dixon, who was Under-Secretary for the Home Office Department.

The contractor for the conversion of the old prison buildings was Mr J. W. Spencer, of St Lawrence Yard, Plymouth. Other local firms and tradesmen involved with the building were: Messrs Penrose and Son, of Mutley Plain, who installed the heating and plumbing; Messrs Vincent J. Pope and Co, who dealt with the electrical work; Messrs Harris and Sons, of George Street, who decorated the premises; the Western Counties Brick Company, who did the brickwork, and the West of England Joinery Company, who carried out all the joinery work.

The police occupied the larger premises of Longfield House, whilst the fire appliances were housed at the purpose-built fire station, built on the site of the old prison. The first floor of the fire station was divided into two flats, one for the superintendent of the fire brigade and the other for his principal officer. The actual fire brigade control room was, at that time, located in the basement of Longfield House, and not within the fire station building.

The site at Greenbank was much more suited for the location of the fire station, as the city was expanding in size and population, and it was more central. The Corporation built several small cottage-style

Plymouth Police Fire Brigade tackling a blaze in the Plymouth Workhouse in 1936. It is interesting to note that the firemen worked with their police colleagues at a lot of fires in the city. This was not a satisfactory arrangement, as it strained the loyalty between policemen and those who elected to be firemen.

Plymouth Police Fire Brigade (Devonport Division) outside the Guildhall in Ker Street 1934. Fireman Tommy Evans is the driver and officers in the middle are William Mead and Ron Smith. This Dennis fire engine remained operational until the 1950s.

houses in Greenbank Road, to house the firemen and their families. Each dwelling had alarm bells fitted, and these were linked to the control room at the police headquarters. Because of the problem of housing at Devonport, reports of fire had to be conveyed to the firemen's homes by runners, therefore causing much delay in turning out of the appliances. The firemen's houses at Devonport had a sign 'FIREMAN' fixed above the front door, so that the runners could quickly identify where the men lived.

Greenbank fire station and headquarters of the City of Plymouth Fire Brigade from 1948 until amalgamation into Devon Fire Brigade in 1973.

CHAPTER THIRTEEN

PLYMOUTH IN WORLD WAR TWO

The Fire Brigades Act, 1938

DURING THE PERIOD of intensified defence activity, the fire brigades in this country were making steady progress, but the problem of overall coordination throughout the country was not being addressed. The first serious attempt at coordinating fire services over a large rural area was made in July 1935, by the newly formed North Derbyshire Fire Board, by which Chesterfield, Sheffield and three other small urban brigades in the region agreed to protect their rural neighbours for an extra penny on the rates. An advisory panel was set up, consisting of chief officers, to inspect the brigades, water supplies and cover schemes. Attempts were made to establish a similar scheme in West Norfolk, but due to apathy and local opposition the plan failed.

The National Fire Brigades Association, and the Professional Fire Brigades Association were thriving, with over 1,000 brigades affiliated. There was talk of amalgamation of the two bodies, and in September 1937 they and the Institution of Fire Engineers held a joint conference at Cheltenham. Proposals were tabled that they should become a British Fire Service Joint Council, on which all three of the associations should be represented. A resolution was passed, asking the government to expedite legislation to deal with the fire service on the lines of the report of the Riverdale Committee.

A Fire Brigades Bill was drafted in consultation with local authorities associations, including Scotland. It stated that every borough, urban and rural district in England and Wales, and every burgh and county in Scotland, must make provisions for fire extinction, by either providing and training a fire brigade, to meet all normal requirements in an efficient manner, or by entering into arrangements for the provision of such services by a neighbouring authority to secure assistance at large fires which were beyond the capacity of their own brigade.

Five years after the passing of the Act, police brigades were not to rely on ordinary constables as supernumeraries. Two years after the passing of the Act, no fire authority was to be entitled to require the owner or occupier of property involved in fire to make payment. The Secretary of State was empowered to appoint inspectors, who would prescribe standards of efficiency for various kinds of localities, to establish a training centre, to require uniformity of appliances and equipment. He was also to appoint a fire service board, to take over an area and precept on its rates, if, two years after the Act, he felt that an efficient service had not been provided.

By April 1938, 30,000 auxiliary firemen had been recruited nationwide. They were all provided with a basic fire kit, comprising cap, overalls, trousers and waterproof leggings, plus a steel helmet. Each man and woman was required to undergo sixty hours' training, which took place exclusively in the evenings and at weekends. The responsibility for training these auxiliary firemen fell on the full time firemen throughout the country. Among the earliest AFS recruits were women, who, in the event of war, were to take over control-room and watch-room duties. They were also required to drive staff cars and perform any work that would release an able-bodied fireman for active firefighting duties.

The Munich crisis of 1938 caught Britain and the whole of the fire brigades almost unprepared. Trenches were dug in public parks, and gas masks were issued. The fleet was mobilised, and firemen and the AFS filled sandbags and piled them against the watch-room windows. As the situation with Germany was worsening, and the invasion of Poland was imminent, the fire brigades in England and Wales were preparing as best they could. Garages, disused factories and all sorts of vacant buildings were commandeered for use as satellite fire stations throughout the city, and men and pumps were posted to them.

The AFS men and women fashioned their makeshift premises into fire stations fit for purpose, and the long wait for Britain and France's ultimatum to Germany to withdraw her troops from Poland expired on September 3rd. Nearly all the fire stations in Plymouth were equipped with some sort of wireless set, and on that fateful Sunday came the announcement from Chamberlain that Britain was at war with Germany.

The Fire Brigade Bill did not apply to London, except for five minor clauses giving them powers not included in the Metropolitan Fire Brigade Act, 1865. The Bill was presented to the House for its second reading on 10th May 1938 by Sir Samuel Hoare, the Home Secretary. The Bill passed its second reading, and subject to some minor alterations, it received Royal Assent on 28th July 1938, becoming the Fire Brigades Act, 1938. It set up no fewer than 1,440 separate statutory fire authorities in England and Wales, and 228 in Scotland, a total of 1,668 fire brigades.

The long period of the Phoney War enabled the AFS to organise itself as much as time and money allowed. Week after week, and month after month, the AFS personnel were on action stations, and no attack. By January 1940, the people of Plymouth, as well as the rest of the country, thought that this Phoney war was everlasting, and their feelings were running quite high. The rigidly maintained blackout was getting on everyone's nerves, and the poor auxiliary firemen were targeted by public antipathy. Once the blitz on our cities and towns occurred, our auxiliary fire service personnel were then regarded as heroes, and the bad feeling that existed prior to this quickly disappeared.

1938 Leyland FK6 cross seat motor pump escape (AJY 747), seen with escape removed. It was sold off in 1950.
© Ron Henderson

1938 Bedford (converted horse box) Emergency Tender (ARD 561). It was sold off in 1964.

Concerns over police-run fire brigades

Advancing firefighting methods and increased responsibilities, plus the gathering clouds of war on our soil, were forcing the issue of separation. In 1936, The Lord Riverdale Committee on Fire Brigades recommended reductions in police firefighting commitments. The latter passages of the Fire Brigades Bill through Parliament in 1938 repeated these recommendations. Sir Samuel Hoare, in reply to a question from Lieut-Commander Tufnell of Cambridgeshire, where there was a police fire brigade, said: 'We have to remember that if a man is doing police duty and fire duty, either the police duty or the fire duty suffers.'

The Fire Brigades Act 1938 required local authorities to make arrangements for establishing brigades, independent of the police, and it was obvious to all that the days of the police fire brigades were numbered. HM Inspector of Constabulary's report for 1939 showed that, at the time, there were sixty-three police brigades in England and Wales, employing 1,055 men full time on firefighting duties, and 2,151 men part-time.

The largest brigades in England were Liverpool and Manchester, which had, respectively, 173 and 200 full-time firemen on their strengths. Among the smaller brigades were Newark and Penzance, with part-time strengths of five and eight.

The outbreak of war threw heavy strains on the members of the police fire brigades, particularly the Chief Constables. They were then in dual capacities of heads of vastly expanding services, which were preparing themselves for the shock of the Blitz in 1940, and 1941. Heavy enemy air raid attacks called for courage and devotion to duty of the highest order.

Following the Riverdale Committee report in 1936, and the 1938 Fire Services Act, there was a tremendous amount of work being undertaken in reorganising and unifying Britain's inadequate, and much understaffed fire services. The Auxiliary Fire Service was formed in 1938, and recruiting to meet the needs of this service was undertaken on a national basis, where over 30,000 auxiliaries were recruited. These men and women were only part-time amateurs. The auxiliaries recruited for Plymouth, after initial training, were guided by a handful of full-time police firemen.

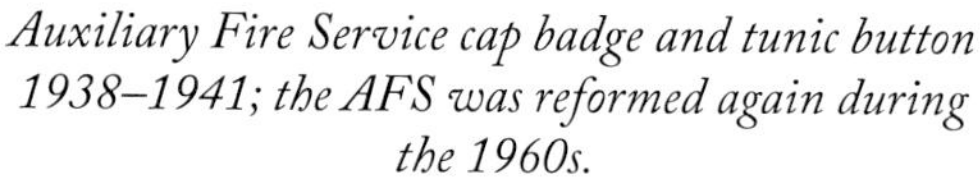
Auxiliary Fire Service cap badge and tunic button 1938–1941; the AFS was reformed again during the 1960s.

National Fire Service cap badge and tunic button 1941–1948.

The Home Office supplied many different types of basic fire pumps, and other fire engines, to meet the demand that was to be put upon them. Trailer pumps were towed by an array of different vehicles, including taxis, which were seconded for use by the AFS; this was more so in London. Over thirty Home Office pumps and a 100-foot turntable ladder were delivered to Plymouth to complement the city's appliances. The Home Office 100-foot turntable ladder replaced the old wooden ladder of 1934 vintage.

There were about fifteen small AFS fire stations located throughout Plymouth, some of which were at Crownhill, Millbay, Lower Compton, Keyham, Camel's Head, Milehouse, Higher St Budeaux, Devonport, Stonehouse and Cattedown, each manned by a team of enthusiastic volunteers. Training was ongoing, but nothing could have prepared them for the devastation to life and property in the raids of March 1941. Plympton and Plymstock were not part of Plymouth at that time, but they did have their own AFS fire stations.

Plymouth braces itself for war

The scale of the risk in Plymouth was greater than in any other town in Devon, mainly due to the fact of the location of the Dockyard, which was a prized target for the German bombers. It was anticipated that about 500 auxiliary firemen and women would be needed in Plymouth. Recruiting proved very difficult, and this figure was never realised, in fact only 267 persons were recruited. Many private companies

Cattedown AFS crew with their trailer pump in 1940.

AFS crew who were stationed at Freedom Park, 1940.

AFS crews from Central Park and St Leven Road stations.

AFS crew at Cattedown fire station in 1940.

AFS firemen at Prince Rock station in 1940.

Area 19 Boat Section at Cattedown in 1942. The officer in charge is Peter Noble.

Children get a chance to clamber over the 1941 turntable ladder at Greenbank fire station open day.

formed their own fire companies, to protect their own properties, but these men and women had no training as such, and were of limited use. The Royal Navy and Dockyard workers formed their own fire parties, and rendered valuable service during the Blitz of Plymouth, and the Dockyard at Devonport.

The first bombs to fall on Plymouth fell on Saturday 6th July 1940, in Swilly (North Prospect), killing a family of three. This was the start of the nightmares faced by civilians, firemen, and everyone involved with the defence of Plymouth. It is difficult to comprehend the devastation and huge loss of life that they faced in the coming years.

The Blitz commences

On Thursday 20th March 1941, an unexpected visit to Plymouth by the King and Queen took place. They were welcomed by a contingent of the military and civic dignitaries. Following a brief walkabout, where they met and chatted to members of the public, they were quickly ushered off to Devonport Dockyard, where they were to meet service personnel, and take tea with other civic and military dignitaries. Within two hours of the royal party leaving Plymouth, the siren sounded at 2035 hours, and for three and a half hours, Plymouth took an almighty hammering from the German bombers.

Communications between the fireground and brigade control were quickly destroyed by the bombing, and the firemen relied heavily upon motorcycle dispatch riders to relay messages to and from the control room. Water supplies were also severely hampered, due to damaged mains; many firemen had to set their suction hoses into flooded bomb craters in order to obtain water.

This was the first heavily concentrated attack, as all the previous air raids were by either single bombers, or small groups of aircraft. These spasmodic raids caused serious damage to Plymouth, but nothing to compare with the raids that night and the following night. More than 35,000 incendiary bombs, and 700 high explosive bombs, were dropped on Plymouth, causing terrible loss of life and property. Charles Church was destroyed by incendiaries on the nights of 20th and 21st March. It is now preserved in its ruined state, as a memorial to the civilian victims of the Blitz. On March 24th, whilst attending to the pump during an enemy raid on the Dockyard, Police Fireman Joseph Gerretty was killed by the blast of a bomb which exploded beside his fire pump; he was forty-one-years old.

On the evening of 22nd April 1941, an air raid shelter in Portland Square took a direct hit, killing seventy-two men, women, and children.

By that time, several outlying fire brigades were drafted into the city to assist in dealing with the huge amount of fires. The Spooners building was a mass of flames, as was Worden's Jewellers in Old Town Street, but that soon collapsed, trapping some of the people inside. Only one unit and four men were ordered to the fire, with the brief to do their best under such circumstances. Despite the massive handicap, they managed to rescue three unfortunate casualties from the burning rubble. Fires were burning uncontrollably throughout the city, and all the fire brigades which were drafted in were working flat out.

Plymouth City Council Rescue Party 1940.

Blitz tragedies

Another huge tragedy occurred in the Devonport Naval Base on the evening of Monday April 21st 1941, when, during the first of a three-night bombing mission, a high explosive bomb hit Boscawen Block, killing ninety-six sailors. Only seventy-eight complete bodies were recovered from the ruins. Identification of the casualties proved to be very difficult, and many of the recovered bodies were buried at Weston Mill Cemetery, without being formally identified. A memorial garden was unveiled in April 2008, outside the Senior Rates mess in HMS *Drake*, to commemorate the sailors who perished during the Blitz of 1940–41.

On the following night, Tuesday 22nd April, a contingent of AFS firemen from Saltash were hurrying into Plymouth, to assist the overstretched firemen in dealing with the hundreds of fires which were burning throughout Plymouth, with very little hope of saving the properties involved. They were using a taxi, which was towing a trailer pump. On their way to Devonport, they hit an unexploded bomb. The resultant explosion killed everyone on board. The men who died were Francis Brooking, Stanley Crabb, Alfred Crapp, Bernard Jasper, John Stanlake and Leslie Tibbs.

The firemen of Saltash were very shorthanded by now, and it is recorded that the 2nd Scout Troop became the only troop in England to be engaged in the Auxiliary Fire Service at that time. Sadly, on 28th April, they were called into Plymouth to deal with a fire in the Railway Goods Yard. They had only been at work for a short time when a German bomb exploded nearby, instantly killing Donald Cummins and badly injuring Sydney Cummins and Bernard Doidge. Douglas Vosper, the crew leader, was later awarded the British Empire Medal and the Bronze Cross (this was the scout VC, which was the highest award given by the scout movement), Donald Cummins was posthumously awarded the scout VC, and the Silver Cross was duly awarded to Sydney Cummins and Bernard Doidge. Fire brigades from surrounding towns and major cities were brought into Plymouth to assist the overworked firemen in preventing Plymouth from becoming totally destroyed.

Never before had the firemen seen so many huge fires burning out of control simultaneously in the city. The need to prioritise which fires demanded their immediate attention was of great importance, as the preservation of life became a priority over saving property. Plymouth was virtually on its knees, contingency plans were failing and chaos was reigning. Brigades from as far afield as Birmingham, Bristol, London, Gloucester, Swindon and Salisbury were dispatched to render assistance in Plymouth. As a result of three nights of bombing, there was reported a total of 171 separate fires to be dealt with: on the 21st, sixty-eight fires; 22nd, forty-seven fires, and 23rd, fifty-six fires. On the first night, a total of 158 forms of fire pumps were used, along with over 90,000 feet of hose. The second night required a total of seventy-eight pumps, and 103,000 feet of hose, and the on the third night a total twenty pumps were used, and 32,000 feet of hose.

There were, of course, hundreds of other smaller fires reported and dealt with almost immediately by fire watchers, wardens, fire parties, etc., as there were over 17,500 incendiary bombs dropped on Plymouth. Most of the small fires were brought under immediate control, whilst others led to big fires as numbered in the above report.

Firemen battling the huge blaze on the oil tanks at Turnchaple following enemy raids on 28th November 1940. Two AFS firemen were burnt to death when a boil-over occurred, and the blazing oil breached the bund wall and flowed to the Cattewater, burning out several boats, including the fireboat.

A black plume of smoke rising from the blazing oil tanks at Turnchaple, following enemy action in November 1941.

Two AFS men perish and some notable acts of bravery

The conflagrations which occurred in Plymouth during 1940–41 will be vividly remembered by everyone who took part in firefighting duties. Two auxiliary firemen were burnt to death on November 29th 1940, at the Turnchapel Oil Depot. The alarm was raised between seven and eight o'clock in the evening, and AFS crews were dispatched from Plymstock and Plympton; Greenbank also sent six pumps.

Upon arrival, there were two tanks on fire. There was a total of six tanks within a bund wall, and the unaffected four tanks were in great danger, as the burning oil, from a severely split tank, was spreading within the bund wall. The tide was low (the Germans always planned their raids on Plymouth when the tides were low), which made it difficult to relay adequate supplies of firefighting water to the tanks.

At about 5.30 a.m. a boil-over occurred, sending flames 200 feet into the night sky, and with a mighty roar, the burning oil breached the bund wall and ran down into the Cattewater, catching two fireboats alight. Other firemen who were on fire-floats had miraculous escapes as the sea became a burning mass, which was spreading with an alarming rate. The fire engine from Plymstock was only saved from a fiery fate by the bravery of her driver, fireman Philip Parsons, who had to cut the hose from the pump, and drive it to safer ground.

The two unfortunate firemen who died were on the bund wall, and were caught by the burning oil. They were fireman Thomas Callicott, thirty years old, and fireman Robert Widger, thirty-three years old; both were firemen sent in from Greenbank. By now, all six tanks were alight. There was very little the firemen could do now but to watch, until the fire eventually consumed all the fuel. The fire was finally extinguished on the sixth day.

Boil-over: When heavy oil burns, a layer of hot oil, up to 500 degrees F. is formed below the surface. Water introduced during fire-fighting lies at the bottom of the tank, and if it contacts the hot layer, will flash into steam and become entrained with the oil, throwing a great wave of burning oil, which might amount to several hundred tons, out of the top of the tank.

Superintendent William Mead supervises fireman Jack Brown and an unknown constable on a roof fire in York Street in 1941. One can see the need for the firemen to be independent from the police force: as this picture shows, it was totally impracticable for the two to be linked.

Great acts of bravery and dedication to duty were witnessed by the citizens of Plymouth, and the men and women of the AFS did themselves and the city proud. I can say, without contradiction, that fire-fighters today will never witness the tragedies and fires that resulted from the Blitz. As a retired firemen myself, I salute them and their memory.

In an incident in January 1941, at the Petroleum Depot at Cattedown, two firemen, named George Wright and Cyril Lidstone, performed heroic acts in fighting a fire on a blazing oil tank. The roof of the Wiggins tank was quite low within its frame, and the fire was in the seal, between the roof and the seal itself. The two men had to haul their equipment up the external stairway, which was attached to the frame, and then climb down about thirty feet, to the roof of the tank. The water supply failed as they were about to commence firefighting, and they had to beat a hasty retreat, as it was incredibly hot without their water spray protection. Once again the water supply was reinstated, and the men climbed down yet again. They fought the fire with a foam jet from a knapsack tank they were wearing. High explosive bombs were still falling around them, making this a very perilous operation, but the two men stuck to their job, and eventually they managed to extinguish the fire, therefore preventing what could have been a major disaster. They were both awarded the George Medal, at a ceremony at Buckingham Palace in June 1942; the medals were presented by King George VI.

Other firemen who received awards during the ceremony were: Deputy Chief Officer Reginald Smith, who was awarded the OBE for his bravery at a big fire in an ammunition depot. Patrol Officer Jack Vale; Watch Room attendant Barbara Rendell; Arthur Larson; William Edgecombe, and Private Leslie Stephens, who was a messenger in the fire brigade. Each was awarded the BEM, for displaying outstanding courage and fortitude in the execution of their duties during the heavy raids in March and April 1941. It is interesting to note that Leslie Stephens was the youngest recipient of that award at that time.

The raids of the 20th–21st March totally devastated Plymouth; its heart had been completely destroyed. The raid on the 21st was more severe than the night before: it was estimated that at least 20,000 incendiary bombs and hundreds of high-explosive bombs were showered on shopping and residential parts of the city. Mr Menzies, the Australian Prime Minister, was in Plymouth at the time of the raids, staying at the home of Lady Astor; he was on an official visit to the provinces. The city centre resembled the scene following a huge earthquake, with shattered buildings, great fires, and a lot of business premises reduced to rubble. Many of the old historic buildings in the old parts of Plymouth were also wiped out. The casualty list was massive, with 590 civilians killed, and the loss of service personnel was not made public at that time. On the night of the 21st, 158 fire pumps, two improvised fire floats, and 143,650 foot of hose were used to fight the fires. Three firemen were killed and eight seriously injured that night.

The firemen were exhausted. Inadequate water supplies severely limited their effectiveness, and they relied heavily on help from brigades around the country, who came to Plymouth to assist in extinguishing the hundreds of fires which were burning out of control.

Firemen protecting the Western Morning News *premises with water curtains to stop the radiated heat from other burning buildings from setting it alight, during the Blitz in 1941.*

The city ablaze – firemen struggle to cope with the mass conflagration caused by enemy action.

Shops ablaze, during the March 1941 raids on Plymouth.

A fire crew from an outside fire brigade damping down following enemy bombing. I hope the ground floor premise was well insured.

There followed a period of respite following the raids on the 20th, 21st, 23rd, 28th and 29th April. The exhausted firemen were kept busy in replenish fuel stocks, repairing and maintaining numerous fire pumps and appliances, washing, drying, and rolling up the hoses, and re-establishing communications which had been lost during the raids.

Devonport was the main target for the German bombers on the night of the 23rd April, but bombs were also dropped on Plymouth. On Monday 28th and Tuesday 29th of April, the Germans concentrated on the north yard of the Dockyard, the ammunition depot at Bull Point, St Budeaux, Camel's Head, and Torpoint. Another forty-three sailors were killed during these raids. Devonport, Milehouse, Keyham and Saltash were targeted on the second night. The water mains were virtually useless, due to the intense bombing, but there were numerous emergency water tanks and temporary pipe work sited in various locations throughout the city to assist in firefighting.

Casualties among the Civil Defence services during the five nights of bombing in March were: Police, seven killed and twenty-seven injured; Fire Brigade, seventeen killed and forty-three injured; Wardens, seven killed and twenty injured; Rescue Service, one killed and one injured. This figure was only speculative at the time, as in a later report it was stated that there were over forty killed and 121 injured.

The fire service in Plymouth came under much criticism for its lack of readiness and general response to the air raids. The Home Secretary, Mr Herbert Morrison, wrote to the Town Clerk regarding the fire protection arrangements within the city. The letter contained a list of recommendations from the Inspector of Fire Brigades, and the Chief Inspector of the South West Fire Division.

One of the main recommendations was for the appointment of a professional Chief Fire Officer, with a proven fire brigade background, and for the immediate separation from police control. The fire service should employ its own fire control and messengers. A legacy from the 'three towns' was the non-standardisation of equipment and water hydrants within Plymouth, Devonport and Stonehouse. The

Another view of the wartime line-up at Sub Area A Station 1, at Greenbank.

The Fire Brigade and the Plymouth Police football teams pose prior to a match at Millbay Park in 1942. Superintendent William Mead, seated with dark gloves on, and Peter Noble, in uniform, are there to support the teams.

Home Office furnished a new standard for fire hydrants and standpipes; these new standards were to be fitted without delay. Even though the fire brigade had various adaptors to meet the needs for the coupling of various hoses, it was many years later that the recommendations were finally installed. In order to oversee the changes, Mr George Drury, a Home Office Inspector, was sent to Plymouth from London Fire Headquarters, to take command and reorganise the fire brigade in Plymouth.

Plymouth's first turntable ladder, which was an Albion Merryweather 75-foot wooden and steel trussed ladder (JY 956), making safe a building in the city centre following enemy action.

Firemen entering a building to knock down a fire in 1941. At the head of the ladder is Jack Mabin; on the centre section is Frank Barcus; feeding the hose at the heel of the ladder is Francis (Jim) Mead, and the officer looking on is Bill Westlake.

National Fire Service formed

Mr Herbert Morrison, the Home Secretary, was pressed in Parliament as to what lessons had been learnt during the past eight months. The national situation, as far as fire brigades were concerned, was not wholly satisfactory, and drastic changes were urgently needed as the blitz upon our cities and ports was intensifying. Parliament was asked to place the whole of the fire brigade resources of the country under the control of the Secretary of State, and the Secretary of State for Scotland. A Bill was submitted to Parliament and great emphasis was put upon a speedy progress of all the stages. As an emergency measure, Mr Morrison presented the second reading of the Fire Services (Emergency Provision) Bill, on May 20th 1941.

He criticised the Fire Brigade Act 1938, in that the Government of the day, even though prepared for war, had kept over a thousand separate fire authorities. The small parish council fire authorities were done away with, which really was not significant, as there were a large number of these parish councils who did not have a fire brigade. An assurance was given to the house that local authorities would regain control of their fire brigades on the cessation of hostilities.

Group of AFS firemen outside Torr fire station, Hartley.

Firemen damping down a fire-damaged building in the city centre the morning after an enemy air raid.

Damping down and clearing debris following enemy bombing in Union Street in 1941.

The first contingent of Canadian firefighters arrived in Plymouth in September 1942; a second group arrived in January 1943, bringing the total number of Canadian firefighters in Plymouth to seventy-four. © John Leete

Torr House, Hartley, the base for the Canadian firefighters from 1942 until 1944. © John Leete

In order to rectify this situation, it was deemed that all fire brigades, no matter how big or small, were to be abolished, and the creation of a National Fire Service was to be implemented on 18th August 1941. The National Fire Service also absorbed the Auxiliary Fire Service, Private, and Volunteer Fire Brigades, therefore creating one single Fire Brigade for the entire country. The country was divided up into regions and fire forces, and Plymouth, Cornwall and part of Devon became National Fire Service Fire Force 19, under Region 7; the remainder of Devon formed Area Fire Force 18.

The man chosen to act as Fire Force 19 Commander was Mr George Drury, who, in April, had been sent to take command and reorganise the fire brigade in Plymouth. One of his jobs was to relocate the control room to Torr fire station in Hartley, which was away from the intensely bombed city centre. His job lasted for a mere eighteen days, as the Home Office asked the Plymouth Corporation to release him to undertake work in connection with the nationalisation of the fire service. A large training establishment was set up at Lee Mill, near Ivybridge, and the fire stations at Plympton, Plymstock, Yelverton, Ivybridge and Tavistock were brought in under the direct control of Plymouth.

Canadian corp of firefighters comes to Plymouth

The Corps of Canadian Fire Fighters was formed, following a visit to England in the summer of 1941, by The Rt. Hon. William L. Mackenzie King, Prime Minister of Canada. He promised the British Government that Canada would be only too willing to assist in the battle of the blitzes, with a corps of Canadian firemen.

A large contingent arrived in this country in May 1942, to serve in various cities. A strong force, comprising of forty-three men of the 2nd detachment, was allocated to assist the NFS in Plymouth. They were self-sufficient, inasmuch as they had their own fire engines, uniforms, etc. After a period of training, at No. 7 Regional Training School at Lee Mill, near Ivybridge, they were initially stationed in station 19-A-1-Z in Greenbank Road, and station 19-A-2-T in Victoria Road, until being consolidated into the large new station at The Drive, Harley. The living accommodation was at the magnificent Torr House in Torr Road.

Opening of Torr fire station on 24th March 1943 by the Duchess of Kent. Also in the picture are the Chief Officer of the Canadian firefighters, Chief Officer of Fire Force No. 19, Mr George Drury, and an unknown dignitary. This fire station, which was located in the Drive at Hartley, was built by the Canadian firemen and a few tradesmen from the NFS; they served there until November 1944, when they returned home to Canada.

First issue of Collector *magazine, issued in February 1940. This was the brigade magazine produced by the AFS, for the AFS.*

Street fire alarm, located at Torr Road, Hartley c.1944.

In March 1943, a new ten-bay fire station was erected at The Drive, Hartley, near to Torr House, where the Canadian firemen were then based. The station was built by craftsmen of the local NFS, and greatly assisted by members of the Canadian Fire Corps. The station number was 19-A-1-L. The station was officially opened by the Duchess of Kent on 24th March 1943. A large crest was put up above the garages, in which the badges of Plymouth, The NFS and the Canadian Fire Badge, were grouped together under a scroll, which read, 'Now are we all of one Company'. This fire station was solely a station for Canadian firefighters, who served there until their departure in November 1944. The station continued being used by the Plymouth brigade until 1959, when a new station was built at Crownhill to replace it.

The ten-bay fire station, co-built by the Canadian firemen, in The Drive at Hartley.

The three badges of the National Fire Service; City of Plymouth, and the Canadian firefighters, above the appliance bays at Torr fire station.

The Canadian contingent worked gallantly and efficiently during the spasmodic raids of 1942–43, and their contribution was welcomed by Mr George Drury and the men under his command. The Canadians began to demobilise in December 1945, and at a moving ceremony at Torr fire station, the Lord Mayor, Mr Mason, bid them a fond farewell and thanked them most sincerely, on behalf of the people of Plymouth.

The Lord Mayor of Plymouth meets with a contingent of Canadian firefighters at Torr fire station in 1942. These firemen were brought over to assist the firemen in various cities throughout the country who were struggling to deal with the aftermath of the German bombings.

Fire Force Commander George Drury, of No. 19 Fire Force, which included Plymouth, paid the Canadians a fitting tribute at a farewell dance prior to their departure, he said, 'These Canadian firefighters voluntarily came to our assistance at the crucial moment.' When difficulties arose about their accommodation, he said there was only one thing to do – to build a station for them. Thanks to them, we then had in Plymouth a fire station which, he thought, might well be a model for the fire brigade to adopt when erecting others in this city.

The citizens of Guelph, in Ontario, and Saskatchewan, donated mobile canteen/kitchen vans to the citizens of Plymouth, as a token of their admiration for the work they were doing. Thousands of cups of tea and lashings of soup were received by the thankful firefighters and other deserving parties of Plymouth.

A barrage balloon which slipped its mooring line flounders in Leigham Terrace, on the Hoe. The firemen struggling with the hose are Jim Mead, nearest balloon, and Fire Inspector Les Downs.

Austin K2 Auxiliary Towing Vehicle GXH 144, bought in 1942.

CHAPTER FOURTEEN

PLYMOUTH'S RISE FROM THE ASHES

PLYMOUTH WAS NAMED as the most bombed city of the war, and the utter devastation and massive loss of life is almost beyond comprehension. The city centre was reduced to piles of rubble, with burnt-out buildings forming a bleak backdrop. Altogether there were 602 alerts; enemy bombs were dropped on fifty-nine different occasions. The official figures covering all the air raids were:

- 1,172 civilians killed
- 1,092 civilians seriously injured
- 2,177 civilians slightly injured
- Seven missing believed killed
- 4,448 total casualties

The official death toll for service personnel was not known at the time, but what was known is that the list was considerable. The largest number of deaths occurred during the raids in March and April 1941. The two Blitzes in March resulted in 336 civilian deaths, and during the five nights of bombing in April, the death toll was 590.

Throughout the war, the resilience of the Plymouth people, and servicemen alike, proved unshakable, and the vast job of clearing up and demolishing dangerous buildings continued, despite the best efforts of the German Luftwaffe. The last bombing raid on Plymouth was on 30th April 1944; this was the final of fifty-nine bombing raids at the hands of the Luftwaffe. The material structure of Plymouth might have been destroyed, but the spirit of Plymothians was unbreakable, and the enormous task of rebuilding Plymouth was about to begin.

Public buildings and famous landmarks destroyed

Pre-war Plymouth was a city laden with a vast array of old and beautiful buildings, some of which were an architect's dream. The utter madness of human beings, inflicting such an outrage upon fellow human beings in the name of war, was a damnation to mankind. Plymouth had its heart ripped out, but somehow, the people of Plymouth, with a strong determination and resilience, began the huge task of rebuilding the city.

National Fire Service despatch rider aboard his Indian motor bike.

National Fire Service personnel outside Torr fire station in Hartley.

Testing the pumps on the D.U.K.W. at Saltash passage in April 1946. This amphibious appliance can travel at 45 mph on land and 8 knots on water. It carried up to a crew of ten, and had two pumps, one fixed and one portable. The term D.U.K.W. is derived from the following: D indicated a vehicle designed in 1942; U indicated utility or amphibious; K indicated all wheel drive and W indicated the two powered rear axles.

Among the notable buildings, businesses and other famous landmarks, which were either destroyed forever or severely damaged, were:

Public Buildings

Guildhall, Municipal Offices, Council Chamber, Council Committee rooms, Lord Mayor's Parlour, Lady Mayoress' Parlour, Western Law Courts, General Post Office, Devonport General Post Office, County Court Offices, Old Guildhall, Promenade Pier, Public Library, Stonehouse Town Hall, Hoe Café, Millbay Drill Hall, Proprietary Library, Plymouth Chambers, Plymouth Argyle Grandstands, Devonport Belisha Hall, The Athenaeum, The Abbey Hall.

Schools

Hoe Grammar, Notre Dame for Girls, Cattedown Road Senior Girls, Cattedown Road Junior mixed, High Street Senior Girls, Hyde Park Boys, Johnston Terrace Senior Boys, Johnston Terrace Junior Mixed and Infants, Keyham College Road Infants, King Street Senior Girls, Montpelier Mixed and Infants, Morice Town Junior Mixed, Morice Town Infants, Palace Court Senior Girls, Palace Court Junior Mixed and Infants, Paradise Road Junior Mixed and Infants, St James-the-Less Junior Mixed and Infants, St. Stephen's Junior Girls and Infants, Union Street Junior Mixed and Infants, Stoke Senior Boys, Tamar Central Boys, Salisbury Road Special Boys, Salisbury Road Special Mixed, Montpelier Girls Secondary.

Churches

St Andrews, Charles, St Saviour's, St James-the-Less, St Peter's, All Saints, St George's, St Aubyn, St James-the-Great, St Thomas, St Stephen's, St Michael's, St Paul's, St Augustine's, The Garrison Church, Devonport Synagogue, Plymouth Unitarian, Salvation Army Congress Hall, Holy Redeemer Catholic Church, Keyham, George Street, Ebenezer (Stonehouse), Morice Square (Devonport), Sherwell Congregational, Courtney Street Congregational, Norley (Ebrington Street), Emma Place (Stonehouse), Wycliffe (Devonport), Whitfield (St Leven Road), Greenbank, Zion, Notte Street, King Street, Ebrington Street, Ebrington Street Mission, Gloucester Street (Devonport), Haddington Road (Devonport), Albert Road (Devonport), Ford (Devonport), St George's Road (Devonport), St Leven Road (Devonport), Central Hall (Devonport).

Clubs

Plymouth Club, Lockyer Street; Royal Western Yacht Club (The Hoe); Plymouth Conservative Club, Princess Square; Plymouth Masonic Club, Princess Square; Plymouth Liberal Club, Russell Street; Devonport Conservative Club, Fore Street; Devonport Liberal Club, Chapel Street; Minima Yacht Club, Promenade Pier; Devon County Billiard Club, George Street; Joker's Club, Athenaeum Lane; Devon Barbarians Club.

Theatre

Alhambra, Devonport.

Cinemas

Palladium, Ebrington Street; Cinedrome, Ebrington Street; Criterion, Cornwall Street; Electric, Fore Street; Devonport Hippodrome; Forum, Fore Street (repaired at a later date); Savoy, Union Street; New Empire, Union Street; Tivoli, Fore Street; Grand, Union Street.

Institutions

Royal Sailor's Rest, Fore Street; Welcome, Fore Street; Plymouth Central YMCA, Old Town Street; Ballard Institute, Millbay; Devon and Cornwall Female Orphanage, Lockyer Street; YMCA, Lockyer Street; North Hill Blind Institution (partial); St Joseph's Home, Harley (partial); Dockyard Orphanage, Stoke (partial); Ford Public Institution.

Hotels

Royal, Plymouth; Westminster, The Crescent; Waverley, Millbay Road; Hackers, The Crescent; Farley's, Union Street; Royal, Devonport; Lockyer, Plymouth (partial).

Prominent Businesses

Messrs Pophams, E. Dingle and Co; Spooners and Co; John Yeo and Co (drapers and outfitters); J. C. Tozer and Co (drapers and outfitters); Costers Ltd (drapers and outfitters); Garratts, Plymouth and Devonport (drapers and outfitters); Goodbodys, George Street and Bedford Street (confectioners and catering); Plymouth Co-operative Society (shops and offices) in Frankfort Street, Drake Circus and Fore Street; Woolworth's; Marks and Spencers (Plymouth and Devonport); Timothy Whites and Taylor's; Harris and Sons (decorators and furnishers); Bowden's (jewellers); Page, Keen and Page (jewellers); Lawleys (glass and china); Perkins Bros (outfitters); Prynn Bros, Plymouth and Devonport (outfitters); Winnicott Bros. (merchants); S. Ball and Co. (wholesale warehousemen); Snell's Motors; Pikes Motors; Army and Navy Stores; Moon and Sons (pianos, music, and furniture); Parker and Smith (music); Turner and Phillips (music); Underhill's Ltd (printers and stationers); Plymouth and Stonehouse Gas Company (showrooms and offices); Mikado Café; Butland and Treloar (tailors); W. H. Smith and sons (books and stationers); Sellicks (books and stationers); Wm Brendon and Son (printers and publishers); Tucketts Ltd (confectioners, shop and factory); London Furnishing Co; Mumford's Motor Showroom; Balkwill (chemist); Rundle, Rogers and Brooks (warehousemen); Dunn and Co. (hats); Hepworth's (outfitters); Lipton's (food); Maypole (food); Willsons (gowns); Whitbread (ladies outfitters); Samuel Edgcumbe (jeweller); Bateman (optician); Randells (footwear); Trueform (footwear); Saxone (footwear); Dolcis (footwear); Red Line (footwear); Austin Reed (outfitters); Jays (furnishing); Thomas Cook and Sons (travel agents); Service and Co. (builders merchants); Wrights (hairdressers); Cousins (hairdressers); Snell and Co. (tobacconists); Limpennys (sports); Wakelings (umbrellas and Sport); Skews (outfitters); Sun Buildings (offices); Plymouth Chambers (offices and public rooms); Old Town Chambers (offices); Corporation Electricity Showrooms; Singers Sewing Machines, Plymouth and Devonport; Edwards (outfitters); Barbers (outfitters); Gieves (outfitters); Fifty Shilling Tailors; Montague Burton (tailors); Williams (café and florist); Breeze's (Plymouth) Ltd (druggists); Andrews Motor Showrooms and numerous others.

Admiral Dunbar Nasmith, together with Lord Aster and other civic dignitaries, inspects the men of the AFS on Plymouth Hoe in 1940.

1951 line-up at Greenbank fire station, L to R: 1942 Austin auxiliary towing vehicle (GXH 144); 1951 Dennis F12 pump escape (GCO 138); 1941 Merryweather 100 foot turntable ladder (CDR 287); 1943 Ford 7V radio van (GXI 43) and 1938 Bedford converted horsebox emergency tender (ARD 561).

Firefighting D.U.K.W. being put through its paces in the River Tamar in April 1946. Fire Force Commander George Drury is beside the driver/coxswain, who was from the army, to teach the firemen how to use it. This appliance was loaned to Plymouth for fire fighting at Torpoint, Saltash, and villages in the Maker Peninsula.

The Fire Service personnel of Plymouth, and the assistance they received from around the country, were very commendable. They too lost good men and women to enemy action, and their sad loss is recorded on a bronze memorial in St Philip's Chapel, located within St Andrew's Church. It reads:

> In Memory of the Personnel of the Fire Service in No. 19 (Plymouth) Area
> Who Lost Their Lives Through Enemy Action in the 1937–1945 War.

M. A. Bartlett	Plymouth
T. Buckingham	Plymouth
T. J. Callicott	Plymouth
A. R. Dent	Plymouth
R. H. Farr	Plymouth
J. T. Gerretty	Plymouth
W. G. Lucas	Plymouth
L. H. P. Oakden	Plymouth
J. Renals	Plymouth
W. A. Roberts	Plymouth
F. J. N. Sandwell	Plymouth
G. Thomas	Plymouth
E. Torr (Firewoman)	Plymouth
R. W. Widger	Plymouth
F. J. Brooking	Saltash
S. R. Crabb	Saltash
A. J. Crapp	Saltash
D. Cummings	Saltash
B. Jasper	Saltash
J. Stanlake	Saltash
L. J. Tibbs	Saltash
G. I. C. Featherstone	Newquay
E. S. Old	Newquay
B. A. Phillips	Newquay
S. H. Vineer	Newquay
W. A. J. Tearle	Lostwithiel
W. H. Northcott	Bristol
C. Chopping	London

1941 Fordson Escape Carrying Unit (GGN 749) seen at Penlee fire station. This appliance was eventually sold in 1954.

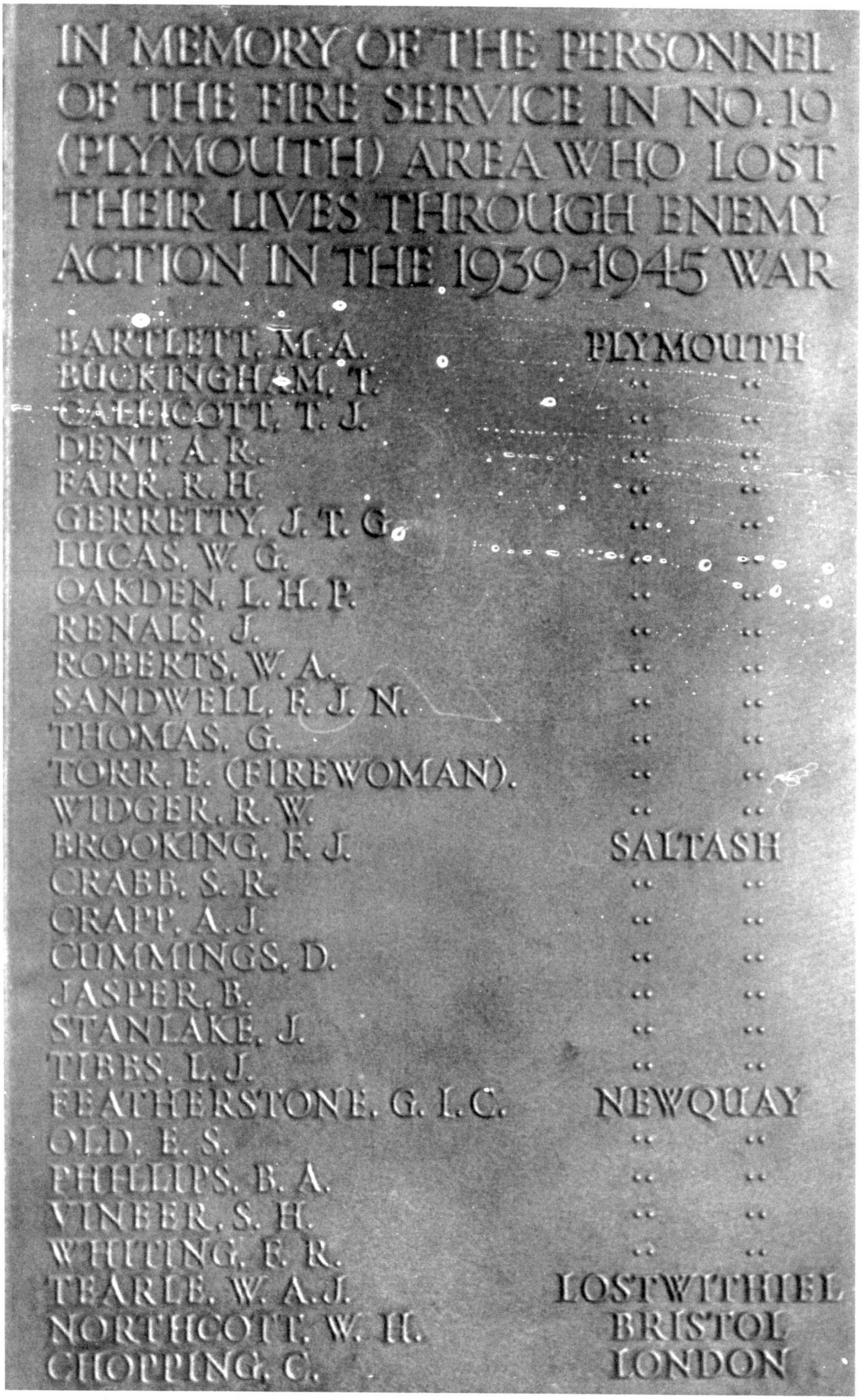

IN MEMORY OF THE PERSONNEL OF THE FIRE SERVICE IN NO. 19 (PLYMOUTH) AREA WHO LOST THEIR LIVES THROUGH ENEMY ACTION IN THE 1939-1945 WAR

BARTLETT, M. A.	PLYMOUTH
BUCKINGHAM, T.	" "
CALLICOTT, T. J.	" "
DENT, A. R.	" "
FARR, R. H.	" "
GERRETTY, J. T. G.	" "
LUCAS, W. G.	" "
OAKDEN, L. H. P.	" "
RENALS, J.	" "
ROBERTS, W. A.	" "
SANDWELL, F. J. N.	" "
THOMAS, G.	" "
TORR, E. (FIREWOMAN).	" "
WIDGER, R. W.	" "
BROOKING, F. J.	SALTASH
CRABB, S. R.	" "
CRAPP, A. J.	" "
CUMMINGS, D.	" "
JASPER, B.	" "
STANLAKE, J.	" "
TIBBS, L. J.	" "
FEATHERSTONE, G. I. C.	NEWQUAY
OLD, E. S.	" "
PHILLIPS, B. A.	" "
VINBER, S. H.	" "
WHITING, E. R.	" "
TEARLE, W. A. J.	LOSTWITHIEL
NORTHCOTT, W. H.	BRISTOL
CHOPPING, C.	LONDON

Memorial plaque in St Philip's Chapel of St Andrew's Church, Plymouth, commemorating the fire service personnel who were killed during the Blitz of Plymouth.

De-nationalisation of the National Fire Service

With hostilities at an end, the fire service found that there was a big surplus of manpower throughout the country and the need for so many men and women was then unwarranted. Many of the tradesmen and builders who joined the fire service in time of war returned to their tools, as there was a shortage of skilled labour in the building industry.

Plymouth was to be rebuilt under a 'Plan for Plymouth', which was prepared by the City Engineer, Mr J. Paton Watson, together with the eminent planner Sir Patrick Abercrombie. As well as all the business and commerce required to regenerate the city, there was a pressing need for 15,000 to 20,000 new homes, as Plymouth stood still for six years, with little or no building work undertaken. New housing estates were planned for Efford, Ham, Ernesettle and St Budeaux.

With the growth of a rapidly expanding Plymouth, serious thought had to be given to the future fire cover of the outlying areas. It was originally intended to denationalise the Fire Service in 1946, but the Government wanted time to determine the future of the British Fire Service. The NFS continued through 1946 and into 1948.

1941 Fordson escape carrying unit (GGN 749) seen at station B, Penlee. This appliance was sold off in 1954.

1942 Leyland/Merryweather 100 foot turntable ladder (EDR 706) seen at Camels Head fire station. This appliance was owned by the Royal Navy and was used in Devonport Dockyard prior to it being loaned to the City of Plymouth Fire brigade, where it served until 1967. A new 65 foot hydraulic platform pump was purchased to replace it.

Fire Services Act 1947

It was deemed, under the new provision, that the National Fire Service would be disbanded, and handed back to the local authorities, but not to the 1668 separately controlled fire brigades that existed prior to the war. These were scaled down to 135 new brigades. Another very important milestone was that the Act stated that never again would policemen be required to undertake firefighting duties. This was the catalyst for a much improved police force, and independent, professionally run fire brigades.

The Fire Services Act 1947, received Royal Assent on 31st July 1947, and came into operation on 1st April 1948. On that day, the National Fire Service in England and Wales was transformed into 135 separate fire brigades, comprising fifty county and seventy-five county borough brigades, and ten brigades serving joint areas under arrangements made voluntarily by the authorities concerned, under Section 5 of the act (Combination Schemes), Section 7 (Joint Committees) or Section 12 (Transfer of Functions).

The following is a list of the ten brigades serving joint areas:

Combination Schemes

- Berkshire and Reading
- Suffolk (East), Suffolk (West) and Ipswich

Joint Committees

- Breconshire and Radnorshire
- Carmarthenshire and Cardiganshire
- Denbighshire and Montgomeryshire
- Newcastle-upon-Tyne and Gateshead
- Smethwick and West Bromwich
- Worcestershire and Worcester

Arrangements under section 12

- Kent and Canterbury
- Leicestershire and Rutland

Approximately 800 new recruits were enrolled nationally. Policemen who were doing full-time fire duties were given the option to remain in the fire service or return to their normal police duties. The AFS was set up again in 1949/50 to meet the threat of the cold war. There remained a need for the Auxiliary Fire Service to remain in force throughout the country. The government did not want the fire service in Great Britain to be caught unprepared should hostilities prevail, as was the case at the beginning of the war. The authorised establishment of the Plymouth Auxiliary Fire Service, at that time, was 236 men and twenty-four women. This was based on the Home Office plan of two auxiliary firemen for each regular fireman.

Plymouth was one of the new County Borough Fire Brigades set up, and once again Mr George Drury was selected as their first Chief Fire Officer. The new fire brigade headquarters was at 'Wentworth' in Dormy Avenue, Mannamead. The four fire stations of the new brigade were: Station A, Greenbank, Station B, Molesworth Road, Penlee, Station C, The Drive, Torr, Station D, Queen Anne Battery, Cattedown. Brigade Workshops was located at Torr fire station.

City of Plymouth Fire Brigade is formed

In April 1949, Chief Officer Drury presented his first annual report to the Chairman of the watch Committee. In it, he stated that during the past year, the brigade had received 611 calls, the number of

Cap badge and tunic button of the City of Plymouth Fire Brigade, 1948–1973.

Greenbank fire station and headquarters of the City of Plymouth Fire Brigade.

The fireboat Cissie Brock, shown in her former livery in 1966. This boat was built in 1942, and was designed for use in estuarial waters. Originally called the Iris after the former CFO George Drury's daughter, she was rechristened Cissie Brock in 1966. The boat underwent a complete refit in 1964, which included fitting two diesel propulsion engines to replace the wartime petrol engines, and a reduction in its pumping capacity from 2,800 gpm to 1,600 gpm, in order to improve the trim of the vessel.

actual fires being 477. The brigade comprised 118 officers and men, this establishment being made up as follows:

- One Chief Officer
- One Deputy Chief Fire Officer
- One Divisional Officer (Fire prevention and general duties)
- One Assistant Divisional Officer
- Five Station Officers (one of whom is the brigade Engineer)
- Eight Sub-Officers
- Twelve Leading Firemen
- Eighty-nine Firemen

The Chief Officer expressed concern about the fire cover afforded to the north of the city, and he said that the matter was one requiring immediate consideration.

Workshops reported that work was completed in removing NFS markings from all the appliances, station signboards and mobilising boards. Thirteen appliances were re-painted from wartime grey to the new Plymouth City red livery.

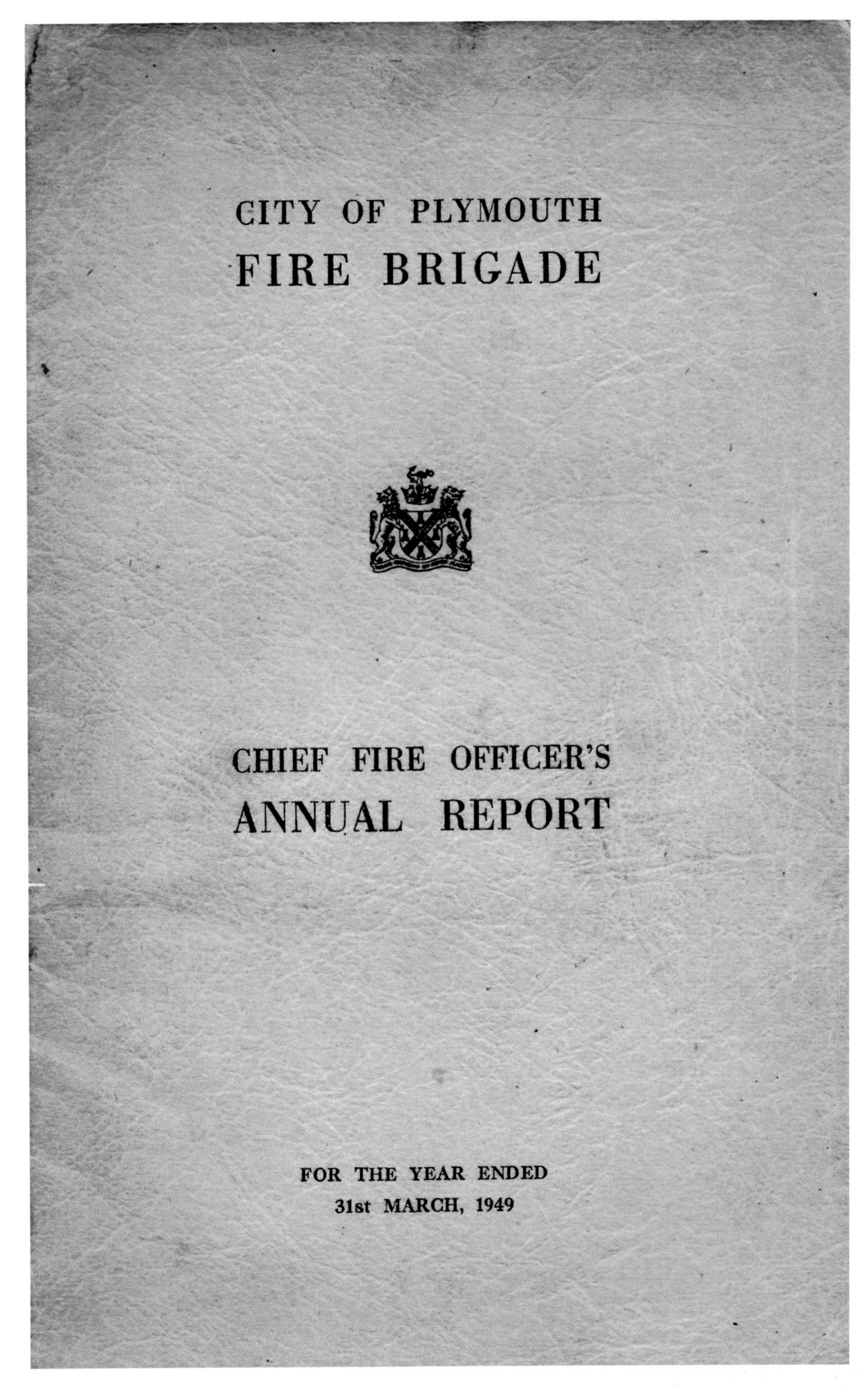
CITY OF PLYMOUTH
FIRE BRIGADE

CHIEF FIRE OFFICER'S
ANNUAL REPORT

FOR THE YEAR ENDED
31st MARCH, 1949

First Annual Report to the Watch Committee by the new City of Plymouth Fire Brigade, year ending 31st March 1949.

The efficiency of the brigade continued to flourish, and in 1951 approval had been obtained from the Council and Home Office to the closing of the combined land and fireboat station at Queen Anne Battery. Arrangements were made for the fireboat to be moored in No. 1 Basin, HM Dockyard. The personnel were dispersed to the three remaining stations, in an endeavour to provide increased fire cover, and at the same time to effect an overall economy in the administration of the brigade.

Priming the trailer pump prior to firefighting on board the SS St Jan, in Millbay Docks on 29th December 1948.

Checking the suction hose whilst pumping in Millbay docks in 1948.

Fireman Dougie Fahey aboard the Dennis Big 6 pump escape (JY 956) at Greenbank fire station in 1950.

Pump escape crew at Greenbank in 1951, L to R: Francis (Jim) Mead, Harry Swift, Ken Bowden, Sid Main, Dougie Walters.

Now that plans had been completed for the extension of the city boundary to the north, the question of the provision of two new fire stations had become of vital importance. The site for one station was earmarked at Crownhill, and a proposed site for the other had been suggested at Camels Head. The two new stations would replace the old wartime stations at Torr and Penlee.

Approval was given to build a further storey to Greenbank Fire Station, to house the executive and administration staff. This would permit the de-requisitioning of the then headquarters building at 'Wentworth', Dormy Avenue, thus effecting economies. The building works at Greenbank was finished in 1953, and the new headquarters for the City of Plymouth Fire Brigade was put to use.

Firemen at work at a fire in Oreston Creosote Plant, in 1949.

Clearing up following a fire in Cattedown school in 1949.

Austin water tender and crew dealing with a small outbreak of fire inside the stage door of the Palace Theatre in 1950.

Inspection of City Fire Brigade

HM Inspector of Fire Services, Mr A. V. Thomas, GM, visited the brigade on 6th and 7th October 1951, to carry out the annual inspection to test the efficiency of the brigade and the Auxiliary Fire Service. Ninety officers and men of the regular brigade, paraded at Station A, Greenbank. HM Inspector was accompanied for the inspection by the Lord Mayor (Alderman H. E. Wright, JP), and the Chairman of the Watch Committee (Alderman F. G. Leatherby) and by other members of the Watch Committee.

Home Office Inspector of Fire Services Mr A. V. Thomas. GM, and the Lord Mayor, Alderman Randolph H. Baker, inspect the men at Greenbank fire station in September 1951. The firemen are (L to R) Francis (Jim) Mead, Joe Wedge, Jack Taylor, Ted Beer, Ronnie Baker and Reg Sinclere.

An Auxiliary Fire Service parade was inspected at the new Auxiliary Headquarters on Embankment Road, and the establishment, which had been totally refurbished, was formally opened by the Lord Mayor and HM Inspector.

Fire engine replacement programmes were operating relatively well back then, and some of the old pre-war appliances were disposed of, even though a lot of wartime appliances were still in use.

The following vehicles had been repainted to the Plymouth City livery:

- Two Austin towing vehicles
- One fireboat (Iris)
- One trailer pump

AFS fire station on Embankment Road, opened in 1952. This photograph was taken during the 1960s.

Spit and polish at the AFS station on Embankment Road.

- One wireless car
- One D.U.K.W. (Amphibious craft)
- One staff car

Work on building a new training tower at Greenbank fire station was completed, therefore affording a much needed training facility, along with a hose drying section.

Maristow House, near Roborough. This picture shows the fire which started on the upper floor, before spreading to the roof, on 11th March 1952. Author's note: they say lightning doesn't strike in the same place twice – another major fire was to occur here again in October 1981.

This dramatic scene was taken at the big fire which occurred in B block of the old Stoke Military Hospital in July 1955. This building was being prepared for the use of Tamar Selective Secondary School. The block was only vacated a month prior to the fire by Devonport High School for boys.

Cover of the booklet for the opening of Crownhill Fire Station in 1959.

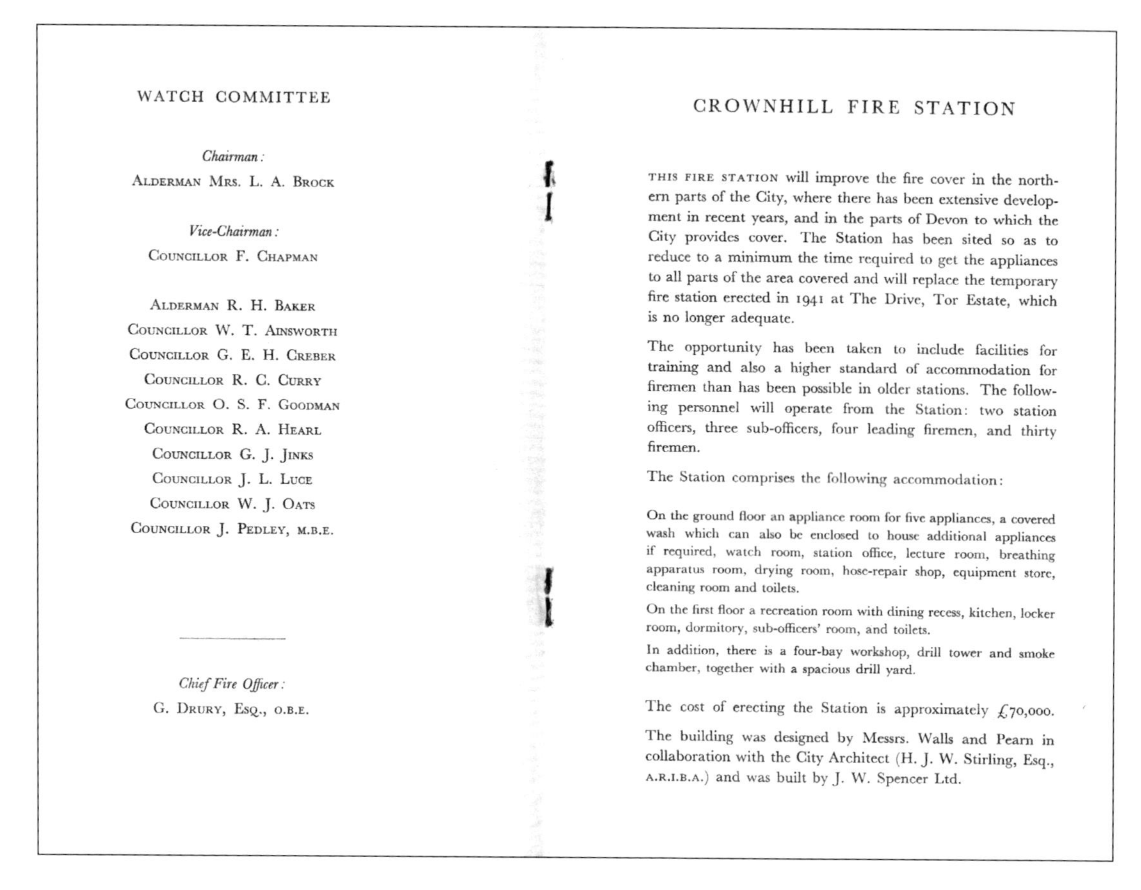

WATCH COMMITTEE

Chairman:
ALDERMAN MRS. L. A. BROCK

Vice-Chairman:
COUNCILLOR F. CHAPMAN

ALDERMAN R. H. BAKER
COUNCILLOR W. T. AINSWORTH
COUNCILLOR G. E. H. CREBER
COUNCILLOR R. C. CURRY
COUNCILLOR O. S. F. GOODMAN
COUNCILLOR R. A. HEARL
COUNCILLOR G. J. JINKS
COUNCILLOR J. L. LUCE
COUNCILLOR W. J. OATS
COUNCILLOR J. PEDLEY, M.B.E.

Chief Fire Officer:
G. DRURY, ESQ., O.B.E.

CROWNHILL FIRE STATION

THIS FIRE STATION will improve the fire cover in the northern parts of the City, where there has been extensive development in recent years, and in the parts of Devon to which the City provides cover. The Station has been sited so as to reduce to a minimum the time required to get the appliances to all parts of the area covered and will replace the temporary fire station erected in 1941 at The Drive, Tor Estate, which is no longer adequate.

The opportunity has been taken to include facilities for training and also a higher standard of accommodation for firemen than has been possible in older stations. The following personnel will operate from the Station: two station officers, three sub-officers, four leading firemen, and thirty firemen.

The Station comprises the following accommodation:

On the ground floor an appliance room for five appliances, a covered wash which can also be enclosed to house additional appliances if required, watch room, station office, lecture room, breathing apparatus room, drying room, hose-repair shop, equipment store, cleaning room and toilets.

On the first floor a recreation room with dining recess, kitchen, locker room, dormitory, sub-officers' room, and toilets.

In addition, there is a four-bay workshop, drill tower and smoke chamber, together with a spacious drill yard.

The cost of erecting the Station is approximately £70,000.

The building was designed by Messrs. Walls and Pearn in collaboration with the City Architect (H. J. W. Stirling, Esq., A.R.I.B.A.) and was built by J. W. Spencer Ltd.

Inside supplement to the opening of Crownhill Fire Station booklet.

New station opens

On Thursday 23rd April 1959, the long awaited opening of Crownhill fire station was officiated by Sir Charles Cunningham, KBE. CB. CVO, the Permanent Under-Secretary of State for the Home Office.

This fire station was built to improve the fire cover in the northern parts of the city. Extensive development had been carried out in recent years, and in parts of Devon to which the city provided cover. This station replaced the temporary fire station erected in 1941 at The Drive, Torr Estate, which was no longer adequate.

The opportunity had been taken to include facilities for training, and also a higher standard of accommodation for the firemen. The new brigade workshops were also opened, across the drill yard.

Coronation displays at Raglan Barracks, 1952

The country was celebrating the Queen's coronation, and Plymouth, not to be outdone, requested that the City Fire Brigade put on a public display. The site chosen was Raglan Barracks, Devonport, where the large drill square and buildings were ideal to show the people of Plymouth how the brigade had become most professional in all aspects of firefighting, and rescuing of casualties. There were also light-hearted displays undertaken, which the big crowd enjoyed, and they laughed heartily.

Crownhill fire station, opened on 23rd April 1959 by Sir Charles Cunningham, KBE, CB, CVO, the Permanent Under-Secretary of State for the Home Office.

Cover picture of the programme for the Coronation displays at Raglan Barracks on 5th June 1953.

PROGRAMME OF DRILLS

MUSICAL INTRODUCTION, 6-30 p.m. to 7-0 p.m.
Musical selections by the PLYMOUTH SILVER BAND
Director of Music: MR. W. F. CLEEVE

1. **COMPETITIVE TRAILER PUMP DRILL**
Two volunteer crews of Auxiliary Firemen will compete in a Trailer Pump Drill. The first crew succeeding in striking the target, with a water jet, will be the winners.

2. **DEMONSTRATION TRAILER PUMP DRILL**
A challenge has been received from "THE AMAZONS" (A female? Pump Crew). They have announced their intention of challenging the accepted principle of male supremacy at Fire Drills.

3. **EXTINCTION OF FIRE IN CRASHED AIRCRAFT**
It is assumed that an Aircraft has crashed and that the pilot is trapped in the resulting fire. A crew responds with a Water Tender to demonstrate the technique of fighting a petrol fire, and using an asbestos suit to facilitate rescue operations.

4. **REVOLVING NOZZLES**
A demonstration of one of the types of nozzle used to fight fires in ship's holds, featuring the Coronation spirit.

5. **RESCUE BY TURNTABLE LADDERS**
Two 100 ft. steel Rescue Ladders will demonstrate two methods used to rescue persons trapped on the roof of a high building.

6. **ANCIENT AND MODERN**
An ancient manually operated Fire Engine and a Fire Engine with steam operated Pumps will be compared with the latest type limousine Fire Engine.

7. **RESCUE BY WHEELED ESCAPE**
The crew of a Fire Engine carrying a 50 ft. Wheeled Fire Escape will demonstrate a rescue by carrying down, using the Fireman's Lift.

8. **AQUATIC FOOTBALL MATCH**
Plymouth Argyle F.C. and Plymouth City Fire Brigade will clash and splash in a "Jet-propelled Ball Game."
Teams:

Argyle	Fire Brigade
Major	Orr
Ratcliffe	Bartlett
Astall—Strauss—Taylor	Taylor—Rundle—Marles

9. **SELF RESCUE WITH LINES AND ROCKET GEAR**
It is assumed that Firemen have been trapped on the roof of a building during fire-fighting operations and they demonstrate a method of self rescue with Fire Brigade lines.

10. **LINE RESCUE? PAST OR FUTURE**
Rescue as practised by Eastern Fire Brigades. Will this become the future rescue technique for the British Fire Service?

11. **FIRE FIGHTING AND RESCUE DISPLAY**
The Brigade has been called to a fire at a hotel. One man is trapped on the top floor and two men on the roof. Rescue and fire operations are carried out simultaneously by Turntable Ladders, Pump Escapes, a Major Pump and an Emergency Tender.

12. **DRIVE PAST**
Units of the Brigade, taking part in the programme, will drive slowly past the spectators and return to the vehicle line ready for inspection.

13. **WATER CASCADE**
Pumps will produce from fixed nozzles a water cascade and coloured water sprays.
(The National Anthem will be played when the coloured sprays commence).

14. **INSPECTION OF VEHICLES**
The Display having concluded, all vehicles will be assembled at the end of the Parade Ground and the public are invited to inspect them.
Crews will stand by to explain the various items of equipment.

Programme of events for the Coronation displays.

A demonstration of a Merryweather steam fire engine during the Coronation Displays at Raglan Barracks in 1953. This steamer was owned by Tehidy House in Cornwall.

Another view of the firefighting displays at Raglan Barracks in 1953.

Fires of special interest

Following the hundreds of conflagrations that Plymouth suffered during the war years, along with the huge loss of life which was inflicted upon the civilian population and firefighters in Plymouth, the 1950s showed an annual rise in fire calls within the city. In 1948/49 there were 611 calls received in Plymouth, and by 1960/61 the calls rose to 1,019. This annual increase was in no doubt attributed to the growing area of Plymouth, with an increase in population.

There were no major conflagrations within the city during the 1950s, but the expertise and professionalism of the Plymouth firemen was often put to the test.

Fires which are worthy of note included:

- The Royal Sailors Rest in Albert Road, in February 1950, where the top two floors and the roof were involved in fire. The call to this service hostel was received at 11.58 p.m. on the 27th February, and by sterling work carried out by the firemen, they were able to bring the fire under control by 1.30 a.m. A pump escape, three major pumps, two turntable ladders and a salvage tender were the appliances engaged at the incident. The fire was limited to a section of the upper floors and roof, and the majority of the premises were undamaged. The rapidity of fire spread was an interesting feature, and it is unlikely that the roof would have been involved had the trap door, leading to the roof space, not been left out of position, allowing free passage for flames and heat. There was no apparent reason for the fire, and the city police were called in to investigate its origin. The external steel fire escapes were of great value for gaining access with lines of hose to the seat of the fire.

- The Boat House, HM Dockyard, in July 1950, where the roof was well alight. The brigade was called to these premises at 5.40 a.m. on the 14th July, and three pumps and a turntable

A trio of Dennis F12 pump escapes at Greenbank fire station.

Ladder were dispatched to the outbreak. On arrival, it was found that the roof of the boat house was well alight, and that a portion of the interior at one end was also burning. The fire was successfully prevented from spreading, either to the boats stored in the premises, or to the remainder of the roof. Nine jets were used to prevent the spread of fire, in addition to jets used by the Admiralty firefighting personnel. The brigade received a letter from the Admiralty thanking them for the work they had done in saving the building.

Firemen at work on the Boat House, H M Dockyard in July 1952.

- Messrs Charles Harding Ltd, House Furnishers, of Mutley Plain, was involved in a serious fire in October 1951. The brigade was called during the lunch hour on this day, and appliances from Greenbank and Torr fire stations were on the scene within two minutes of the original call. However, despite their prompt attendance, they found that a serious fire was in progress. The fire involved offices on the first floor, and the stairway leading into the showrooms. The fire was eventually controlled in approximately forty minutes by the use of four jets from the three pumps. Fire damage was confined to the first floor and stairway. The particularly interesting feature of the fire was the rapidity of spread, especially as several of the firm's staff were on the premises, at lunch, when the outbreak occurred. There is no doubt that had the fire been unobserved for a further fifteen minutes or so, a large fire would have confronted the brigade on arrival. This fire particularly illustrated the tremendous advantage of an immediate call to the fire service at the first sign or suspicion of a fire. A salvage tender was in attendance and waterproof sheeting was used to protect furniture on the ground floor from excessive water damage.

- Maristow House, Roborough, was the scene of a serious fire in March 1952, where the top floor and roof were involved. The brigade was called to this fine old house, which was used as a home for retired clergy, at 1.28 p.m. on the 11th March. Appliances from Torr and Greenbank fire stations responded, and arrived within twelve minutes of being called. It was immediately apparent that an extensive fire was burning in the roof and third floor of the premises. An assistance message was sent back by wireless, for an additional three pumps and a turntable ladder.

  Seven jets, including one from the turntable ladder, were eventually brought to bear on the fire, before it could be considered under control. The difficulty which confronted the brigade arose from the Mansard roof construction of the building. This type of construction results in concealed spaces, above and to the side of the attic rooms, with the result that fire travel is difficult both to locate and to stop. Owing to the limited amount of water available from the hydrants surrounding the premises, it was necessary to relay water from the River Tavy, which necessitated the laying out of long hose lines, from the river to the fire.

  The fire was brought under control at approximately 3.30 p.m. Owing to the great amount of heat, and to the extensive nature of the damage to the roof and top floors, crews remained in attendance until the following morning, to assist with clearing up operations and to ensure that no further outbreak developed.

  Despite the extensive use of waterproof sheeting (salvage sheets) on the ground floor, to prevent water damage, the size of the fire at roof level inevitably resulted in water draining through to the lower floors. The efforts of the brigade, however, resulted in the fire damage being limited to the roof and top floor and a large portion of the premises was habitable immediately following the fire. A letter of thanks for their efficient work was received by the brigade from the Bishop of Plymouth, the Rt. Rev. Norman H. Clarke, M.A. It was thought that the outbreak was caused by the overheating of an electric appliance in a room at roof level, which eventually ignited combustible material in the room.

- In November 1954 a large fire was fought at the Timber Yard at Cattedown, premises owned by Messrs Cole Brothers (Plymouth) Ltd. The year had once again been remarkable for the absence of large fires, only one being classed as a major outbreak, which was this one, at Messrs Cole Brothers Joinery Works and Timber Yard.

  At 2.37 a.m. on the 24th November, a call was received, via 999, for a large fire in the Cattedown area. The caller stated that it appeared to be in the industrial area. Several repeat calls were received for this fire within the following minutes, including one from the Breakwater Fort. Upon arrival at 2.40 a.m., the brigade found that a building measuring

100ft by 100ft, used for storage of joinery, timber, etc., was involved. A message received from the fireground, by radio, indicated the serious nature of the fire, and additional appliances were dispatched. The total comprising five pumps, one turntable ladder and one emergency tender, eleven jets being utilised to extinguish the fire.

The main hazard was the possibility of the intense, radiated heat igniting the timber structure of the adjoining main saw mill, the gap between the fire and this building being about twelve feet. A concentration of jets to form a water curtain set up between the buildings confined the fire to the building of origin. The contents of the building were very severely damaged by the fire. At the height of the fire, a notice board across the road, some fifty feet from the fire, was scorched by radiated heat, and the asphalt road was smoking with the heat. Although a night watchman was employed, no fire call was received from this source. It was apparent that the telephone lines had been burnt through before an attempt was made to call the brigade.

- Devonport High School for Boys was involved in a serious fire in 1956. On the 19th July at 11.32 p.m., a call was received to the above premises from a passing motorist, having observed flames coming from the roof of the school. A predetermined attendance was made, consisting of two pumps, a turntable ladder and a wireless car. The fire was visible from a considerable distance, and immediately a message was radioed back to fire brigade control, requesting additional pumps. On arrival, it was found that the roof and top floor of the building were completely involved, and a total of five pumps with the turntable ladder were necessary to control the fire. The roof of the building was destroyed, and extensive damage was caused to the upper floor. The fire was prevented from spreading to the lower floors of the premises.

Two turntable ladders at work during a serious fire in the top floor and roof of Devonport High School for Boys, in Regents Street on 19th July 1955.

A turntable water monitor is got to work to deal with the fire at Devonport High school for Boys in July 1955.

FDR 706 in use as a water tower, the fireman at the controls was Dougie Fahey.

Enquiries into the cause of the fire revealed that the premises were under reconstruction for occupation by the Tamar Secondary Modern School. The fabric of the roof was being treated by Pest Control Operatives, using portable flame equipment to eliminate woodworm. The workmen had ceased operations at about six p.m. and it was thought that some smouldering particles of timber had been left unobserved at roof level. The burning particles gradually fanned into flame, resulting in a serious fire. The fact that the building was remote from the road meant that the fire had been burning a considerable time and gained a firm hold before it was discovered and reported.

Fire Brigade Long Service and Good Conduct Medal

Under the Royal Warrant dated 1st June 1954, a medal, styled The Fire Brigade Long Service and Good Conduct Medal, may be awarded as a mark of Her Majesty's appreciation of long and meritorious service, rendered by members of fire brigades in Great Britain, who have completed twenty years service.

The Fire Authority imposed a condition upon the granting of this award, to the effect that no other long service award is now recognised by them as applicable to their brigade.

On the occasion of the Annual Inspection by Her Majesty's Inspector, Mr A. V. Thomas, G M, the deputy Lord Mayor, Councillor P. D. Pasco, accompanied by the Vice-Chairman of the Watch Committee, Councillor W. J. Oats, presented the first medals to the following members of the City of Plymouth Fire Brigade:

G. Drury OBE	Chief Fire Officer
F. H. J. Danniells	Deputy Chief Fire Officer

E. G. Dawe	Divisional Officer
F. A. Windebank	Assistant Divisional Officer
R. W. Lee	Station Officer
G. S. F. Pike	Leading Fireman

This medal is still awarded to members of the British Fire Service today who meet the qualifying standards.

Long Service and Good Conduct Medal, issued by Royal Warrant on June 1st 1954. This medal was awarded as a mark of Her Majesty's appreciation of long and meritorious service rendered by members of the Fire Brigades in Great Britain who have completed twenty years' service.

Dennis F12 pump escape, JCO 224, bought for Plymouth in 1953.

CHAPTER FIFTEEN

MORE SIGNIFICANT EVENTS AND FIRES

Rooftop rescues in Devonport and brave deeds in Swilly

IN THE EARLY hours of 11th January 1959, the City Fire Brigade was called upon to perform their biggest rescue operation for many years, when they were called to the Polonia Club in Morice Square, Devonport. On arrival, they were confronted with a serious basement and ground floor fire, which forced the occupants to make their escape through an attic window. Five people, along with their pets, were perched precariously on a narrow parapet high above the pavement. A fifty-foot escape ladder was pitched to the parapet and everyone made a safe descent, with the assistance of the firemen. The fire, which completely gutted the basement and severely damaged the bar area, was allegedly started by defective wiring in the basement.

More good work was done by the brigade at a severe blaze in a council house in Swilly (now called North Prospect) on 22nd March 1959. The brigades received a call to 30 Dingle Road at 3.04 a.m., and were on the scene within minutes. They were confronted with much alarm and panic in the street. It was quickly established that a man was trapped in the first floor bedroom of this heavily smoke-logged house. Firemen wearing breathing apparatus quickly located the man, who was found collapsed on the bed, and brought him to safety. The rescued man was Mr Frederick Hext, who was taken to hospital for treatment. Mr Hext lived with his sister, Mrs Ellen Howard, who along with her children managed to escape down the blazing staircase. Mr Hext was seen smashing the windows of the upstairs bedroom, and despite calls from his neighbours to jump, he refused, even though the flames from the downstairs windows were curling up towards him. He was apparently overcome by the thick smoke and collapsed back across the bed.

The alarm was given at about 3 a.m. by Mrs Daphne Cretch, Mrs Howard's seventeen-year-old daughter. She woke her husband when she could not breathe because of the smoke in their room. Mr Philip Cretch, nineteen years old, woke his mother-in-law, and with her two children, made their way down the blazing staircase and into the front garden. A fire officer later stated that he didn't know how they did it, as conditions were terrible. Neighbours had to restrain Mrs Howard from running back into the house, in an attempt to save her brother, as they said it would have been suicide to do so. The fire brigade took about thirty minutes to bring the blaze under control.

The following morning Mrs Howard, in borrowed clothes, watched her family carry the few remains out of the gutted house, and she described the loss of her budgerigars as the saddest thing of all. She used to breed them, and the birds and twenty-five eggs were worth about £100, she stated. She had an aviary at the back of the house, and they were brought in because of the cold weather. Also brought out of the house were the charred remains of a puppy called Prince, who was found in a downstairs room. The firemen who donned breathing apparatus to enter to rescue Mr Hext were none other than Divisional Officer Fred Danniells and Station Officer Jim Mead. This would have been a very rare occurrence for two supervisory officers to become involved with the rescue; this would indicate to me that they were very short-handed for the job in hand, and they could have only had one fire engine in attendance at that time. It is good to know that, no matter how detached senior officers are from operational work, they are still firemen, and when needed, they get stuck in where it matters. Chief Fire Officer George Drury said afterwards that the firemen had worked magnificently under very difficult conditions of heat and smoke.

Severe floods in Plymouth

It is not only fires that the fire brigade responds to, but also a diverse amount of special service calls, including flooding. On Monday 10th August 1959, more than an inch of rain fell in Plymouth, during one of the most violent thunderstorms the city had known for years. Flooding caused absolute chaos within the district, and the Plymouth Fire Brigade were hard at work hours after the deluge, dealing with storm-damaged property.

The storm in the Plymouth area seemed to be centred over a triangle, formed by Plympton, Yelverton, and Plymouth, while Dartmoor had nothing unusual. Holidaymakers along the Bigbury Bay coastline knew nothing of the storm that struck Plymouth. Months of hot sunshine had brought Plymouth Fire Brigade one of their biggest problems of the year – coping with numerous grass fires. Within less than half an hour of the storm breaking, an even greater problem presented itself: how to cope with the sixty calls that had jammed the telephone switchboard. In all, the firemen dealt with eighty-two flood calls and their devotion to duty won the praise of their Chief Fire Officer, George Drury. The months of May, June and July had been three of the driest months in thirty years recording at Mount Batten. The average rainfall for 1959 was 3.65 inches, the lowest except for 1921 and 1934, when the averages were 3.53 inches.

Big fire at Butt, Vosper, and Knight

Plymouth's worst fire for five years occurred on 30th June 1961, when fire swept through the warehouse of Messrs. Butt, Vosper, and Knight, clothing wholesalers, near the Octagon. The intensity of the fire left only the walls of the building standing. A call was received at 5.14 p.m. via the 999 telephone. When the first appliances arrived, all three floors were well alight, with smoke and flames pouring out of every aperture. Chief Officer Drury took control of operations, and a total of eight jets were used to deal with this outbreak. The fire was got under control in ninety minutes, mainly due to the efforts and courage of the firemen at the scene. One fireman received a severe cut to his arm caused by a falling slate from the roof; he was treated in hospital for his injury. The building was locked at five p.m. when the staff left, and nine minutes later the serious fire ensued.

The cause of the fire was never ascertained, and due to the very rapid spread of the fire, an officer from the South Western Forensic Laboratories was called in. Following a thorough investigation of the debris following the fire, he was unable to establish a definite cause.

The Chief Fire Officer directs his men at this serious fire at Butt, Vosper and Knight clothing warehouse in June 1962.

One hose line working from a Dennis pump escape, at a fire at Butt, Vosper and Knight clothing warehouse in June 1962.

Firemen at work

Fireman Ken Irvine damping down following a serious fire in Shaldon Crescent in January 1955; note the glum looks on the faces of the two station officers, Jack Hollingsworth and Vic Watson. As per normal, the Duty Officer looks on, without any fire kit on!

Crews dealing with a shop basement fire in Embankment Road in 1949.

Firemen search the area for possible casualties after an explosion of gas cylinders in a workman's hut, on a site on North Hill in 1972.

Scene of a fatal fire in Emma Place Stonehouse, in the late 1960s.

Turntable ladder (VJY 44), used as a water tower at Nicholls builders yard in Valletort Road, Stoke, in the early 1970s.

Fireman John McCoy (Mac) on hook ladder drills at the former recruit centre in Reigate, a walk in the park for a former Para!

Multi-purpose appliance with four lines of hose from its deliveries. This incident was at Conoco Petroleum Installation near Hooe Lake.

Station Officer briefs his B.A. Control Officer on where his men are working during a fire above a city centre shop.

Long Service Medals for Plymouth firemen

One of the more gratifying duties performed by Chief Officer George Drury was to oversee a ceremony at Greenbank fire station on 15th September 1960. The event was to award thirteen firemen with their Long Service and Good Conduct Medals, for twenty years' meritorious service. The Chief Fire Officer was accompanied by Mrs Cissie Brock, and two other members of the Watch Committee, Messrs W. T. Ainsworth and R. C. Curry.

The awards went to Sub-Officers F. J. Briggs, H. N. Page, H. J. Smith; Ldg. Firemen F. T. Bird, F. H. Ripley and Firemen L. A. Hooper; W. E. Horstead, G. S. King, T. W. Martin, J. H. Minhinick, R. A. Sinclair, B. J.Tonkin and E. Warring.

Senior Brigade Officers with pump competition winning team in 1956. Top (L to R): Wilf Edwards, Ron Baker, Jack Taylor, Ron Hooper, Pete Gregory and Gordon Strike. Front (L to R): Peter Noble, Fred Danniells, George Drury, Ernie Dawe and Francis (Jim) Mead.

Big fire at B Power Station

Molten metal and a temperature of more than 3,000 degrees Fahrenheit turned the Prince Rock power station into a raging furnace on the morning of 7th January 1962. Firemen braved sulphur fumes, cascading sparks and steam to fight the blaze, which broke out at the Plymouth B power station at 4 a.m. and took nearly six hours to extinguish. Before it was brought under control, the fire caused between £20,000 and £40,000 worth of damage to a 95ft air heater; it was three days before it was cool enough to be repaired. About twenty members of the night staff tried to tackle the fire when it first started, but the blaze was out of control, and they then called the fire brigade. Fire appliances were sent from all over the city, and thirty-five firemen, used twelve lines of hose, with powerful jets, to train water on to the heater. An accumulation of overheated oil residue was believed to have been the cause.

Thousands of copper pipes melted in the fierce heat and fell to the bottom of the heater, where they burnt the asbestos-lagged outer casing. At one point, there was danger that the whole heater might collapse. Firemen reported that it was like working in a giant foundry, with thousands of sparks flying everywhere. One fireman stated that this was the hottest fire he had ever been to since he joined the brigade, and it was one of the biggest he had known in Plymouth. Mr George Drury, Chief Fire Officer, directed operations, and he said the biggest difficulties were the gases, and terrific heat from steam generated, as water was poured in. The heater, which was sixty feet long and twenty feet wide, was, back then, a recently completed part of the power station.

Chief Fire Officer George Drury retires

The City of Plymouth Fire Brigade's first Chief Officer, Mr George Drury, retired from the brigade in July 1962. Mr Drury served for fifty-one years in the fire service; he was the holder of the OBE, MBE (awarded for distinguished wartime service) and the Queens Fire Service Medal. He first came to Plymouth in April 1941, to reorganise the city's fire service and direct operations during the raids of that month. He was appointed Chief Fire Officer in July and was released within a few weeks to become Fire Force Commander of No 19 Area, National Fire Service. Services associated with the allied invasion of France, brought him the OBE in June, 1945. In 1949, he went on a three-month advisory visit to the Sudan.

He joined the fire service in November 1911, and later became Chief Officer of the Fire Brigade at Kingston-on-Thames, Surrey. In 1923, Mr Drury was awarded the diploma of The Royal Society for the Protection of Life from Fire for saving three lives at a fire in Kingston-on-Thames. At the beginning of 1939, he was seconded to become Fire Brigade Inspector on the Headquarters staff of the Home Office. He remained there until October 1940, when he went to Bristol as Regional Fire Brigade Inspector, in a temporary capacity to do certain reorganisation.

While in Bristol, the Blitz on that city broke, and for his work in connection with this, in November 1940, he was awarded the MBE; he returned to London in March 1941. He assumed his appointment on the headquarters staff of the Home Office, until, in April 1941, he was instructed to go to Plymouth, to reorganise the fire service there. He arrived in Plymouth a few hours before the raids began on April 21st 1941. Just over two months later, he was offered the job of Chief Fire Officer. But eighteen days later, the Home Office asked the Plymouth Corporation to release him to undertake work in connection with the nationalisation of the fire service, as he had been appointed Fire Force Commander-designate for No. 19 area.

Mr George Drury had transformed the fire brigade in Plymouth into a well trained and professional organisation. When he took command back in 1941, there were only fourteen full-time Police Firemen in Plymouth, the rest being made up of auxiliaries. When he retired, the actual establishment of the brigade was 137 full-time officers and men, and 100 men and women of the Auxiliary Fire Service. During his time in command, he oversaw many changes in fire engines, and bought a fleet of three Dennis F12 pump escapes, and three Dennis F8 pumps. In 1961, the old turntable ladder was replaced with a new £12,000 AEC Mercury, with a 100-foot Merryweather automatic ladder.

Dennis F12 pump escape, GCO 138, bought for Plymouth in 1951.

Dennis F8 pump (LCO 318) outside Crownhill fire station.

A real fire engine! This Dennis F12 pump escape (JCO224) was bought in 1953 and sold off in 1969.

New Chief Fire Officer for Plymouth

With the retirement of George Drury, it was decided that Plymouth needed a Chief Officer who would be dynamic enough to take the City Fire Brigade to a new level of excellence. The man who was chosen was Mr Ralph Havery, who at thirty-five-years of age was the youngest chief officer in the country. Mr Havery, a native of Newcastle, joined the fire service at the beginning of 1949 after serving in the Merchant Navy.

He joined Durham Fire Brigade in 1949, and by 1956 he was a Station Officer. In 1960, he moved to the Central Area Fire Brigade in Scotland as a Divisional Officer (III); by 1962, he was the Acting Firemaster of that brigade. He quickly established himself in his new job at the headquarters at Greenbank, and set about the task of improving efficiency and modernising some of the old appliances and equipment.

Prior to Mr Havery's arrival, there was industrial unrest throughout the ranks of the brigade, as the Fire Brigades Union was pressing for a reduction in hours, from a fifty-six hour week to a forty-eight hour week. The National Joint Council for the Fire Brigades accepted the principal of a forty-eight hour week in 1955, but its introduction was a matter for local determination.

As well as a reduction in working hours, the firemen were also demanding a substantial increase in basic pay, a telescoping of incremental scales from five to fourteen years, and the abandonment of cadet corps (some brigades ran a cadet scheme within their brigade).

The firemen of Plymouth sent a letter to the Home Office in October 1961 explaining that the intended absence of off-duty members at the annual parade the following week should not be regarded as a deliberate discourtesy to Her Majesty's Inspector. The decision to boycott the parade, where off-duty men are concerned, was decided upon by a meeting of Fire Brigade Union members, who voted to work to rule in support of their forty-eight hour week claim.

The opposition to the granting of a forty-eight hour week was the recruiting of an extra twenty-two men, which would add a penny to the rates. Finally, in September 1962, the introduction of a forty-eight hour week for Plymouth firemen was accepted in principal by the Watch Committee, but it would cost

Off-duty Plymouth firemen on an FBU demonstration in the early 1960s, they are, from L to R: Ken Bowden (half hidden), Trevor Rawlings, Jock Orr, George Pike, Les Hockaday, Charlie Babbage, Brian Sullivan, Pete Gregory, Mel Hughes, John Evans, Jack Pester, Wally Rider, Reg Sinclere, Ron Baker and Ken Slade.

an additional £20,000 a year. The Committee asked for the start of recruitment from April the following year, in order to implement the forty-eight hour week in 1963/64.

Baby thrown to safety in Plymouth blaze

A life or death situation occurred on 4th February 1962, in a blazing tenement in the North Road West area of the city. Trapped in the blazing living room of a Plymouth tenement, a thirty-year-old mother of four children threw her baby daughter to safety, and then jumped out of the window herself, fracturing her leg badly in the fall. Firemen rescued her younger son, who had been overcome by smoke.

The fire broke out at 12.45 p.m. on the first floor of 28 Wolston Street, which was near to the Roman Catholic Cathedral. It was established that a lit oil heater had been knocked over, which accounted for the fire. The mother, Mrs Catherine Gomer, was apparently preparing lunch for her family; her husband was out at work for the day. Three of her children were in the tenement when fierce flames and acrid smoke forced her to the window. Her neighbour, Mr Frank Thorne, was just putting his car away when he heard her cries for help. He was forced to break open the back yard door, as it was locked shut, he then ran to beneath the first floor window. He saw the terrified lady hanging out of the window clutching her six-month-old baby Jacqueline, with smoke and flames licking around her. He shouted to her to drop the baby down to him, which she eventually did, and the baby was safely caught by Mr Thorne, who then handed the baby to his wife. He then told Mrs Gomer to jump, which she did, but sadly she fell awkwardly and received a complicated fracture to her left leg. She also had burns to her arm, incurred in trying to douse the flames.

A passing ambulance was flagged down and the crew tended to Mrs Gomer. The first fire engine was soon in attendance, along with a radio car, and their top priority was to establish whether all persons were accounted for. It was quickly learned that two of her other children had managed to flee the burning

Cover of booklet for the opening of Camel's Head Fire Station in 1965.

tenement, but Mrs Gomer's three-year-old son was still missing. Firemen entered the choking smoke in a bid to find the young boy, and their bravery and diligence were soon rewarded, as one of the firemen, Patrick Manley, found the little boy, who was overcome by the smoke, in an empty tin bath at the top of the stairs. He was taken to hospital along with his mother, where they eventually made good recoveries. The Deputy Chief Fire Officer, Mr Frederick Danniells, stated that it was a very difficult and brave search by his men, and he was pleased that the incident concluded without any fatalities.

New Fire Station and improvements

Permission was finally granted in September 1962 for the erection of a new fire station at Camels Head. This station was needed to replace the old wartime station at Molesworth Road. The finance committee of Plymouth City Council approved a tender for £100,000, but subject to some minor adjustments, work was due to commence within the current financial year.

After long delays and red tape, the station at Camels Head was finally built, and it was officially opened by the Lord Mayor, Alderman T. H. Watkins, on 6th January 1965. Because the station was built on reclaimed land, it was necessary to build the station itself on concrete columns, which were sunk into the ground. The station boasted some ultra-modern features, including a state of the art watchroom and a large drill yard, with a smoke chamber, hydrants, and an underground static water tank.

The appliance bays were fitted with up and over doors, which were electrically operated from the watch room. When fully opened, they lay horizontally along the underside of the roof, thereby leaving the whole of the doorway clear, thus achieving ideal operational conditions. The establishment of the new station consisted of three Station Officers, three Sub Officers, three Leading firemen and thirty-seven

WATCH COMMITTEE

THE LORD MAYOR

Chairman:
ALDERMAN W. J. OATS

Vice-Chairman:
COUNCILLOR R. C. CURRY

ALDERMAN R. H. BAKER

COUNCILLOR W. T. AINSWORTH
COUNCILLOR B. F. BROCKINGTON
COUNCILLOR D. G. CARTER
COUNCILLOR C. C. COLEMAN
COUNCILLOR J. J. COWAN
COUNCILLOR A. R. GLINN
COUNCILLOR F. S. KELLAND
COUNCILLOR J. L. LUCE
COUNCILLOR A. G. H. METTERS

Chief Fire Officer:
R. HAVERY, Esq., A.M.I. FIRE E.

CAMEL'S HEAD FIRE STATION

THIS NEW STATION replaces an old hutted Fire Station situated in Molesworth Road, Stoke, which was erected as a temporary wartime measure and which was completely inadequate for the modern large appliances and greatly increased number of firemen necessary to maintain the appliances and deal with the ever-increasing demands made upon the Brigade by the public.
The Station has been sited in conjunction with the Brigade's other two Fire Stations in order to provide a fast, efficient attendance of fire engines to any emergency incident within the City.
The establishment of the Station consists of three Station Officers, three Sub-Officers, three Leading Firemen and thirty-seven Firemen, who are responsible for the manning of one Pump Escape, one Pump, one Turntable Ladder and one Fireboat, these different types of appliances being necessary for the many varied and complex fire and life risks which exist within the Station area.
There are a number of ultra-modern features incorporated in the design of the Fire Station, amongst the most important are the following:

APPLIANCE ROOM
The Appliance Room is fitted with 'up and over' doors which are electrically operated from the Console Desk in the Watchroom. These doors, when open, lie horizontally along the underside of the roof and therefore leave the whole of the doorway clear, thus achieving ideal operational conditions.

WATCHROOM
Situated centrally within the Watchroom is a Console Desk containing the Exchange telephone and private line telephone direct to Brigade Control, also all the operational switches for operating the fire-bells, doors, lights, loud-speaker system, etc. The Console is so designed and situated that the Duty Man has a commanding view of both the Appliance Room and the large forecourt, and so can immediately observe any member of the public who may approach the Station in search of assistance.

Inside supplement to opening of Camel's Head Fire Station booklet.

firemen. They were responsible for the manning of one pump escape, one pump, one turntable ladder, and one fireboat; these different types of appliances being necessary for the many and varied fire and life risks that existed within the station area.

As well as having a new fire station, other important work was undertaken in that year to modernise the brigade. The control room at Greenbank was completely remodernised and re-equipped, making it one of the best in the country. The AFS station on Embankment Road was much improved, with new steel folding doors fitted to the appliance bays. Some of the outbuildings were either rebuilt or modernised, to include lecture rooms and new cooking facilities. The ten firemen's houses at Greenbank were completely modernised; this included converting one of the three bedrooms into a bathroom and toilet. The house occupied by the Deputy Chief Fire Officer was also completely rewired and generally renovated, before being reoccupied by the new Deputy Chief Officer.

All the pumping appliances and staff cars were now fitted with wireless in place of the previous system of having wireless cars on each station. This change released the cars for other duties, and en-

Fireboat Iris sunk at her moorings as a result of her sea cocks being left open during the 1960s.

abled brigade control to contact the appliances direct, and redirect them to other incidents as necessary. Permission was also granted, from the Home Office, for the brigade to operate its own radio frequency, instead of the practice of sharing the police wavelength.

On taking command of the brigade in August 1962, Mr Havery formulated a five-year modernisation programme. It was designed to introduce modern techniques and equipment into the brigade, and dispense with the wartime, or pre-war, appliances and equipment, both operational and non-operational, which were still in everyday use. The main principle of the plan being that renewal of as much of the equipment as possible should be effected within the normal financial estimates. Also, that the anticipated lifetime of the new operational equipment, should, as far as possible, be of the same duration as the appliance on which it was carried. This ensured that excess money was not spent on equipment so constructed that it would last indefinitely, and so prevent advantage being taken of any new developments in the future.

Pump escape crew slipping the escape prior to a rescue drill at Greenbank fire station in 1967.

Crews manage to get the Iris afloat again with the aid of ejector pumps and hauling lines.

Pump crew getting on board a Dennis F8 at Greenbank fire station.

AFS pipe laying drill being carried out on Dartmoor.

'Come on lads, only another 180 lengths to add': another picture of a pipe-laying exercise on Dartmoor during the 1960s.

The Snorkel showing its 65-foot reach at Camel's Head fire station.

Given below are some of the main improvements that Mr Havery had effected:

Appliances and vehicles

Emergency salvage tender: was purchased in 1964 and replaced two appliances, one an emergency tender, which was a home-made appliance using a horsebox of 1938 vintage, and the other, a salvage tender, which was a 1942 wartime towing vehicle. The new appliance, which was extremely well equipped with modern equipment, was designed to deal with any type of disaster, such as road, rail, aircraft crashes, and fires involving ships, chemicals, or radioactive substances. It also carried a good range of salvage equipment, in order to mitigate damage by water and dirt during firefighting operations.

1964 Bedford/Mumford emergency salvage tender (YJY 999) based at Greenbank fire station, sold off in 1980.

Water Tender: was also purchased in 1964 and replaced a twenty-year-old home-made appliance, which was, in fact, a lorry carrying a 500-gallon water tank, and a war-time 120 gpm light pump. This also allowed a 1955 pump to be taken out of regular service, and used as a spare appliance, in order to permit the other appliances to be regularly withdrawn from service for maintenance purposes.

This appliance, in addition to carrying a supply of 400 gallons of water, was fitted with a 500 gpm high pressure pump, capable of supplying two fog guns at 500 psi pressure. This high pressure enabled the extinguishing of fires with much greater efficiency, by making more use of the latent heat of vaporisation of water, and, therefore, reducing the likelihood of water damage. It also had built-in equipment for generating up to 2,800 gpm of foam, for fighting fires involving flammable liquids.

Hose Foam Tender: was placed in commission in 1965 and replaced a 1941 wartime hose-laying lorry, with a 1944 trailer pump, and a 1943 wartime towing vehicle, which also towed a 1943 trailer pump, and was used as a foam tender. The new appliance carried 310 gallons of foam compound, which is over 200 gallons more than carried on the previous appliance, and could produce up to 7,200 gallons of foam per minute. It could also mechanically lay twin lines of hose, each of 1,500 feet, or a single line of 3,000 feet. It also carried an additional 900 feet of hose for hand laying. This appliance was designed to attend ship fires, and other fires which may involve flammable liquids, or incidents at which there is a known shortage of fire hydrants. Its value as a hose layer proved invaluable in rural areas.

1965 Bedford/Mumford hose foam tender at Crownhill fire station, sold off in 1986.

Snorkel Fire and Rescue Appliance: a new type of fire appliance of American design, the main feature of which was its hydraulic platform with a working height of sixty-five feet. It enabled it to operate over the top of parked cars, concrete canopies, etc., and approach right up to the face of a building to effect rescues, or fight fires with greater accuracy than the turntable ladder. This appliance had been on order for approximately a year and a half before it was finally delivered in October 1967. This appliance replaced the 1942 100-foot turntable ladder, which was the property of the Admiralty, and the last wartime land fire appliance in commission within the city.

Leyland Carmichael 65 foot pump hydraulic platform (HCO 999F) bought in 1967 and sold off in 1982.

Multi-Purpose Appliance: this appliance was designed to undertake several different roles. They were built on a Leyland Beaver chassis and were much larger than the old pumping appliances. They were called 'multi purposes', because they were capable of performing the functions of a pump water tender, a pump escape, salvage tender, and ET/rescue tender. They were the first appliances to carry the new forty-six foot light alloy extension ladder (Lacon), which replaced the fifty foot wheeled escapes. They also carried a thirty-five foot wooden Bayley ladder, a roof ladder and a short extension ladder. The appliance also carried hydraulic rescue equipment (Epco), power cutting equipment (Partner Saw), and powerful electric lighting. It also carried twenty gallons of foam compound together with a pick up tube and a foam branch pipe. The first of these appliances arrived in 1967, and it replaced a sixteen-year-old Dennis pump escape. The concept of this appliance, which was the brainchild of Mr Havery, was that it was the first of its type used in the fire brigade, and placed the City of Plymouth Fire Brigade firmly among one of the best equipped fire brigades in the country.

Leyland Beaver multi-purpose (HDR 999F), bought in 1968 and sold off in 1984.

Fireboat: was an estuarial type of vessel built in 1942, originally named the *Iris* after the daughter of Mr George Drury, ex-Fire Force Commander for No. 19 area and first Chief Officer of City of Plymouth Fire Brigade. Her name was changed again in 1966, to *Cissie Brock*, in appreciation of ex-Alderman (Mrs) L. A. Brock, who was the first Lady Chairman of a Watch Committee in the country. The boat underwent a complete refit in 1964, which included the fitting of two diesel propulsion engines, to replace the wartime petrol engines. This resulted in a reduction of its pumping capacity, from 2,800 gpm to 1,600 gpm, in order to improve the trim of the vessel. During 1963, a fireman was posted to the fireboat on permanent day duty, since when he had qualified as a coxswain, and took pride in the efficiency, condition, and appearance of the boat.

The fireboat Cissie Brock in Sutton Pool.

Operational equipment

Breathing apparatus: thirty-two sets of Roberts, Mark 101, high-pressure compressed air breathing apparatus, together with the necessary spare cylinders, etc. were purchased during the year 1966/67. This equipment replaced the oxygen equipment, most of which had been in service for nearly thirty years, and proved to be very expensive to maintain.

The one major disadvantage with compressed air equipment was the limited cylinder duration, which, for all practical purposes, was restricted to approximately twenty minutes. Much design and development was devoted to this problem for at least ten years, with the result that a new, high capacity, ultra-lightweight cylinder was produced early in 1966 and issued to certain fire brigades, including the Plymouth brigade, for field trials. After much testing and consideration, the trials substantiated the maker's claim that the cylinders would last one hour. The brigade was re-equipped with the new cylinders, and so became the first fire brigade in the world to be completely equipped with the ultra-lightweight cylinder.

Resuscitation Equipment: all pumping appliances and the emergency tender were equipped with automatic resuscitators (Minuteman). This equipment had proved itself on numerous occasions, both at fires and special service calls, and had been responsible for saving many lives.

Branch Pipes: all branch pipes and nozzles were replaced by hand-controlled, variable branches (Hughes Noble), capable of producing a firefighting spray, or up to a one-inch jet, with an output ranging from 0 to 300 gpm. These branches enabled the water streams to be varied or completely shut off by the operator. It was not possible with the old branch pipes to shut off or reduce the size of the jet, without sending a runner back to the pump operator, which could be some distance away. This branch proved very effective in reducing water damage during firefighting operations.

Foam Equipment: the brigade increased their stock of foam compound from 700 gallons to 3,000 gallons; this was to meet the need because of the ever-increasing use of flammable liquids. All the old wartime foam-making equipment was replaced with modern foam branch pipes.

Experiments were conducted in the 1960s into the use and effectiveness of a new type of foam, known as high expansion foam. This material is a detergent compound, which is aerated by blowing it through a nylon mesh net, by means of a fan, and has an expansion ratio of 1000:1, against the normal type of foam which had an expansion ratio of approximately 8:1. It can quickly produce vast quantities of foam, which can be used to fill basements or compartments on ships. The one big downside of this type of foam is that there is no way of telling if the fire is out, without committing firemen into the flooded areas to confirm the fact.

Considering the fact that Mr Havery did not take control of the City Fire Brigade until 1962, the rapidity of his modernisation programme and the professionalism he installed within the brigade, was there for all to see. One can only commend his ability to command a fire brigade, and to strike up such a good working relationship, which he undoubtedly had, with the Watch Committee and other Civic Dignitaries.

Not everyone agreed with his man management techniques! If an individual fell foul of him, he made it clear in no uncertain terms, but he also had a very warm and understanding side to him. It would be right to say that he was a hard but fair man, who commanded the respect of all who served under him during his eleven-year reign as Chief Fire Officer of the City of Plymouth Fire Brigade.

The following is a list of personnel who received their Long Service and Good Conduct Medal during 1966:

> Station Officer F. J. Brimacombe. No. 19/32; Station Officer J. Donaldson. No. 19/31; Station Officer J. F. Hollingsworth. No. 19/29; Station Officer L. D. Marles. No. 19/38; Sub Officer A. G. Joslin. No. 35; Leading Fireman J. N. Denton. No. 101; Leading Fireman C. T. Rule. No. 34; Leading Fireman R. C. Williams. No. 118; Fireman C. H. Babbage. No. 59; Fireman E. J. Bartlett. No. 73; Fireman W. P. Brown. No. 107; Fireman H. Dixon. No. 94; Fireman H. C. Doddridge. No. 37; Fireman D. R. Fahey. No. 38; Fireman W. H. Faye. No. 110; Fireman D. R. Glass. No. 117; Fireman A. W. Halcrow. No. 120; Fireman L. D. Henwood. No.120; Fireman J. D. Irvine. No. 106; Fireman F. Nunn. No. 78; Fireman D. C. Prynn. No. 74; Fireman R. E. Smith. No. 28; Fireman A. H. Stephens. No. 98; Fireman A. J. Taylor. No. 121; Fireman A. E. Wherry. No. 61; Fireman J. Youde. No. 59.

It is interesting and commendable to note that Station Officer Ken Welberry was awarded the Royal Humane Society's Testimonial on Parchment, combined with the Resuscitation Certificate, for the part he played in the rescue of a drowning man from the sea, off the Hoe foreshore, on 2nd July 1966. Ken was a well-known all year round swimmer, and could always be found at the Lions Den, on the Hoe foreshore. He once persuaded some of the watch at Greenbank to partake in this activity one frosty Christmas morning. Among the takers were two ex-Paras, Mac McCoy and Zipper Ferrand. They both recounted later that it was a full day before they stopped shivering and stuttering. On future excursions, Ken only singled out ex-RAF types, as they were much harder!

Torrey Canyon disaster

On 18th March 1967, a major disaster struck the south-west of England, with the floundering on the Seven Stones Reef, between the Isles of Scilly and Lands End, of the *Torrey Canyon* oil tanker. Thousands of tons of crude oil from her tanks headed towards the coastline of Cornwall and Devon. She was sailing for Milford Haven with 120,000 tons of crude oil from Kuwait. The immediate response was to try to salvage the ship, but over 30,000 gallons of oil had escaped, and the tanker was starting to break up. Prime Minister Harold Wilson held a cabinet meeting at the Royal Naval Air Station at Culdrose, and it was decided to order the setting on fire of the remainder of the oil, to try to avoid a total environmental disaster.

The Fleet Air Arm sent Buccaneer aircraft from Lossiemouth, to drop forty-two 1,000lb bombs onto the wreck. This was quickly followed by the Royal Air Force sending Hawker Hunter jets, to drop cans of aviation fuel, to make the oil blaze. In all, 75% of the bombs were on target, and both sections of the

A City of Plymouth fireman wearing a Roberts Mk 101 B.A. set, c.1971.

'Where are all the trophies?' Fire brigade football team in 1963 who did very well in the local Devon Wednesday league during the 1960s . They are, from L to R rear: Ray Rounsfull (Manager), Cliff Cox, Ted Pascoe, Paddy Manley, Alan Hicks, Ted Wright, Ray Yabsley. Front L to R: Brian Harrison, Eddie Reburn, Bob Russell, Mick Little and Ken Hooper.

wreck were on fire. The sea state hampered the operations, and it took further attacks by Sea Vixens from Yeovilton, and Buccaneers from RNAS at Brawdy. The Royal Air Force sent more Hunters with napalm to ignite the oil.

Emergency meetings of the officers who were responsible for the protection of Plymouth Sound and the immediate surroundings were called, under the chairmanship of the Town Clerk. The necessary plans, which involved the City Fire Brigade, were formulated to combat the danger. Fortunately, no oil reached Plymouth, but our neighbours, Cornwall County, were badly affected by large deposits of oil on their lovely beaches. This necessitated very long cleaning operations, which involved HM Forces, local authorities and fire brigades.

Firemen and appliances from many parts of the country were sent to the aid of the Cornwall County Fire Brigade, and over thirty officers and men, both professional and auxiliary, together with seven fire appliances, were sent to their assistance from Plymouth. Thousands of gallons of detergent were sprayed on the 270 square miles of contaminated sea. In all, ninety-three miles of Cornish coastline was affected. The men spent several weeks dispersing the oil, and all returned to their normal duties once the situation was remedied.

Chief Fire Officer Havery demonstrates the workings of the control room at Greenbank fire station to members of the Watch Committee.

CHAPTER SIXTEEN

CITY OF PLYMOUTH FIRE BRIGADE LEAVES ITS MARK

Plymouth expands

AS FROM 1ST April 1967, due to local government reorganisation and boundary changes, the size of the city was increased by over 50%, and the brigade took over the day-manned fire station at Plymstock, and the retained fire station at Plympton, both of which were former Devon County Fire Service stations.

The City Council decided to improve the standards of fire cover in the added areas, which, in turn, provided an increased standard of cover in the existing city, in order to deal with the increasing demands made upon the brigade. The decision necessitated an increase in the establishment of sixty personnel, both uniformed and civilian, and the dispensation of retained (part-time) personnel at both of the fire stations. The increases, which were phased in over two years, were as follows:

- April 1967: Increased by thirty-six
- April 1968: Increased by eighteen
- April 1969: Increased by six

Neither of the fire stations taken over was suitable for use as a fully manned station, and consideration was given to the replacement of both stations. A recommendation was also put in at the same time, for the erection of a new brigade headquarters. The existing premises at Greenbank, which housed both the headquarters and a fire station, were badly overcrowded, and unsuitable for their joint role.

Lawson's fire creates city centre gridlock

On 13th May 1968, Plymouth city centre was brought to a virtual standstill, as firemen fought one of the largest fires of the year at F. T. B. Lawson Ltd., Tool and Cutlery Merchants, in New George Street. The fire required the attendance of a total of ten fire appliances. There was a serious fire burning on the mezzanine floor, between the ground and first floors, and the building was heavily smoke-logged. Initially, getting to the seat of the fire proved very difficult, due to the fact that the fire was between floors. The use of a smoke extraction unit, which was relatively new to the brigade, made for much easier working conditions for the Breathing Apparatus teams working inside. The loss was estimated at £23,000, however, as the store needed to be closed for many weeks following the fire, to enable repair and redecoration work

Smoke extraction unit being taken aloft during the fire at Messrs Lawson's in 1968.

John McCoy and Ray Hargreaves take a well earned breather after tackling a fire at Messrs Lawson's, New George Street, in May 1968.

Crowds gather to witness the fire at Lawson's in May 1968.

to take place. It was obvious that the indirect loss caused by the fire, e.g. loss of business and employment, was quite considerable.

Non-fire calls

Special Service calls, i.e. incidents not connected with firefighting, accounted for approximately 25% of all calls received; this figure had been rising slowly over the years. There was no legal obligation to perform such operations at that time, hence no additional funding to cover the costs of extra equipment or specialised training. In 1968 alone, the brigade dealt with 586 such calls, ranging from cutting casualties out of crashed vehicles, releasing persons trapped in lifts, cutting rings and other jewellery from various appendages, etc. Plymouth's Chief Fire Officer considered it a moral responsibility to undertake Emergency Special Services. He was not alone with his views. Nearly every Chief Officer in the country made their feelings known to the government, who, at a much later date, did make it a legal responsibility, which in turn attracted better funding.

Dockyard Fire Brigade disbands

Even though Plymouth City provided back-up to the Dockyard Fire Brigade at Devonport, and other military establishments throughout the area, it was decided that the Admiralty Constabulary would no longer provide fire cover in Her Majesty's Dockyards around the country. Devonport Dockyard officially came under the protection of the City of Plymouth Fire Brigade in 1969, ending hundreds of years of

Road traffic accident in Exeter Street c.1968.

protecting their own property. The fire engines and other equipment were taken from Devonport, and the part-time police/firemen returned to full-time police duties once again.

Pay and conditions

There was much unrest and debate during the late 1960s between members of the Fire Brigades Union and the employers, regarding pay and conditions. In May 1967, the Prices and Incomes Board issued their report on Fire Service Pay. In addition to recommending a general increase of pay of 7.5 %, it also recommended that the size of all fire brigades be reduced. This was to be achieved by the working week of the lower ranks being increased from forty-eight hours to fifty-six hours. After much negotiating and consultations with the workforce, it was agreed to accept the recommendations. How ironic, that back in 1962 the firemen fought for a reduction in hours, from fifty-six to forty-eight, and now, they voted to work longer hours once again!

The establishment of the brigade was cut by twenty-four men. This meant that a number of personnel became supernumerary, and also that the third phase of the brigade's expansion programme, scheduled for 1st April 1969, would have to be modified. The enrolment of six Sub-Officers was changed to the promotion of six Sub-Officers from within the existing ranks, without the enrolment of six additional personnel. It was anticipated that the supernumerary personnel would be absorbed, due to normal wastage, by the early part of the following year.

At a City Council meeting held in January 1969, the Council accepted the Fire Brigade Committee's recommendation that a new brigade headquarters be built. Such headquarters was to be large enough to cater for the needs of a brigade, to cover the type of local authority area which was anticipated following the recommendations of the Royal Commission on local government. It was hoped to commence this project during 1970, and Mr Havery stressed the importance of an early start. The serious lack of accom-

The Magnificent Leylands: this line-up was used to publicise Plymouth's fleet of Leylands.

Special Equipment Tender, 1970 Bedford (MDR 999H), stationed at Crownhill fire station. This appliance was known among the men as the Bread Van!

modation at brigade headquarters was preventing the brigade from its forward progress and in no field more so than fire protection does an organisation which stands still, in fact, move backwards.

In the Chief Officer's annual report for 1970, he wrote how disappointed he was with the decision taken to postpone the commencement of work on the new brigade headquarters project, due initially to financial and technical difficulties. There then followed a suggestion by the Home Office, to have a waiting period, until the results of a report on reorganisation of local government and the fire services were evaluated. The brigade attended 2,716 emergency calls during 1969; this was 181 more than the previous year. Mr Havery stated that it appeared that a yearly increase of emergency calls was here to stay, and he envisaged that the 3,000 mark was just around the corner. In addition to providing fire protection for the 31.2 square miles of the City of Plymouth, the brigade was also responsible for providing complete fire protection for 36.5 square miles of Devon County, i.e. portions of the parishes of Bickleigh, Sparkwell, Brixton, Wembury, Ermington, Newton and Noss, and Holbeton. The brigade was also responsible for providing part of the first attendance for fifty-eight square miles of Devon County.

The total number of emergency calls attended in the first year of the formation of the City of Plymouth Fire Brigade was 611. With the size of the population, and city expansion, there was a steady increase in the number of call outs; the figure for the year 1971/72 was 3,412, which was yet another increase on the previous year by 449.

Fire Precautions Act 1971

During the late 1960s and early 1970s, much concern had been expressed on the increasing fire risks, and losses, of both lives and materials. As a result, in the early part of 1971, Her Majesty's Government placed on the statute book the Fire Precautions Act 1971. The main purpose of this Act was to make further provisions for the protection of persons from fire risks, and for purposes connected therewith. The new Act was designed to bring virtually every type of premises, not previously covered by fire regulations, under its control, and in future, premises, with certain exceptions, put to any of the following uses would require inspecting by the fire brigade, and issuing with a fire certificate:

- Use as, or for any purpose, involving the provision of sleeping accommodation
- Use as, or as part of, an institution providing treatment or care
- Use for purposes of entertainment, recreation, or instruction, or for the purposes of any club, society, or association
- Use for the purposes of teaching, training, or research
- Use for any purpose involving access to the premises by members of the public, whether on payment or otherwise

This was a very welcome piece of legislation, as far as the fire authorities were concerned, and it had a marked effect upon the standards of safety available in all buildings to which the public have a right of access. After studying the comprehensive report, and its increase in workload on the brigade, Mr Havery recommended to the City Council, that the brigade's establishment be increased during 1972/73 as follows:

Operational: three Leading firemen and fifteen firemen – to man an extra appliance at Station A Greenbank.

Fire Protection: two Station Officers and one Sub Officer – to inspect the premises covered by the First Designating Order, issued under the Fire Precautions Act 1971, i.e. hotels and boarding houses.

Training: one Station Officer, two Sub Officers and one fireman – to meet the increasing training required of Brigade, and Merchant Navy personnel.

Administration: one Clerk/Typist – to meet the increasing commitments due to the introduction of the Fire Precautions Act, and extension of training commitments.

Whilst every recommendation was not implemented right away, the increase in operational and training staff was approved forthwith, and commenced early in the new financial year. Mr Havery stated that the early approval of these recommendations was a good example of the City Council getting its priorities right, i.e. firefighting before anything else – after all, an inspection of a building can be delayed, but not the extinction of a fire.

The brigade used to send its recruit firemen to Birmingham, and then to Reigate, in Surrey, for initial training. But in 1971, they conducted their own recruit courses, of three months' duration, at Camels Head. This fire station and training school was only a temporary arrangement, as the new Headquarters and training facilities were granted approval by the City Council; building work began during the next financial year. The degree of excellence afforded to the whole training set–up, duly impressed other fire brigades from around the country. The likes of Cornwall County Fire Brigade, Bath Fire and Ambulance Service, Berkshire and Reading Fire Service, and Exeter City Fire Brigade sent their recruits to Plymouth for initial training. Plymouth also trained over 1,000 Merchant Navy personnel each year.

Large fire at Earls Acre, the Barbican

The first of five calls to the above premises was received at 05:04 hours on 1st December 1971, and because of the very high fire risk of the area concerned, an initial attendance of five appliances was sent.

The first pump arrived within four minutes, and the officer in charge was confronted with a large range of interconnected, warehouse-type buildings, of two and four floors. The two-storey section was well alight on both floors, and flames issuing through the roof had entered the windows of the top floor of the four-storey section, and set fire to the rooms at that level.

An assistance message was radioed back to the brigade control at Greenbank, and jets were got to work to extinguish the fire in the four storey warehouse in Southside Street, which was also connected to the premises, and which were also well alight.

All the premises involved were used as toy and stationery warehouses, and were very well stocked with Christmas supplies. A large proportion of the stocks consisted of plastic toys, etc. The smell of burning plastic was noticeable many streets away from the actual incident. Due to the intense heat given off from the mass of burning stock in the two-storey section, the walls of the premises began to collapse, and all the firemen had to be withdrawn from the front part of the building.

The fire in the four-storey section was confined to the top floor, and it was also cut off just inside the two-storey warehouse in Southside Street. The two-storey warehouse in Friars Lane was completely destroyed by fire and was later demolished.

A total of eleven jets, one turntable ladder monitor and one snorkel monitor, together with a large number of breathing apparatus sets, were used in extinguishing the fire. One fireman suffering from heat exhaustion was removed to hospital, where he made a complete recovery.

A fire of particular interest occurred on 16th February 1972, at Hareston Farm, Yealmpton, which was situated in that part of the administrative County of Devon covered by the City Fire Brigade. When the first appliance arrived, the officer in charge discovered that a severe fire was burning in a large range of one- and two-storey buildings, which were used for the storage of hay, corn, and general farming equipment. Because of the intensity of the fire, shortage of water supplies, and the amount of manpower required to move all the hay, etc., from the burning buildings, pumps were made up to six, and the hose layer requested. The fire was extinguished after the brigade had been in attendance for more than twenty-four hours, by the use of six main jets, and two hose reel jets, but only after the first floor and roof, together with more than 3,000 bales of hay, had been severely damaged by fire.

Recruits' course at Camel's Head in September 1972; the author, Finbar 'Baz' Nolan, is on the far left of the front row. The course instructors were: Dennis Woolwright, Peter Kerr, John Donaldson and Les Smith. Other Plymouth firemen in the photo are, in rear: George Ungells, Ray Mass, Roger Smith. In centre: Jimmy Hargreaves, Keith Cooper, John Vincent. In front: Baz Nolan, Neil Handley, Paul Elliott.

This fire was unusual, in that immediately following the incident, twenty-two of the personnel who attended it reported sick, and were off duty for a total period of 151 days. As a result of this very high sickness rate, the Chief Fire Officer contacted the Medical Officer of Health, who carried out a thorough investigation into the circumstances. He came to the conclusion that one of the firemen must have had a virus infection at the time of the incident, and because of the hot, damp, enclosed conditions in which the men were working, the virus infection had developed and spread very rapidly, and so affected most of the men who attended the incident.

End of an era

Changes within the whole of the British Fire Service were due to commence in April 1974. The number of fire authorities in England and Wales was to be reduced to fifty-four, including London (which was not affected by the local government changes). All the county borough fire brigades, which were formed in 1948, were also to lose their identity, and be absorbed into the new County brigades; this of course, included the City of Plymouth Fire Brigade. Fire brigades in Scotland and Northern Ireland changed in 1975.

For the first time since 1838, when the West of England Insurance Company formed a fire brigade in Plymouth, the brigade would lose its links with the City Fathers, and come under the jurisdiction of Devon County Council. Due to local government circumstances, Plymouth faced amalgamation before the nationally accepted date for reorganisation of Local Governments on 1st April 1974. It transpired that Plymouth was to change twelve months before any other fire brigade changed.

The Fire Brigades of Exeter City and Devon County Fire Service were also in a position of early change, and 1st May 1973 was to be the amalgamation date. One of the most important tasks to be done was to appoint a new Chief Fire Officer, to command the vast area that the new brigade dictated. There were many senior officers, from all three fire brigades, who were very worthy contenders, and the unenviable job of electing the right man began.

Finbar (Baz) Nolan, the author of this book, about to make entry into a fire in an exotic reptile and creepy crawly shop in Buckwell Street in 1973. Note the look of horror on his face, as he is terrified of anything wriggly.

Some members of Blue Watch at Greenbank join senior officers in presenting Deputy Chief Officer Ernie Dawe with a retirement gift, L to R: ADO Alex Harvey; ADO John Donaldson; Sub.O. Brian Read; Stn.O. Alfie Banks; Fm. Joe Dolphin; DO John Corbett, half hidden; Fm. Ken Wood; DO John Fiddeman; CFO Ralph Havery; Fm. Derrick Baker and Fm. Trevor (Zipper) Ferrand.

The most obvious and deserving candidate was Mr Ralph Havery OBE MIFireE, who, in his eleven years in command of the City of Plymouth Fire Brigade, totally transformed it, and left a legacy of modernisation and professionalism to be proud of. He was duly elected as the first Chief Fire Officer of the newly named Devon Fire Brigade, where he continued to modernise and set standards that other fire brigades sought to achieve. The City of Plymouth Fire Brigade was no more, and the firemen of this fine city transferred their allegiance to their newly appointed fire brigade, as did the firemen of Exeter City and Devon County.

Written histories of Exeter City Fire Brigade, and indeed Devon County Fire Service, have been published in the past, and it is to be hoped that *Risen from the Ashes* reflects a true account of the terrible tragedies and the proud history of the former fire brigades, that served the three towns of Plymouth, Devonport, and Stonehouse.

Insignia of the following fire brigades that served the three towns: No. 1, Stonehouse Fire Brigade; No. 2, Devonport Fire Brigade, No. 3, Plymouth Police (Borough & City); No. 4, AFS; No. 5, NFS; No. 6, City of Plymouth Fire Brigade.

The last HMI inspection of the City of Plymouth Fire Brigade was carried out at Greenbank fire station on 3rd May 1972.

Deputy Chief Fire Officer Ernest Dawe.

Firemen A. M. Orr (Jock); T. A. Lowe (Ted) and Sub. Officer. S. G. Strike, displaying their long service medals, which were presented by Alderman J. C. Porter in 1973.

BIBLIOGRAPHY

Plymouth, Devonport, and Stonehouse Town's accounts and public records

Western Daily Mercury

Plymouth Weekly Journal

Plymouth Independent

Plymouth, Devonport, Stonehouse Herald

Western Evening Herald

Western Morning News

Numerous editions of the *Fireman* magazine 1840–1900

Various Merryweather and Shand Mason trade catalogues of the late 1800s

Phoenix Assurance Company Ltd

Plymouth Reference Library

Annual Reports of Plymouth City Fire Brigade 1948–1973

History of the British Fire Service. G. V. Blackstone, Routledge and Kegan Paul, 1957

Plymouth Fire Brigade Stores Book 1886

A Stonehouse Century. Bruce Firth. The Devil's Point Press, 2002

Plymouth and Devonport in times of War and Peace. Henry Francis Whitfield. 1900

Devon Firefighter. Edited by Iain Rice. Halsgrove Publishing 2000

Metropolitan Police/Fire Brigade Handbook. 1869

Personal written accounts from retired Plymouth Firemen

The Great Fire of Devonport Dockyard 1840. George Dicker

A History of the Police at Devonport Dockyard. Alfred Wigmore.

Stranger's Handbook to the Western Metropolis of 1841

Policing the Peninsula. Forest Publishing, 2000. Simon Dell, MBE

Police in Plymouth. Ernest Dickaty

Plymstock during the second World War 1939–1945. Arthur L. Clamp

Diary of a Fire Fighter. Fm Brooks. 1940–45

A History of Devonport. Chris Robinson. Pen and Ink Publishing, 2010

Under Fire. John Leete. Sutton Publishing, 2008

ACKNOWLEDGEMENTS

I WOULD LIKE to express my sincere thanks to the following institutions and individuals, for their assistance in providing photographs and information for use in this book:

Plymouth and South Devon Record office; Plymouth Reference Library, for their use of their micro film archive; Ron Long; Ron Henderson; John Leete; Chris Robinson; ex-City of Plymouth Chief Fire Officer Mr Ralph Havery, for kindly writing the foreword to this book; Mel Hughes; Michael Lucas; Mac McCoy; Pete Hooper; all the lads of The West of England Fire Heritage Museum (formally known as Devonport Naval Base Fire Museum); the late Jim Mead; my dear son Garry, for assisting with the technical side of formatting the book and securing the proofreading talents of Andrew Ross, and of course my darling wife Pat, for putting up with the countless hours over many years I was researching records and old newspapers at the city library, and for the months that I was tied to my computer.

I would also like to thank the other members of my family, and friends, for their encouragement. Thanks also go to a former colleague and friend, Barrie Dibble, who many years ago, when the idea of a historical account was first mentioned, gave me much encouragement to write this book. Well here it is Barrie, albeit thirty-two years late!

DOWN MEMORY LANE

Mass jets as a finale to Baz Nolan's recruits' course in 1972.

Her Majesty's Inspector Mr G. R. H. Payne, OBE, BEM, MIFireE, talks with fireman Keith Burridge during his visit to Greenbank in 1972. Peter Martin is on the left of the picture. The other inspecting dignitaries are CFO Ralph Havery; Deputy Chief Ernest Dawe; Alderman J. C. Porter and Councillor Mrs M. Robb.

Group Photograph at Camels Head in 1972, Rear L to R: Barry (Biffo) Cann, Jock Cameron. Front L to R: Dave Brooks, Dave Hendy, Buzz Inglis, Sid Main, Trevor Mole, Garth Herd, Peter Chaffe.

Senior officers of the City of Plymouth Fire Brigade in 1973. Back row L to R, ADO John Donaldson; ADO Alex Harvie; ADO Victor Watson. Front row L to R, DO John Corbett; Deputy CFO Ernest Dawe and CFO Ralph Havery.

Re-naming the fireboat Iris to Cissie Brock, on 22nd October 1966.

Divisional Officer John Corbett and Alderman Mrs L. A. Brock, after the re-naming ceremony of the fireboat from Iris to Cissie Brock, on 22nd October 1966.

Chief Fire Officer Ralph Havery congratulates Fred Barker on getting his long service medal in 1973.

Fireman Ted Lowe receiving his long service medal from Alderman J. C. Porter in 1973.

Members of the brigade outside the Council Chambers, following presentations of IFE certificates and Long Service and Good Conduct Medals in 1973.

The fireboat Cissie Brock welcoming the Royal Yacht Britannia in Plymouth Sound.

'Yet another trophy!' The brigade football team receiving the Devon Wednesday league cup from Mr Maurice Williams, the league president during the 1970s. The team is, from L to R: Ray Yabsley, Eddie Taylor (Manager), Pete Davis, Johnny Hoyle, Bernie Talling (rear), Steve Wavish, Peter Martin (Captain), Ron Smerdon, Baz Nolan, Ken Mulville, Maurice Williams, John Griffiths, Roger Johnston and Bob Vinnecombe.

Deputy Chief Officer Ernest Dawe introducing Alderman Porter to Station Officer Alf Le Count at Greenbank fire station.

Well done son! Fireman Jock Orr congratulates his son Don on winning the silver axe on his recruits' course in 1971.

Chief Fire Officer George Drury, HMI. A. V. Thomas and Deputy Chief Fire Officer Fred Danniells inspect the stowage on a Dennis pump escape in 1953.

Fire Brigade Committee inspection at Plympton fire station in Market Road in 1969. Lined up for inspection are Dave Ritchie, Jock Orr, Ray Yabsley and Ginger Sandell.

HMI parade at Greenbank fire station in 1952.

HMI inspection at Greenbank in 1971.

HMI Inspection at Greenbank fire station in 1966.

Station Officer Ken Welberry taking a crew on Salvus breathing apparatus training at Camel's Head.

Pieces of Eight! Mel Hughes entertaining the children at a Christmas party at Greenbank fire station in 1966. Mel went on to become an ADO, and he went to Morton in Marsh as a BA Instructor before returning to Devon where he ran the BA school at Exeter for a period.

Derek Davies and Mel Hughes keep the children entertained at the Christmas party at Greenbank fire station in 1966.

Civil Defence training at Millbridge in 1968. This training was undertaken by all newly appointed firemen within their probationary period.

Fireman Ted Beer displaying a new-style fire tunic. This tunic was trialled, but not adopted, and Plymouth continued to use the lancer-style tunic.

(L) Carrying down drill on a fifty-foot wheeled escape.

(R) Fireman Garth Herd at the controls of the 65 foot snorkel aerial platform at Camels Head. Note the old Southern Railway bridge, which was later pulled down, and the area used for housing.

Lined up for inspection at Greenbank 1970. One crew in Plymouth lancer tunics and the other crew in American-style tunics, which were on trial, but not adopted.

The purpose built ship's structure at Camel's Head was a first class training facility for ship fire fighting, and was used by fire service, merchant navy and general industry personnel.

Training an industrial course in the art of ship fire fighting at Camel's Head fire station.

Line up at Camel's Head fire station, L to R: Dennis F8 pump (STT 317), an ex Crediton pump used as a reserve; Leyland Pump Hydraulic Platform (HCO 999F); Leyland Multi-Purpose (KCO 999G); Leyland Multi-Purpose (OCO 999J), this appliance was involved in a fatal road accident in 1979 and was written off the fleet.

Dennis F8 pump (LCO 318) bought for Plymouth in 1955; it is currently owned by Devon & Somerset Fire & Rescue Service and is on loan to the West of England Fire Heritage Museum.

Leyland multi-purpose. The rolled canvas hose was later replaced with Duraline hose, flaked into carrying containers.

Pump Hydraulic Platform (HCO 999F) at Camel's Head fire station.

1964 Bedford J5 water tender, 210 TTA. This appliance was transferred to the City of Plymouth Fire Brigade from Plympton fire station, which was formerly part of Devon County Fire Service, until amalgamation in 1967. This appliance was known as the 'Silver Bucket'.

Fireboat Cissie Brock on drills at Queen Ann's Battery in 1968.

Plymouth's former turntable ladder (CDR 287) which was sold off in 1964, is seen here in private ownership, at a fire engine rally in Oxfordshire in the 1970s.

Leyland Beaver multi-purpose fire engine, HDR 999F, bought for Plymouth in 1968, and sold off in 1984.

1961 AEC Mercury Merryweather turntable ladder (VJY 44) at Greenbank fire station, sold off in 1981.

Another view of the mighty Leylands at Camel's Head.

Blue Watch at Greenbank fire station in 1973. Watches of this size were a joy to serve on, with plenty going on, and good camaraderie. L to R: Ken Mullville, Neil Handley, Jimmy Boyle, Dave Whitehead, Roger Hoskins, Bernie Talling, Hedley Richie, Baz Nolan, Jan Raddan, Trevor Ferrand, Derrick Baker, Brian Livingstone, Dave Thomas, Eddie Taylor, Brian Knott, Alan Phillips, Dave Brooks, Alfie Banks.

ABOUT THE AUTHOR

FINBAR NOLAN WAS born in Plymouth in 1948, and was brought up in St Budeaux. After leaving Camel's Head Secondary School in 1963, he began an apprenticeship in HM Dockyard as a shipwright. Failing to be impressed with that vocation, he moved on, and took other work as a steward on the Golden Hind express train, with the Pullman Company, and later as a hairdressing sundries man with Flairway Ltd, in Millbridge. Having been a keen member of 2171 squadron, with the Air Training Corps for four years, he was naturally guided into joining the Royal Air Force.

He started his fire service career in January 1966, when he joined the Royal Air Force as an Airfield Crash Rescue Fireman. After successfully completing his six weeks' square bashing at RAF Hemswell, and a thirteen-week basic firefighting course at RAF Catterick, in Yorkshire, he was posted to RAF Northolt in Middlesex. He quickly got to grips with the banter and comradeship which is unique among firemen. Finbar served all of his service time in the RAF on the Crash Line at various operational airfields, at home and overseas. Upon leaving the service in September 1972, he joined the City of Plymouth Fire Brigade, where he remained operational for his entire service.

He was promoted to Leading Fireman in 1980, Sub Officer in 1981, and served on Blue, Red, and White Watches on all five current fire stations in Plymouth, these being Greenbank, Crownhill, Plymstock, Plympton and lastly Camel's Head Fire Station. Finbar served the City of Plymouth Fire Brigade, Devon Fire Brigade and Devon Fire and Rescue Service until he was retired on ill health grounds, after nearly twenty-seven and a half years' service.

It had been his intention to write this historical account for more years than he cares to remember and he is pleased that, after many hundreds of hours researching old newspapers, books and other documents, as well as bending the ears of numerous retired firemen, his research is now complete. It is hoped that this record of the history of the fires and the brigades and firemen who have served Plymouth, Devonport, and Stonehouse will be enjoyed by all who are interested in our proud heritage.